BITTER
SUGAR

Maurice Lemoine

BITTER SUGAR

Slaves Today in the Caribbean

Photographic Reportage by the Author
Translated from the French by Andrea Johnston

Banner Press

Originally published as *Sucre Amer: Esclaves aujourd'hui dans les Caraïbes* ©1981 Nouvelle Société des Éditions Encre, Paris

Banner Press, Chicago

Zed Books Ltd., London

Library of Congress Cataloging in Publication Data

Lemoine, Maurice.
    Bitter sugar.

    Translation of: Sucre amer.
    1. Contract labor — Dominican Republic. 2. Sugar
workers — Dominican Republic. 3. Haitians — Dominican
Republic. I. Title.
HD4875.D44L4513   1985   331.5'42'097293   85-7457
ISBN 0-916650-18-9 (pbk.)

Approaching the city, they encountered a Negro stretched out on the ground having no longer but half his clothing — that is to say, blue canvas underdrawers. The poor man was missing his left leg and his right arm. "Oh, my God!" Candide said to him in Dutch, "what are you doing there, my friend, in the horrible state in which I see you?" "I'm waiting for my master, Mr. Vanderdendur, the famous merchant," replied the Negro. "Was it Mr. Vanderdendur," said Candide, "who treated you this way?" "Yes, sir," said the Negro; "it's the custom. We are given a pair of blue canvas drawers twice a year for clothing; when we work in the refinery and our finger gets caught in the millstone, they cut off our hand; when we want to flee, they cut off our leg; I found myself in both these situations: it is at this price that you eat sugar in Europe."

Voltaire. *Candide* (Chap. XIX)

This book is dedicated to the memory of
Millien Beaubrun, Haitian cane cutter,
murdered on July 7, 1980,
shot in the back
with 15 bullets of an M-1 rifle,
at the Palmajero military post
on the Catarey sugar factory property
in the Dominican Republic.
His crime was unpardonable. He had
refused to continue to work without pay.
He said no to slavery.

Preface

In the following pages, mention is often made of "the Dominicans."

An explanation is imperative.

It is not a matter of the Dominican People, who often, to a great extent, are unaware of what goes on in the sugar cane plantations in their name.

By "Dominicans," we mean all those, from the lowest echelon to the highest, sometimes very low, and often at the very top, who participate in one of the most despicable processes of exploitation known, in a time when it is nevertheless not uncommon.

May the rumblings of this book reach the others.

In the words of a Haitian exile — Jean-Claude Bajeux — recently expelled from the Dominican Republic for having opened an "Ecumenical Center for the Rights of Man," through which he meant to sensitize and mobilize public opinion to the drama lived by his compatriots in the hell of the "bateys": "experience has shown that the public's ignorance of the state of affairs is a guarantee of impunity for the transgressors of the Rights of Man. The weapon of public opinion can mean the difference, for thousands of people, between prison and liberty, life and death, humiliation and respect."

Such is the meaning that I give this book, written without hatred, but with great anger.

There is, in this account, alas, no fiction.

Only the names of some principal figures and that of the "batey" in which much of the action takes place have been changed. One will easily understand why.

My thanks to *Le Progrès de Lyon*, whose financial aid made possible the realization of a portion of this investigation.

I thank all those who... they know who they are.

Moreover... when a journalist lands in a foreign country, he moves among the people like a fish in a junkyard. If he remains isolated all by himself, he can accomplish nothing. Especially when everything is done to camouflage the truth. Thus, a reportage of this sort is always in a certain way, and to a certain extent, the result of confidence and collective effort.

To all those who helped the progress of this investigation, *a todos los compañeros que me ayudaron... Fanmi-yo, jodi-a m ap salué nou.*

PART ONE:

A SEASON IN HELL

CONTRACT

In accordance with the agreement on the hiring in Haiti and entry in the Dominican Republic of the Haitian temporary day laborers, agreement reached on 14 November 1966 between the Governments of the two countries in order to determine the financial clauses of the implementation of the above-mentioned agreement related to the hiring operations of the Haitian day laborers entering the Dominican Republic for the 1978-1979 sugar season:

Article 1: The "State Sugar Council" (CEA) solicits from the Haitian Government for the 1978-1979 sugar harvest, by letter addressed to the Haitian Embassy in Santo Domingo, the hiring of 15,000 (fifteen thousand) day laborers for the needs of the sugar factories of the Dominican State.

Article 2: The "State Sugar Council" agrees: a) To recruit the 15,000 Haitian day laborers according to the current Haitian laws. The recruiting operations will take place in Haiti, by agents of the State Sugar Council (CEA) in the hiring centers established for this purpose by the concerned services of the Haitian government. The duration of these operations will not exceed 30 (thirty) days...

Article 10: In order to cover the expenses brought about by the hiring of the 15,000 agricultural workers and their transportation from the hiring centers in Haiti to Malpasse, the State Sugar Council agrees to pay the Haitian Government the sum of one million two hundred and twenty five thousand dollars ($1,225,000) in American currency. This sum will be paid in two equal issues: the first payment will be made immediately after the Haitian Government's acceptance of the request submitted by the State Sugar Council has been communicated to the above-mentioned Council; the rest will be paid within fifteen (15) days from the opening date of the hiring operations or before this deadline if the State Sugar Council has already hired half of all the solicited agricultural workers.

Clusters of men had been overloading the wall for too long, overhanging the multitude, craning to see what was going on, attempting to understand how to go about getting hired. The wall caved in. Cries were heard. Now four bodies lie motionless in the dust and, all around, wails fill the air. One of the dead, in a crumpled heap, has a strangely disconcerted look. But it was an accident.

Losses and gains, and so be it, forever and ever, Amen. The day continued.

A strange maelstrom of madness was whirling over Croix-des-Bouquets, but also over the mornes,* as well as over the plains, traversing the island and its tormented lands, buffeting men with starving bellies, transiting through the masses in the streets of Port-au-Prince, shantytown of Haiti.

November sixth, nineteen hundred seventy-eight. They were hiring to cut sugar cane in "Dominicanie."

Already the day before, and the days before that, everywhere, they were mobilizing.

Through the absence of a door, the commotion outside penetrated the shop in sharp waves. Estimé Mondestin had stopped staring at the bolts of material stacked up along the peeling walls.

"Well, my friend?" the usurer was saying.

"I tell you, it's worth it," Mondestin had said, a little tense. "I'm leaving for Dominicanie. I'm going to work. I'll be making good

---

Morne: bluff or hillock in the West Indies. — Trans.

money." The Syro-Lebanese had nodded, flicked his tongue over his lips. He knew. He'd heard the radio.

"Ah, yes, cut cane..."

Mondestin was hopping from one foot to the other. He didn't know a whole lot about it, but it had been explained to him. Fortunately, there was no lack of well-intentioned people to explain everything to you. And not just anybody. Influential people.

He, at first, hadn't been particularly interested in leaving. He'd had his opinion changed.

Sugar cane is a comprehensive industry, *ou konprann?* It starts with the cultivation, the harvest of course, but there are also all sorts of jobs. If you're a painter, you don't need to cut. Not if you're a mechanic either. Not if you're a driver either. And Estimé Mondestin was a driver, a driver out of work, but a driver he was. He'd do all right; maybe wouldn't even have to cut cane. He'd been told so.

"They also told me the employees can make as much as fifteen dollars a day!" He stopped and tried to calculate. About two hundred days at fifteen dollars a day... At fifteen dollars a day and for two hundred days...

"There's money to be made. I don't want to leave empty-handed. I'll need a little something for the initial expenses, and you know me."

A short silence had set in.

"Besides, my family is staying, and they live down the street."

The usurer had agreed, and was coming around to the front of the counter.

"How much?" he asked.

"I'll need eighty dollars."

"For how long?"

"In six months I'll be back, after the *zafra,** and I'll be able to pay it back easy. Easy."

The usurer had wrinkled his forehead, squinting his eyes, as if absorbed in a difficult calculation. Mondestin had noticed a beggar. What was left of the man was hobbling on his stumps in front of the entrance to the shop. He was hideous.

"You'll have to give me one hundred sixty dollars when you get back."

"But, you're only lending me eighty," gasped Mondestin.

It was a rude shock.

"It's only reasonable."

"Reasonable? It's not at all reasonable, I'd say! You're killing me!"

Zafra: sugar cane harvest.

16

"Non, monché. Sé pri m fè pou ou spésial.* I'm even making a special deal because it's for you. The going rate is usually twenty to thirty percent interest a month."

"Ah...," murmured Mondestin feebly, nonplussed.

"You go to a lender, you tell him, 'I'll have my hundred dollar paycheck at the end of the month,' and he'll lend you eight."

Mondestin shrugged. A hundred dollar paycheck at the end of the month didn't exist. In any case, not in Haiti. The average income of a Haitian amounts to two hundred dollars a year. A quarter of the population, a million persons, have to try to stay alive with sixty-one dollars for the same period. For 17 percent of the rural inhabitants, the annual income is only thirty-three dollars!

"Look, I'm only asking a hundred sixty for an eighty dollar loan, and six months later at that!" By this time, the indigent had settled into the inside right angle of the doorway as if he meant to take root there. This daily vision settled it for Mondestin. "I'm leaving Haiti because life is very hard here," he mused. "There's nothing for me to do here. Over there, in Dominicanie, I'll make it. I must leave."

He had accepted.

As usual both sides of Dessalines Avenue were awash in a sea of human misery. Not really knowing why, he'd headed towards the marketplace at Croix-des-Bossales. (In this same spot, in another time, when Haiti was a French colony called Saint-Domingue, thousands of slaves torn out of Africa by the slavetrader disembarked.) The muck and debris were piling up. Trodden upon by thousands of bare feet, the teeming throng was packing down the accumulated waste of the central fruit and vegetable market of Port-au-Prince. He'd threaded his way with some difficulty through the crush — vaguely worried. Clutched in his sweaty fist, jammed deep in his pocket, were four hundred Haitian gourdes, the equivalent of eighty dollars. Never in his life had he had so much money.

Seething, wretched humanity — a swarming mass of human misery. He'd emerged at the cesspool that is La Saline without really noticing the horrifying reality. He was used to it. He'd taken a look around, and not knowing why, had thought of his President, President for Life of the Republic of Haiti, Jean-Claude Duvalier. The one that foreigners called Baby-Doc. Seated randomly, in unhappy disarray, were women, waiting to earn the few coins that would allow them to get through the day. Legs spread, they mechanically lifted the torn remnants of their dresses between their thighs. Comatose, overcome by the broiling sun, they offered emaciated bosoms to in-

---

*There are two official languages in Haiti: French, which is learned and spoken by the middle and upper classes; and Creole, an authentic Romance language based on French, used by the entire population.

different eyes. Further on, all around, ahead, behind—braziers, corn, oranges, wooden planks, cardboard crates, the dense teeming multitude. Men in rags, sweating blood, were hammering out pieces of scrap iron. Survive one more day. And make it to the night.

All this had hit Estimé Mondestin like a ton of bricks. His decision reinforced, he'd gone home.

The woman, not comprehending, had regarded the small packet of bills that her companion placed on the table in the shack. He'd counted it out proudly.

"Four hundred gourdes,* my dear, eighty dollars! Here's half for you." Then, anxiously: "But careful, it's to last six months."

"*Ki sa ginyin?* What's going on? Where did all this money come from?"

He'd looked down, brows knit. The time had come to tell her.

"I saw a shark." (She jumped.) "I borrowed it."

The silence that fell obliterated even the roar from outside.

"I'm leaving tomorrow for Dominicanie. This money is for you; to make do with until I get back."

The first sob was one of surprise, the second of despair. He pretended not to hear.

"You can't leave."

"Tomorrow I'm leaving."

"You are the man in this house."

"A man with no work and no hope."

"But the only man."

"Who cannot feed you."

"You don't leave for that! The country would be empty long ago."

"No, I'm leaving." And in a quieter voice: "I'm leaving."

"You've got three little girls I gave you. You can't leave us."

"I'm not leaving you, I'm going to make a life for you. They say that over there, in Dominicanie, it's fifteen dollars a day. I'm going to make a fortune. Then I'll come back."

"But what if you don't come back?"

"I will come back."

She thought she'd heard him say fifteen dollars a day. For an

_____

*In this book, sums of money will be expressed in the following currencies: the U.S. dollar, accepted everywhere in Haiti without obligation to exchange; the gourde, Haitian unit of currency; and the Dominican peso. Approximate exchange value of these currencies [in 1981—Trans.]: 1 dollar = 5 gourdes; 1 gourde = 20¢ U.S.; 1 peso = 5 gourdes = 1 dollar. The gourde is divided into 100 centimes; the peso, in 100 centavos. Centimes and centavos are both called "Kob" by the Haitians.

instant her reason had faltered. Immediately her heart took the upper hand.

"You can't. You can't."

"I'm going to make a life for you," he repeated, stubborn.

He had no other hope; he was leaving Haiti to work. She didn't want him to, but he was leaving anyway. It was decided. Besides, now they didn't have any choice.

Thus, he was left with two hundred gourdes, forty dollars. In Haiti, the dollar is accepted everywhere, no need to exchange. An "official" currency. He'd gone out again, his throat tight. He would be needing a few things for the trip. He wasn't going next door. It was another country. He'd been to buy himself some "Kennedys," used clothing imported from the United States, sold under the arcades on Dessalines St. and everywhere else. He'd chosen an old flowered shirt, an old pair of dark pants, an old pair of shoes, and had suddenly felt newly outfitted, very rich, very excited. Next, a small suitcase, a toothbrush, the first in his life, but at thirty he wasn't that old, some toothpaste, nothing more than the luxury of the barest essentials. Then, he'd counted his money again, his chest tight. Of the eighty dollars borrowed, he only had twenty left to cover his initial expenses in Dominicanie. He smiled to himself. In the Dominican Republic, he was going to earn a good living.

He had returned home to his wife. She was slumped in the only chair in serviceable condition in the dwelling. "What will become of us?" she'd demanded. The little girls, their noses running, were playing in the dust. He caressed their woolly heads, their swollen bellies. They were hungry, but said nothing. In Duvalier's Haiti, it doesn't do any good to complain when you are hungry.

Estimé Mondestin and the woman had secluded themselves, drawing the torn and frayed curtain hung on a string which separated their bed from the view of the nine other people living in the two dark rooms. They had held each other very tight, trying to be quiet, but had made some noise anyway. They perspired profusely.

He didn't know it, but he spat a new baby deep in her belly. She didn't realize it either. Who can say why things happen that way?

At dawn he left for the hiring center. But these details are of little importance. Haitians like him, there are thousands.

They had solicited fifteen thousand workers. Sixty thousand showed up at Croix-des-Bouquets and Lèogane. Basic food production has been cruelly deficient in Haiti for years. The peasants, dispossessed, emigrate to the city. The urban dwellers, unemployed, are on a treadmill in the slums. They are ready to seize the first opportunity that comes along. It's easy to buy a starving man.

By ten o'clock in the morning, it was no longer possible to get past the police barricades around Saint Rose's church in Lèogane.

In his shop, across from the Simone Duvalier Marketplace—which if it hadn't been named after the First Lady of the Republic, would have borne the name of Jean-Claude Duvalier, her son, of François Duvalier, her loathsome late husband—a skeleton-like old man with a fixed gaze sat stiffly behind his long counter and apprehensively surveyed his cans of condensed milk, his sacks of flour, his supply of privy paper, stacks of big yellow soaps, two cases of Heineken on the ground, the overloaded shelves, the pump marked "kerosene" stuck outside on the sidewalk, and the enormous metal strongbox set way back on his left in an obscure corner. All around, everywhere, the rabble were pushing and shoving. He did not begin to breathe again until the forces of "order" had impassively fractured a few collarbones and gouged a few eyes—but only a few—with blows of rifle butts and *rigoises** distributed forcefully on the roaring, undisciplined crowd.

As for Estimé Mondestin, he headed for Croix-des-Bouquets. At first light he left Port-au-Prince. At the public fountain on Fronts-Forts St., the women were already fighting among themselves to fill a measly container of water. One out of four houses has running water in this capital. He caught a "tap-tap" on Dessalines Ave. and managed to find himself the semblance of a place—*bonjour mésyé dam*—in the jammed public transport. The vehicle crawled along the avenue, unusually encumbered for the early hour, and as always in such a case, the driver was overdoing it. Nineteen persons were already crammed into the back platform of the Peugot 404 and he was stopping to take on more passengers. "*Pa gin plas anko*," someone protested. "There's no more room!" He stopped anyway. "*Ki koté ouap mété lot moun yo chofé? Eské sé sou potchay la ouap mété yo?* Where are you going to put them, driver? On the baggage-rack? On the roof-rack?" The driver snorted with distinction and continued to load. He'd never seen so many passengers for Croix-des-Bouquets. Besides, at the price they were paying, he wasn't going to allow them to piss him off!

He continued to pack them on. "And if you don't like it, you can walk."

They finally got started—having given up protesting—rolled along the slums of Mama Simone, crossed a desert which anywhere else would have been covered by an industrial zone, veered right at Croix-des-Missions, passed along fields of sugar cane—"You're going

---

Rigoises: riding crops.

to Dominicanie?" "Yes, and you?" "Yes, me too!" "And you, and you, and you?" "Me too, me too, me too"—caught a glimpse of a few banana trees and a woman on the road with a large basket. "There's money to be made there, the crop will be real good this year." Less than thirty minutes later they arrived, mildly stunned, at the Croix-des-Bouquets.

Estimé Mondestin dove headlong into the crowd. So did the Tonton-Macoutes, the bastards. The vicious henchmen of the militia were roaming everywhere, in conquered territory. As usual. But first, he took a look at the crowd. Peasants from Bainet, Jacmel, Thiotte, Plaine des Gonaïves (the desolate savannah), from Ouana-minthe, Mont-Organisé, from all the godforsaken corners of the country, obviously hit with cursed economic problems; as well as the chronically unemployed from Carrefour, Saint-Martin, Brooklyn, Bel-Air, and other slum quarters in Duvalier's capital. They'd left a wife, a fiancée, their mistresses. They'd pronounced the magic word to persuade their families and to persuade themselves: Dominicanie. And they were leaving. I'm going to get together a small sum to buy a little land. To not starve anymore. To buy some tools. To build a house with sheet metal on the roof like the gro-nèg* nearby. They were leaving: small farmers, poor but independent, sons who work as hired hands of other poor peasants, unsalaried domestic help, marginal coffee producers adrift. One-fifth of the total agricultural surface of the country is exploited by only three per cent of the farmers. These were the conditions in which they were leaving, flee-ing, running; pushing and shoving at the exit of the country, their country, the pearl of the Caribbean, so some say, considered by cer-tain economists to be a veritable laboratory of underdevelopment, and by others, more optimistic, to be the prototype of a country in the process of regression. They were leaving.

Croix-des-Bouquets, taken by storm by a multitude of Haitians adrift, was ready to explode. The hiring had not yet begun and there were four dead due to a section of the wall that had crumbled.

Right from the start of the "hiring," Estimé Mondestin had a lot of trouble. First of all, he got himself billy-clubbed by a Tonton-Macoute that he'd inadvertantly jostled. He should have been more careful. The VSN† seemed very agitated. Rifles slung over the shoulders, automatic pistols in hand, machetes stuck in the belts,

---

*"Gro-nèg": "Big-Man," a term used by the Haitians to designate other, wealthy and/or important Haitians; also used, less frequently, to mean a large, powerfully built person. — Trans.

†VSN: Volunteers of the National Security, official designation of the "Tonton-Macoutes," the Duvalier regime's militia.

they were making their rounds, looking defiant in their bright blue uniforms. Mondestin had taken the blow in stride; like everyone else, he was afraid of them. Lackeys, mercenaries, torturers, killers, they have made "their order" reign in Haiti ever since their creation by François "Papa Doc" Duvalier, dictator. They crisscross the country thoroughly and systematically: violence, arrests, reprisals, rapes, assassinations, massacres of entire families — these fascist Creoles easily live up to a comparison with Hitler's Gestapo or Mussolini's militia. Recently, their most visible outrages have somewhat disappeared from view. "A little discretion, Gentlemen," Carter had demanded, a bit ticked off. "What about Human Rights? Do what you have to do, but do it quietly." Lesson learned.

The regime: Jean-Claude "Baby Doc" Duvalier, democratically elected President for Life of the Republic by his father, François "Papa Doc" Duvalier. He himself democratically elected President for Life in his day. By himself, naturally.

Estimé Mondestin did not falter. He made his way to the end of the line which was already stretched out over a few hundred yards. Others were piling up behind him. He didn't know anyone. He waited, listened. A muffled buzz was rising from the long line of men. "I was carrying cinder blocks from one end of a site to another," piped up a voice lost in the crowd, "I never had a nickel to my name." "I don't have a father, I don't have a mother," chimed in another unknown. "I've got five little sisters, I'm the oldest in the family. My aunt said 'you're big now, you are nineteen years old, you can't sit down at this table without doing anything.' " "You can't sit down at this table without doing anything," his aunt had told him, and ten heads were agreeing.

After this story, there was the misfortune recounted by another anonymous voice. It wasn't clear just exactly what it was all about. "Radio Nationale announced fifteen dollars a day, that's why I'm here." That, on the other hand, they could all understand. And the litany continued.

A brutal convulsion shook the whole throng. The line writhed like a crushed snake. A few yards away, no one knew why, the unleashed Macoutes were savagely lashing into the crowd. It was very heavy. The wounded were taken away.

The day stretched on, implacable and fierce, awash in a flood of humanity, sun, and guns. People were climbing trees. The branches were so overloaded they snapped. The people too. About twenty gesticulating men scaled a statue — in whose glory they did not know. The statue collapsed and they with it. Estimé Mondestin was not terribly inspired by all this. You could read it in his tense face. His neighbor grimaced a smile. "I'm here, I want to go, but I don't know if my name will get on the list. Last year people were beaten up."

"This year too, I believe."

They had all decided to get hired no matter what. Even if it meant getting clubbed.

He went all day without eating. Now and then, by stretching his neck, he could make out the makeshift hiring office, surrounded by important-looking Macoutes. You could see leaping shadows pass behind the windows. This business was, without a doubt, a veritable affair of state. Everyone was there. Except Duvalier, of course. He must have been playing with his motorcycles in the courtyard of the National Palace, in Port-au-Prince. The Departments of the Interior and of National Defense were drafting the travel documents. The Foreign Affairs Department was registering the cards which were to be sent first to the Chancellery, then on to the Haitian Embassy in the Dominican Republic. The Department of "Social Affairs" (!) was preparing and drawing up the individual work contracts, making out the list of those hired, and was organizing the shipping of the herd to the Dominican Republic. The Macoutes, put there to club, were clubbing. In short, the entire Duvalier machine, from the smallest cog to the biggest, was involved up to the neck. Just for the record, just in case someone dared to pretend one day that he didn't know.

The Haitians weren't saying anything. "Once we get to Santo Domingo all that is going to change," stated an optimist calmly, with a little bravado.

It was a rough moment to get through.

There were more beatings. No one dreamed of keeping count. The Macoutes were having a good old time, really going at it. The human livestock bellowed and balked. Shots were heard. The horde howled, roared, and reeled. The Macoutes were screaming, drunk with power and arrogance. Estimé Mondestin was violently shaken, jostled, swept away. Desperate, he felt one of his moccasins being wrenched from his foot.

"My shoe! I lost my shoe!"

Big deal. Others were losing their lives. Some guy looked at him without seeing, too busy trying to keep his balance. Mondestin, furious, gathered his forces, both arms outstretched, pushed the body in front of him out of the way, and dove head first into the heap of human flesh reeking of sweat and dust.

"I see it! Good God, I see it! Don't push! Help me get it!"

The pressure became intolerable. The man next to him was no longer the same one, already replaced by another the current had dragged along. He panicked. If I bend over, they are going to trample me to death. They are going to trample me. Seething with rage, he gave up. He lived barefoot from that moment on.

At six o'clock, or five of, maybe seven minutes of six, he let out a moan. He was no more than a few yards from the providential window when they closed the offices. The inscriptions were all over for the day. He clenched his fists; which changed nothing. In order not to lose his place, in order not to have to start all over the next morning, he decided to stay right where he was. He hailed a peddler who was present for the festivities, dashing about, wheeling round, opening bottles and hastily giving change, bought a hunk of bread and a bottle of Kola. A little later, he made himself a place among the other bodies already stretched out and went to bed on the ground on the spot where the wave had left him.

Little by little a carpet of starving men covered the ground at Croix-des-Bouquets, like a multiform and motley human plague.

Thus Mondestin spent the night cold and sleepless.

The first Tonton-Macoute had an old rifle in hand. He was advancing stiffly, his face expressionless. Other bastard-blue uniforms were following like a shadow, shoulders held back; in addition, there were two soldiers who were flanking a "gro-nèg" in civilian clothes. An official to be sure. Behind this doubtful aristocracy trailed several dozen ill-assorted individuals, in a state of disorder. The latter, except for their gait, at once hesitant and determined, arrogant and ill-at-ease, looked exactly like all the half-awake men who, groaning and stretching, were awkwardly starting to reconstruct the line interrupted the day before. A bit of the night mist still hung in the soon-to-be-immaculate sky.

"*Sa pa pi mal,* no," smiled Estimé Mondestin's neighbor, indicating with his chin the still-closed office, almost within an arm's reach. "Things aren't going too bad for us. We'll get by this morning." He opened his eyes wide, delighted: "Thank Goodness! I'm almost out of money — I wouldn't be able to wait much longer."

Mondestin didn't answer him. He was watching the strange troop moving toward them, a seed of unexplainable anxiety growing inside him.

"Who are they?" asked his neighbor, who had finally detected Mondestin's worried look.

"*M pa konin,*" breathed Mondestin. "I don't know." Then, in a half-whisper: And I don't really want to know.

No one asked for his opinion. The first VSN had just stopped, casting a very professional glance over the line. The "gro-nèg" came to a standstill at his side. Hands on his big hips, he eyed the procession up and down, scornfully and with disgust, noting with his beady eye those who were up, those who were not, those who were seated, those who were still camped out. One big dunghill. A veritable pile of ordinary shit.

"And what is this line?"

As if he didn't know, the bugger!

He spat with scorn before this living resumé of the miserable People of Haiti, and addressed a Macoute:

"What are these people doing on the ground?"

"*N ap atann*! We're waiting," cried a voice, strong and determined. "We're waiting for the offices to open!"

"Yes! *N ap atann*!"

"They are waiting," sniggered the bigwig with a nonchalant gesture, a gesture to humiliate them, as if he were wiping an ass with toilet paper! "They are waiting lying on the ground!"

"Well, yes, we're waiting."

"But this is not a flophouse here, my friend!"

A reproving buzz rose, made up of indignant whispers, uneasy gasps. "Is it our fault if we don't have money to sleep in hotels, which don't even exist anyway? Spend the night all hunched up. To sign up nice and early. Yes, camping out. Not to lose our place, sir, to not lose our place! You understand?"

"Their places! Ah, ah, their places! But as far as I know this place doesn't belong to anybody! Who then claims to appropriate this piece of national territory without permission from the proper authorities? This place doesn't belong to you, you are nothing but vagabonds!"

The man turned theatrically toward the military thugs, who straightened up, knowing their time of glory had come on this memorable day.

"Where do we stand, faced with this new generation that takes the liberty to engender an attitude which belittles the glorious past of our Duvalierist Revolution, undermines national dignity? Where do we stand?"

Unconsciously, they lowered their heads. The more grandiloquent the speech, the more vicious the beatings — they all knew by instinct and by experience this primary and immutable truth of the Duvalier mafia. The man took a step forward, very certain of his power, and spat once again. One could make out a lump in the right-hand pocket of his impeccably pressed suit jacket. He pretended to be angry.

"Toussaint Louverture and Jean-Claude Duvalier, noble heros for whom the whole world envies us, have the right to the respect of all generations, black and white. By your pernicious disorder, you dishonor them."

He planted himself facing the Macoutes who suddenly advanced, rifles first.

"What is needed in this country, gentlemen, is some order!" He screamed, "Order! Disperse this riffraff and let an orderly line be installed here! A line of civilized people! A line that does not bring shame upon us in the eyes of the generations to come! Let there be order, gentlemen, order! Order!"

He could have spared himself all the theatrics.

With blows of rifle butts and clubs, the riffraff was dispersed. Under this pressure they ran, they set off in every direction, sometimes going very far, they shouted, and crossed the anemic public garden facing the yellow and green stained church whose heavy doors were closed. Mondestin, his mouth wide open, was neither the first nor the last. He gave way under the avalanche, backing up, backing up, caught a glimpse of the faces of the Macoutes, and said to himself that someday, it will be necessary to kill them. They have been there since 1957, and no one yet has been able to dislodge them. They think their shit doesn't stink. For the hired thugs, coming, for the most part, from the hoodlum population, Duvalier's pseudo-revolution means possessing arms and the license to use them without restriction. Mondestin, enraged, tried to make himself small; "It's not Jean-Claude who's doing this," he choked; thinking of his president for life, Jean-Claude Duvalier, who wouldn't permit it, who couldn't know about it, who must not know — shut away in his palace where he works without respite for the happiness of the Haitian people — and at counting his four hundred million dollars stashed away in Swiss banks. "It's not Jean-Claude, it's the Macoutes, the VSN, that scum of the earth! If only someone could inform Jean-Claude! He wouldn't permit it! He's a good fat cat, that fat cat there!"

No one informed Jean-Claude.

"The department heads in my district told me that it would be a great life," moaned a boy, still almost a child, holding his broken arm, before fainting into the chaos of the contracting crowd.

Estimé Mondestin noticed something. As soon as the terrain was clear, a new line formed, with those individuals brought by the authorities at the head. For a moment he asked himself if there wasn't some kind of cause and effect relationship: who the Devil were these privileged persons? He asked himself the question sincerely. Then he plunged back into the crush.

Behind those protected by the Macoutes, the line was re-forming in the most perfect anarchy, each one trying to get himself as close as possible to the front. You had to be quick, and fight to win a place.

Mondestin was not among the speediest. He cast a sickened look at the whole mess. The coveted building was right back where it was when he started. Having almost reached his goal the night before, this morning he'd have to start from scratch.

To recount what happened this second day would be perfectly useless. It was just like the first. There were fights and disputes; there were clubbings and injuries. Mondestin drank a syrupy Kola and ate a piece of bread. All around him, the great majority were already suffering, completely penniless. He congratulated himself for having taken the loan.

He plunged into a torpor, surrounded by noises and confused rage, overcome by the sun and the effort of standing up. He gave a start. An energetic hand was pulling his arm violently.

"Mondestin, my friend, what are you doing here?"

He recognized Petit Pierre Déroseaux, from Pétionville, and thanked the dear Good Lord for finally sending him a familiar face.

"Eh, well, I'm waiting in line, my friend, and it's no good at all."

"No good at all?"

"I left Port-au-Prince two days ago. In two days they haven't taken me. They made us get in line, one behind the other, there was a commotion, they broke us up. I lost my place."

"Better not stay here, my friend."

"But I want to get hired!"

"Exactly! Me too; I want to get hired, too."

"And you're not waiting in line?"

Petit Pierre Déroseaux from Pétionville smiled and shook his head; Mondestin hadn't changed, still a little countrified. He leaned towards him, continuing in a confidential tone.

"It's useless to wait here. It's the surest way not to be taken. Me, I don't wait, and I'll be hired tomorrow."

"*M pa konprann*," blurted Modestin, who, in fact, did not understand at all.

Déroseaux stared at him as if he were observing a friendly halfwit. He moved a few steps away, looking around for someone or something, pointed in the direction of a Tonton-Macoute making his rounds a few yards from the flock.

"If you want to get through, go and see one of these people in charge, or the other over there."

Mondestin's gaze followed his finger, and he recognized with surprise — none other than...the "gro-nèg" from this morning.

"What should I tell him?"

Déroseaux couldn't help laughing — a bitter, grating laugh.

"Nothing! You don't ask them anything, you give them

something."

"Give them something?"

"Money, of course!"

"Money...how much?" asked Mondestin, who after all wasn't really that surprised at the turn of events.

"Ten will do it."

"Ten gourdes?"

"Ten dollars! You have some money? Because if not, it can be very long."

Mondestin nodded.

"You've got to pay, my friend, in order to be among the first in line in the morning. *Ou konprann?* Understand?"

As a matter of fact, Mondestin believed he did understand.

"And if I give, I get by for sure?"

"Normally, yes. Although in this country you can never be sure of anything."

Estimé Mondestin left the long line, the long line that stretched on and on, painted in colors of weariness, and moved slowly towards the center of the square. In Haiti, the mafia that lives off the traffic of Negroes started there, among the officials of the Haitian regime.

Estimé Mondestin was terribly ashamed, but what could he do about it?

As the rising sun just skimmed over the bell tower of the church, the Macoutes tore into the dazed crowd, clubs and rifle butts raised, to make a clean sweep, to make a clean sweep for him, as well as for all the others who had "participated in the expenses." Among those who fled screaming in anger and in pain, he recognized several familiar faces, who the day before had run side by side with him, fleeing the avalanche of blows. He felt bad, closed his eyes, very tired. He'd paid ten dollars, a fortune, in order to be among the happy few. Even if he'd wanted to give it up now, he couldn't. Almost all the money from his loan was spent. He was condemned to succeed. All he had left was forty poor little gourdes; the equivalent of eight dollars. How long must those have waited who had nothing to give? How long? He shrugged. What good did it do to torment himself? He already had one foot in Dominicanie.

"Here we go—there's the beginning of our good fortune," joyously cried Petit Pierre Déroseaux, from Pétionville.

"A fortune that was mighty expensive," muttered Mondestin bitterly. "I hope we'll be paid soon!"

Someone behind him snickered. He wheeled around. The man avoided his look, lowered his eyes, seemed to think better of it.

"Me, I've already been, but I only stayed fifty-nine days and I got out of there." His mouth twisted in an ironic smile. "It's not all that great, Dominicanie, you know! It's not all that great!"

A man burst out laughing, then suddenly fell silent, vaguely worried.

"Well then why are you going back, my friend, if it's not so hot?"

"I went in '75 and in '76," added another voice on the left. "It's true. Under Balaguer, it was different, but with Guzman things are going to change. It's another story."

Guzman, Balaguer — these illustrious unknowns passed Estimé Mondestin right by; he'd never even heard of them.

"What do you mean, it's another story?" cut in the pessimist, disenchanted.

"Another thing altogether. Balaguer was a bad president, an old friend of the dictator Trujillo. With Guzman, the new president of the Dominican Republic, it's even better. He's going to do big things for the Kongos."

"For the what?"

"For the Kongos."

"*Sa sa yé sa?* What's that?"

The veteran burst out laughing. There are those who are in the know, who've been three or four times already, but for the others it's the first time. You have to explain to them.

"The Kongos, that's us. Over there, they call us the Kongos."

"What does it mean?"

"*M pa konin.* That's the way it is."

Kongo, kongo. Kongo. Estimé Mondestin repeated the word softly to himself. Kongo. He found it beautiful.

Kongos: the name of the last slaves torn out of Africa by the slavetraders and brought to the distant Caribbean, as far as Santo Domingo, possession of France and of Spain, whose territory is divided today between the Dominican Republic and the Republic of Haiti. Mondestin found the word very beautiful.

A push in the back propelled him suddenly into the building. Petit Pierre Déroseaux from Pétionville and twelve other vigorous fellows made up the same batch. They passed a torn memorandum hanging on the open door without seeing it, or read it without understanding. (Seventy-five percent of the Haitians are illiterate and, out of a hundred children entering the first year of the rural primary public schools, only ten obtain their diplomas issued after completion of the first seven years. An elementary school teacher earns between fifty and sixty dollars a month.) The memorandum read: "*The agricultural worker chosen by the hiring officials will appear before an employee of the Center in order to furnish all information necessary for the preparation of his documents. He will then be dispatched, in possession of a form, to the medical service where he will undergo a medical examination. If he is found in good health, he will be sent to the photographer. After these formalities, the Haitian day laborer will be informed of the date of his departure for the Dominican Republic."* "Next!" bawled a voice about as pleasant as an outhouse. Estimé Modestin stepped forward and realized he was trembling. At ten minutes past eleven, he stood up proudly and stopped trembling. Or if he still trembled, it was perhaps from excitement.

The game was won. He was on the list.

Still crowded. Not even a chair to sit down and rest for a moment. Not even a bench. Not even nothing. Not even a way to sit on the ground. The Macoutes were keeping a ferocious watch over them, just to keep busy. The heat. The edginess. They were all feeling very tense, really tense.

"What exactly are we waiting for?" a little man asked Petit Pierre Déroseaux.

He was probably a farm worker, perhaps a *maléré*, poor peasants owning a tiny handkerchief-plot of land, unable to survive, sharecropping for others, occasionally working for wages. A guy from the back-country. Or something like that. Certainly not a member of one of the two hundred families, dollar millionaires, the richest of the rich in Haiti. Nor was he a cousin of one of the thirty-eight hundred families whose annual income is assessed at more than ninety thousand dollars, not counting what is in foreign banks. Someone else. One of those who each day sink deeper and deeper into destitution, while the aforementioned get richer and richer. No, there was no doubt about it. He was just a poor wretch, like practically everybody else. That was for certain.

"We're going to get a medical checkup," answered Déroseaux. "To see who's sick and who's not."

"What difference does it make if you're sick or not?"

"If you're sick you can't go."

"Me, I'm fine, I'm not sick," said the little man, buoyant.

When they were told to take off their clothes, it was no problem — they didn't have much to take off.

The doctor wiped his brow wearily, then contemplated the sweat on the back of his hand. "Next!" he yelled. "Hurry up!" From the adjoining room he could hear himself echoed by a colleague. "Next!" He smiled. They weren't sitting around idle. No, they certainly were not. "Well, come on!" They were twelve in all, recruited by the state, and each with a contract.

A small man entered, another peasant. He saw almost two hundred of them a day. Two minutes a head, including the rest of the body. Sufficient time to eliminate the worst dregs. And there were some. Handicaps of all kinds, lung pathologies, cardiac deficiencies, venereal disease, varicose veins, hypertension. They ran the gamut.

"Come here," he barked to the peasant who was waiting, a little awkwardly.

General impression, extreme weakness, he diagnosed immediately. This guy is undernourished. Next, he picked up the man's penis, examined it from every angle with a rather disgusted air. You'd think they could find some means to wash themselves before the examination, he said through gritted teeth, exasperated. "Turn! Bend over!" An inquisitorial glance at the anus, the legs, the spine. Especially watch out for venereal maladies. The Dominicans must have some problems, they make a fixation out of it. It would appear that the Haitians spread venereal disease! Completely exaggerated! Those who are afflicted, in my opinion, must have caught it from the Dominican prostitutes that invade Port-au-Prince! We send them cane cutters and they send us prostitutes. It's a funny world. That's the international division of labor. If they're so short of manpower, they could take back their *bouzins*, their prostitutes, and put them to work on the plantations! In Brazil, one-third of the labor force are women, in spite of the reputation that cane-cutting has.

"Turn. Come here. Breathe."

The stethoscope wandered, cold as destiny. General weakness, exactly what I . . . uh oh, another one! What is wrong with them all?

"You're sick, my friend. You can't go to the Dominican Republic."

The man let out a cry like that of a tortured animal.

"But I feel fine. Really! I'm fine."

The doctor shook his head. "No, my friend." The morning was coming to an end, and this was the thirteenth he was rejecting. He wasn't a statistician, he didn't draw any conclusions. He could have. He could have quickly calculated that 15 percent of adult Haitian males are unfit for prolonged physical labor. A lot for one People. He could have come up with some comparisions. In Haiti, malnutrition is the second cause of hospital admissions and death. (There are practically no hospitals.) In the one- to four-year-old age group, it is the primary cause of hospital admission and death. Dietary deficiencies in protein, 25 percent; in calories, 23 percent. Et cetera. But really, he wasn't paid to do that. He sat up. Our job is to do our work conscientiously and to furnish our client with men who will be productive. The contract has to be respected and the Dominicans kept happy. After all, they are paying — and well. One million, two hundred

31

twenty-five thousand American dollars! A pretty little sum! Eighty-six dollars a head.

"You're sick, and the sick ones can't go. I have to eliminate you."

The man shrank, took his head in his hands, and murmured almost inaudibly:

"I've got to go, I've got to go and work! If not, it's *Grangou** gonna kill me!"

"I'm sorry. Those are my orders, there's nothing I can do for you. Let the next one come in."

"But Doctor, isn't there any way I can facilitate matters?"

"Facilitate, facilitate! What does that mean, facilitate?"

"You know, Doctor, facilitate."

The doctor threw up his arms and sat down on the edge of the creaky table.

"That, my friend, is very delicate. Very delicate."

"Couldn't I give you a little something anyhow to pass me? I've absolutely got to get by."

"It would be a risk, my friend. I find you very fatigued."

"I've only got forty gourdes, doctor, eight dollars, but if that can help..."

"As far as I'm concerned, I'm speaking in your own best interests, you know that. Now if you absolutely insist upon leaving, that's your problem. You'd simply have to take it easy. But normally, I shouldn't do it."

Quickly, the peasant dug into the pocket of an old shirt, placed with his pants on a green chair near the entrance to the small, over-heated room. He pulled out a wad of crumpled bills, completely faded by sweat and time.

"Here Doctor, take it! Take it!"

The doctor casually held out his hand. One can do one's job properly and make a few exceptions nevertheless. At times, one finds oneself faced with a veritable human drama. All the more so since the Haitian, even in a state of general weakness, has exceptional endurance and stamina. You can still get some work out of them.

"My friend, I accept your offer because I'm putting myself out for you; however, we must consider it a rather token gesture in as much as it is a matter of only eight dollars. You may not be aware that what I am doing for you has no price. I ask you simply not to talk about it. Or, except to those friends of whom you are very sure, and who might possibly have a little health problem. And even at that, I would prefer... If this were known, you would be obliged to stay here. Do you understand?"

---

*Grangou: hunger

32

The peasant understood, and did he ever. Thanking, thanking, thanking the doctor, he received his medical card and the two regulation pills. Now irritated, the doctor dismissed him with a wave of the hand, and looked mechanically at the box of pills. What exactly they were for, he didn't know — malaria maybe — but in any case, he couldn't care less. They told him to give them out, he gave them out. He carefully smoothed out the bills with the edge of his hand. Industrial medicine is a specialty relatively new in Haiti, he thought absently, but one which shows great promise. He put away the banknotes in his pocket with the others. His glance fell on a portrait hung clumsily on the wall. Jean-Claude Duvalier, President for Life, was looking down at him amiably. He didn't look shocked. The doctor returned his stare without batting an eyelash. After all, how much does he put in his pocket out of the 1,225,000 dollars paid by the Dominican Republic?

Petit Pierre Déroseaux, of Pétionville, was standing at attention, his chest thrown out. The business was quickly settled.

"You're in excellent health. Next."

Estimé Mondestin, as usual, was a little tense. Good for the system. The machine functions well.

"Thank you, Doctor."

"Have a good trip, my friend, work hard."

The one who came next had two big varicose veins and was anemic. He didn't have a penny. He was eliminated.

It was rough. The police clubbed the Kongos. A lot of people died. Mondestin had been lucky, as they say. The next day they took his picture. He knew now. It's rather expensive to leave the country. You have to pay to get to the offices, to obtain the medical certificate, the identification papers. You have to pay a lot.

The hiring lasted several more long days. On the last of these, at precisely 11:15, the forces of order intervened brutally and demanded that the premises be immediately vacated. "It's all over, gentlemen, finished!" A long moan rose from the crowd of those who were still hoping. The life seemed to ebb out of their pale, defeated faces. They left in silence. Those who didn't move away fast enough were manhandled by the Macoutes, who were moving around rather more slowly than usual, however, their pockets loaded with coins and bills. Near the livestock market, where the players line up against the wall, fighting cocks under their arms, a man sat down on the ground and wept silently. Two women with baskets on their heads stopped and contemplated him at length, exchanging words in lowered tones. He looked up, stared at them uncomprehendingly, and sighed.

"If only I'd had some money I would have given something to the members of the police to facilitate my inscription. If you pay something, you get enrolled the same day. But I had nothing. I had nothing." Then he began a low monologue in a very weary voice. "Usually it never rains. This year the rain wiped out the gardens. The floods destroyed everything. They swept away the dwellings, the cattle, the goats, the pigs, everything carried away to the sea. A lot of people lost their homes. President Duvalier had asked that something be done at Bassin-Bleu. The foreigners helped, gave clothing. We never received it."

The man got up, and his movements were slow.

"I lost five oxen, I lost five children — dead of starvation and the bloat. The pigs, the goats are dead. I had some chickens, I brought them to Port-au-Prince to sell to leave for Dominicanie. Many of them died en route. I sold one chicken for four and a half gourdes. I spent it all here to eat."

He wept again. Now he had nothing left and he was going home.

Article 2: The State Sugar Council agrees:

b) To provide transportation for the Haitian agricultural workers from Malpasse (Republic of Haiti) — Jimani (Dominican Republic) to the work centers in the Dominican Republic, in busses offering all the guarantees of comfort and security. It is understood that the transportation from the hiring centers to Malpasse will be provided by the Haitian government.

c) To cover the food and lodging expenses for the duration of the trip from the hiring centers to Malpasse, as well as during the trip from Malpasse to the work centers in the Dominican Republic.

The officials set the time and place. They were told to come back the next day. Some of them waited still another day, on account of the insufficient number of *machines.** Transporting fifteen thousand laborers to the border was no small affair. Estimé Mondestin stayed put for forty-eight long hours. Petit Pierre Déroseaux, from Pétionville, exasperated, could keep still no longer. At long last the moment came to board the vehicle. They were all very excited. Each carried his own baggage, whether a small suitcase, a bundle of clothes, or an awkwardly tied up parcel. Some were clutching a little change. Others left with nothing.

There were sixty-five seats on the bus. Sixty-five persons took their seats, not one more. To each a seat. This was not the least of the

---

*Machines: automobiles, buses.

35

day's surprises. When the sixty-sixth, a tall strapping fellow, hauled himself up on the first step, ready to jump aboard, he was summarily ejected. He objected that he was with his friend, that they were from the same village, that they had no intention of separating. As far as everyone present was concerned, the case was closed; there was no doubt in their minds. Haitian buses, the famous "tap-taps," ordinarily agree to start only when they are loaded with twice as many passengers as there are seats. Unexpectedly, the driver appeared quite intransigent, he even called for an inspector, as inflexible as himself.

"If the seat holds three people, you put three people," he declared, smacking his palm on the fender.

"But I'm going to..."

"Standing is forbidden."

"But it's just that..."

"Get off immediately, or else your name will be crossed off the list."

The sixty-sixth was floored. And the others with him. In no Haitian's memory had such a thing been seen. It was incredible. One passenger per seat, one seat per passenger!

The bus started up, filled with young boys, and some not so young too. Not to mention the oldest. The Japanese Isuzu, all daubed with red paint, forced its way through the crowd, its horn blaring. Like a ship leaving for a far journey plays with its siren. Estimé Mondestin was smiling, delighted to leave Haiti to go to work in Dominicanie. He was so happy that he hadn't been able to sleep the night before. Also because the hard ground of the Croix-des-Bouquets had been uncomfortable. It was over now. He knew that he would make it. He gave free rein to his joy as the vehicle lumbered towards Ganthier and Ford Parisien. Then he shut his mouth. They were swallowing poisonous dust on a bad section of unasphalted road. Then they started to sing. They struck up protestant hymns because the driver, who had started, belonged to one of those sects. Three times they took up a stirring tune dealing with the Good Lord, rain, and sun. The bus was running very fast, swallowing the miles and the familiar landscape scattered with shacks, huts, and tumbledowns. They were singing. They were singing. Then they stopped singing. The road was getting really bad, it was actually caved in.

Estimé Mondestin and Dieudonné Labelle became acquainted. It was inevitable. First, because they were sitting side by side. Second, because he'd launched into telling his "war stories" in a loud, strong, and practically all-pervading voice. He'd already been to Dominicanie. This immediately won him the respectful interest of the entire bouncing and jouncing assembly. Questions were flying. "When are we going to start working?" "Who's the boss?" "What does he do?"

"Sometimes the *capataz* knocks on the door at three o'clock in the morning to wake the Kongos."

"Three o'clock in the morning! That's some early, my friend!"

"Except for the smarter Kongos," cut in Labelle. Then, a bit condescendingly: "Me, I never had to worry about those things. I myself am an early riser. *Mwin sé youn nonm ki rinmin lévé boneu*...I'm in the habit of getting up early."

"Oh yeah? At two o'clock then probably," hooted Petit Pierre Déroseaux from the seat behind Mondestin, and whom the seniority of Dieudonné Labelle seemed to irritate.

"And the bosses — are they bad?"

Labelle shook his head, twisting around in his seat.

"The capataz and the majordomo don't give us any trouble, on the contrary, they pamper us. They're paid by the work we do."

Dead silence — except for the noisily backfiring engine. The Haitians were bug-eyed. It was certainly the first time in their lives that someone was going to pamper them.

"And how do you cut the cane?"

Estimé Mondestin's query provoked an hilarious uproar. How do you cut the cane?...Ah ha ha. They whooped with mirth. Where did they find that one, anyway!

Mondestin shrugged. The migration of Haitians to the Dominican Republic, formerly the prerogative of the peasants, has in the past few years included more and more city dwellers in search of subsistence. There are even young people possessing a high school education among the migrants. (They are nevertheless greatly outnumbered by the illiterate.)

"I don't see what's so funny," retorted Mondestin. "I never picked up a machete in my life, I'm a driver! How many of you know how to drive? So don't laugh. I'm from Port-au-Prince, and before, I was driving a van. But for two years now, everything's gone wrong. All my relatives are unhappy — myself, my wife, and my children too. So...how is it — the cane?"

"It's pretty tough," conceded Dieudonné Labelle, "but it all depends if you're gifted or not. Me, I was good at it!"

"Is that so?" snorted Déroseaux. "You don't..."

"The very first day, I worked so good that by noon I cut a 'round-trip.' A *viajé*!"

"What part of Haiti are you from?" marvelled Déroseaux.

"I'm from Gressier."

"You'd cut before?"

"No, I was a beginner," swaggered Labelle, "a rookie, but when you gotta work, you gotta work. If you're Haitian, you better know how to do any kind of work. That's what I came for. When I feel like it, I work without ever looking back." He fell silent for a minute, then pointed heavenwards with an air of authority. "Sometimes the Dominican bosses come out to the fields and cut a piece of sugar cane that comes up to the belt, as a sample measurement to the cutters. Me, I never paid attention to that measurement. I cut however I feel like it. It was so good that the Dominicans themselves said to me: 'My friend, you're an ace!' "

Labelle sat up, discreetly glancing around to assure himself that he'd gained the desired effect.

"I'll never be as good as that," worried Mondestin, sombered by the account of these exploits. He turned towards Petit Pierre Déroseaux. "You think I'll be able to?"

At that moment he almost doubted it, and suddenly felt like turning back.

"Don't worry," rejoined Déroseaux in a low voice, "this guy is a braggart, he's embellishing his stories to sound interesting. It's nothing but a bunch of bullshit!"

Estimé Mondestin sighed. Little by little, the scenery was changing. They were penetrating deeper and deeper into the desolate countryside not far from Saumâtre Pond. Looking south, you could make out the massive bulk of La Selle Peak, carpeted by the dark Forest of Pines. A grassy savanna, bristling with cactus, streamed by in the low-angled light of the setting sun. They were dreaming now. Cows, pigs, calves, baby chickens. Each one already investing his future profits. Cloth, shoes, a roof for the house, some land, some livestock. In the air, thick with dust, floated cattle — or maybe a goat or a pig. A *carreau* of land.* Not in the plain, where the price can get up to more than a thousand dollars per *carreau*; no, not in the plain. But in the mornes, on the side of a hill. "*Tè a ti kal, éritié yo anpil*," murmured a peasant, his head bobbing in time to the jouncing of the bus. "The earth is small but many are the heirs." Then he smiled, without realizing it. He was headed towards his fortune.

But night was already falling.

Estimé Mondestin walked along at a brisk pace, but in a way he was disappointed. The warm breeze caressed his cheek, and in the obscurity of the night, the curving shadows of palms were overhanging a few scattered buildings. He'd imagined a border to be

---

Carreau: approximately 3 square acres.

much more impressive and ceremonial. This one, which separates the island in two, looked sort of dilapidated, almost pathetic. Malpasse, the last locality in Haiti, stretched out under the pallid moon, squashed on the horizon. Further on, a few fragments of mornes, still further, Jimani, the first Dominican city. He had expected better. Flickering lights, scattered in the translucence of the fallen dusk, were blinking weakly. With each step, his little suitcase banged his knee, bounced and landed back along his leg. The group was marching along, all around him, disorder punctuated by nervous exclamations. The conversations, like the men, were moving along at a good clip. They'd been told to get off the buses, and were continuing on foot.

All of a sudden the animation turned to confusion, shouts collided with cries; they'd come to a standstill and didn't quite know why. Someone pushed Estimé Mondestin, a white to be sure, the way his face loomed out of the shadowy domain of obscurity. The stranger flung a few words at him. Mondestin looked urgently at Petit Pierre Déroseaux from Pétionville, who seemed at ease in this confused fog.

"*M pa konprann sa li di!* I don't understand what he's saying!" It was Deiudonné Labelle who responded.

"*L ap palé pangnol monchè!* He's speaking Spanish!"

By this insignificant detail, Estimé Mondestin understood that he'd arrived in Dominicanie. He turned around, a lump in his throat, and felt a warm glow permeating his being.

A few dozen yards further back, an armada of rifle-toting Macoutes was vanishing into the pitch-black night.

There was food, it seemed, for sale. Skinny Dominicans were passing back and forth in front of the Kongos, crouched at the foot of a long white wall. "*Lemonada, lemonada! Pollo, pollo, a medio peso, a medio peso...* Lemonade, sugar, cooked chicken, cookies and sweets." The troop of Kongos waited in silence. They hadn't embarked upon this adventure to spend money, but to make it!

"The Haitian authorities told us they would give us something to eat," grumbled someone. "Well, where is it?"

"And what are we doing here — without any place to sit down or rest?"

"Well, we're sure not going to spend the night."

"You said it!"

"I'm hungry," someone permitted himself to suggest, and that about summed up the situation.

"Yeah, I'm hungry."

The situation, in effect, was this: they were parked in some kind of a pen, illuminated by nothing other than the twinkling stars; several hundred penned in and pacing the ground around a building without walls, a corrugated metal roof hanging between the earth and the sky.

"What kind of warehouse is this?" a Kongo whose stomach was contracted with hunger asked himself out loud.

"It's a warehouse for men," spat an anonymous voice. "I left with clothes," chimed in a face with dry, cracked lips, "but without a penny in my pocket." "Without a penny," complained an echo. "And those guys are selling food."

A little later, there were suddenly promising noises: a rumor of hope, an unhoped-for lift, reverberated through air redolent with sweat. They had seen someone preparing something.

Those who had caught a glimpse of the cauldrons before they were placed on the uneven ground in front of the hastily formed lines of famished men, claimed afterwards that there had been some fish in the rice. Those who had received their meager portion on a piece of paper, and who, in consequence, knew better, burst out laughing and objected with vehemence that there certainly hadn't been any. Questioned on the truth of the matter, Petit Pierre Déroseaux from Pétionville, who through simple curiosity had witnessed the entire operation, did not hesitate to say what he'd observed.

"It was the Dominicans who stole the fish. They took out all the fish and left us the rice. The Dominicans ate the fish. I saw them. They took it all. All we got was rice! They ate the fish!"

The rice had been very badly prepared; it wasn't cooked. Only those who were really very hungry had swallowed it. The food was so bad that Estimé Mondestin, who may be a lot of things but certainly not dainty, left it.

It was true that the Dominicans had eaten the fish.

Mondestin took a few hesitant steps. He had a little money left, why not buy something? He approached a small group where he had already noticed a hawker, and walked smack into a heated argument. A Haitian was gesticulating.

"We want to buy something, you know, buy something. We know how much it costs. But you have to pay in American dollars. We have gourdes, but they don't want them. They want Dominican pesos or American dollars! Are we Dominicans or Americans? Are they going to go and get Americans to cut their cane? Aren't we at the border? Isn't our country a country? Isn't our currency a currency? But no! They don't want it, these Dominicans!"

No one was accepting gourdes, and gourdes were all they had. Theoretically, it seemed that a Haitian inspector was going to conduct the exchange the next morning. In the meantime, nothing.

Except to go through a middleman. There, near a lush mango tree, was a small man who was ready to conduct the operation, but at what a rate! He was offering one peso for ten gourdes. Mondestin launched into an almost rapid calculation. One American dollar is worth five Haitian gourdes. One Dominican peso is worth one American dollar. So, a peso is worth... No. A dollar equals a peso, and five gourdes equal a dollar. Thus, a peso equals... It seemed to him that it was a peso for five gourdes, six at the most, for the transaction; it seemed to him also that ten gourdes for one peso...that was overdoing it. He couldn't have sworn to it, but that's what it seemed to him... It's at school that you learn to count correctly. In doubt, he let it drop. Still...The little man was busy. It was inevitable. Even at that exorbitant rate.

Next, they went to lie down on the ground, since, for a few days, those were apparently the only accommodations that had been reserved for them.

"They told me everything was arranged," sighed a Kongo, propping his one and only treasure, an extra pair of pants, under his head. "They even said, 'you're not going to sleep in just any hotel...' "

"But my friend, what are you complaining about?" quipped Petit Pierre Déroseaux, curling up as best he could on the bare ground. *"Otel Splendid la li bon, li fré, épi li pa tro chè!* This Hotel Splendide is fine, it's nice and cool and it's not too expensive! We're really lucky!"

He was thinking bitterly of the humid chilliness soon to attack them.

They were resigned.

Some even managed to sleep.

The Kongos were getting in line to go into the clinic, a stable from which the horses had been removed.

The hapless peasant was shouting, crying, explaining, begging, and spluttering. The two Dominican gendarmes were dragging him firmly towards the open door — in the direction of the border. The stupid Haitian could work himself up all he liked, they didn't understand a word of Creole, his language. And they didn't give a goddamn. He did.

"I paid!!!" he screamed. "I paid thirty gourdes to the National Security Volunteers, I paid forty gourdes to the doctor, you've got to let me work! There's nothing wrong with me, you've got to let me pass!"

"Callate, Haitiano grosero!"

A violent shove propelled him several yards and he shut up, the wind knocked out of him.

"What's going on?" demanded Estimé Mondestin. "Why are they sending him away?"

"The Haitian doctors accepted payoffs from some of the Kongos, but the Dominicans reject them when they see the diseases."

"Will they get their money back?"

Déroseaux burst out laughing.

"Not a cent! And he's not the first, either. There's already been several sent back. A lot of them, even."

The Dominican doctors weren't fooling around. X-rays, malaria check, detection of venereal disease. Those who'd paid off the Haitian doctors had been royally screwed.

When Mondestin arrived in the vicinity of the table where the male nurses were bustling about, he cried out at the sight of the syringe. Déroseaux frowned. The others, intimidated, kept quiet but were no less troubled. Two Dominicans leaning against the wall doubled over, laughing at their fright.

A man screamed in pain, his mouth wide open and his teeth bared as they punctured him with the needle. "Let's not exaggerate," said a Haitian, with dignity. "In my opinion, he's a little squeamish."

The speculation was flying thick and fast.

"It's to get rid of venereal disease," suggested someone. "No, it's to drug us." "Not at all, it's to make us work harder," corrected another, who didn't know anything.

"*Qué es eso?*" asked Dieudonné Labelle, who knew a little Spanish, of two Dominicans who were watching them.

One of the men responded, then they both sniggered nastily.

"What does he say?"

"He says it's a sterilizer to prevent us from screwing the Dominican women!"

The guy put his hands in his pockets, turned toward his companion and rattled off a few words in Spanish, his eyes glittering.

"What did he say?"

"He says anyway it's useless because the Dominican women wouldn't sleep with us. He says they don't like nègres* and that they're absolutely right."

"Let him keep his *bouzins*," growled Déroseaux, his fists clenched. "We've got our own women and they're not whores."

He glared at the Dominican and his eyes flamed with barely suppressed anger.

Nègre: In this translation, the term *nègre* has often been left in the original French in an effort to retain authenticity. In Creole, spoken by a Haitian, it simply means "man." Used otherwise, it has a somewhat pejorative connotation, ranging from the outdated use of "Negro" to the more derogatory "nigger." — TRANS.

"*Raza de maldición*," the latter belched slowly, and his face twisted with disgust. "Cursed race!"

Mondestin regarded him with surprise. Why did this Dominican with almost white skin appear to be insulting them?

Pretty soon there was a rumor going round, its origin unknown. "Watch out! The shot is horrible, like the kind they give to animals. Anybody who can't take it gets sent back. If you don't fall over, you've made it. Grit your teeth!"

Estimé Mondestin did not fall over, but he really hurt.

"I don't know if it's a drug or what," groaned a Kongo, "but this is the kind of a shot they give to horses!"

Mondestin resigned himself to his fate. After all, he was lucky. He was in Dominican territory. Things would certainly get better.

Once again they were photographed. A not-very-friendly Haitian inspector changed gourdes for pesos. He didn't have much work to do. They were made to line up again. This they were used to. They took away their passports, their identity papers. Petit Pierre Déroseaux from Pétionville objected to parting with his documents. Without them, he felt naked. It was as though he no longer existed. The Dominicans insisted, yelled at him, insulted him, and finally went to look for a "gro-nèg" who arrived furious. A Haitian inspector.

"What's going on here?"

"They want to take my papers."

"Well then give 'em to them! Give 'em to them!"

"But what are they going to do with them?"

"Your documents will be sent to the Haitian Embassy in Santo Domingo. You have nothing to worry about."

"But what if I need them?"

"You don't need them any more."

"But I might need them!"

"No more, I tell you. Don't you understand?"

"And what if I want to get them back?"

The inspector was getting irritated; he raised his voice and stamped his foot.

"Look, you don't have any reason to want to get them back. From now on, you are completely in the hands of competent organizations. The Embassy will return your papers when the Dominican government tells them to, after the *zafra*."

"But," rebelled Déroseaux, "what if I want to leave before?"

"Leave before! You're not here to go sightseeing, my dear friend, you are going to work! You'll leave when you are told to. And not before."

"So I'm a prisoner, then?"

"You are not a prisoner. Besides, you'll be given a new identity card, a Dominican one."

He should have said so. In that case it was different. Déroseaux calmed down.

All the same he was a little worried.

He shouldn't have been. Soon after, they were each given a magnificent card with their photograph affixed.

But he should have been. This card was not a "residency" card, but a piece of paper issued by the sugar factories without any legal value whatsoever. Outside of the plantations to which they were destined, they had no further legal existence.

They were very careful not to explain that to them.

They were piled into trucks, the "Cataré." They hardly had the leisure to admire Lake Enriquillo, one hundred thirty-three feet below sea level (its caymen* and its iguanas), which they passed alongside, however, for a number of miles. Nor did they see, arriving in Barahona, the spectacular palm-fringed coastline, the one they say is dazzling, (the Caribbean's Most Bewitching). All that was not for them, but for the tourists. Descended from the trucks, they were put in a barbed wire enclosure with soldiers and dogs. There was no watchtower. There they spent the rest of the day, and when night came, they were shown a large building, without beds, without a mattress, without walls, but with a concrete slab. By these distinguishing characteristics, they recognized a dormitory. For the first time since their departure, it occurred to some of them that they were being treated like livestock. They were distributed some sugar, for they were very hungry. "Not like livestock," protested Petit Pierre Déroseaux from Pétionville, who liked precision. "Like dogs."

Granulated sugar, thus, was what they had for dinner. It was given to them in total darkness. Blackout.

They spent the night, again, on the bare ground, and some of them started to cough. The next morning they were brought some water, and some more sugar, the same as the night before. Now they understood why the power had been cut. The sugar was filthy, full of dirt, germs, and god knows what. "Not like dogs," corrected Déroseaux bitterly, "like pigs!" With that, he took off in great strides toward a Dominican who had the well fed look of assurance of those in charge.

"We demand something to eat other than this filth," he began,

---

*Cayman: Central and South American reptile similar to the alligator but often resembling the crocodile. — TRANS.

in a strong and determined voice.

Someone had to translate for the "authority," just what he was talking about. His face hardened, his muscles tensed. He flung a few curt words in their direction before walking away as if nothing had happened.

"What did he say?" stammered Déroseaux, disconcerted.

"He said that all the Haitians have been sold to their government. He says they paid for us. He says we only have one right, and that is to keep quiet."

Petit Pierre Déroseaux's features seemed to contort. He spun around on himself unconsciously, caught a glimpse of his companions standing silently, their arms hanging down at their sides, and the soldiers, arms cradling their rifles. He stopped, looked down at his feet. Dirty sugar for every meal! Sure, he'd vaguely heard talk about the one million, two hundred twenty-five thousand dollars paid to Duvalier; but. . . but what?

And what if they really had been sold?

Plantations all around. Miles and miles of plantations. Sugar cane, in undulating waves, for as far as the eye could see, all the way to the distant bluish hills. At the foot of a gentle slope, a darker spot marked the shadow of a white cloud hanging between the fierce sun and the green *zafra* carpet. Far away, the purring of a motor rose softly, grazed the long graceful stalks engorged with sugar, lost momentum in a small valley, emerged once again at the edge of the immense expanse, and alighted on the first of the barracks. Antoine the *viejo* looked up, took a few steps, and stopped at the edge of the trail. His wrinkled face and his gray-white hair stood out for a moment from the leprous rectangle of the camp. He blinked his eyes. He could just make out the first truck of the season, a tiny, wobbly black spot in the distance.

"Here come the Kongos!" he cried softly, then louder and louder, "The Kongos are coming!"

He spun around running.

The news quickly made the tour of the barracks. Heads appeared in the doorways of the shacks, at first hesitant, then questioning, exclaiming at the response; there were many men, a few women, a horde of children, many Negroes, few whites. An observer would have been surprised. Right in the heart of the Dominican Republic, while the Kongos had not yet arrived, the great majority of the inhabitants of this miserable place seemed to be Haitian.

"The Kongos are coming! The Kongos are coming!" The cry took off in every direction, took flight in light circles, spread out over the expanses, caught its breath and the wind, soon extending beyond the limits of the camp, caught hold of a pueblo that seemed to hear nothing, swelled in the valleys, reached other villages, a few cities, emerged at the highest mountains in the Caribbean arch, resounding in a single blast over all the territory of the Republic whose inhabitants were listening to the news, heads held high. "Here come the Kongos, on whom depend the wealth and prosperity of our country! Here come the Kongos!"

Up and down the hills and dales, and over the plains, wagons crammed with men, old wagons for young men, young men who'd only been given sugar and water, were clanking and clamoring along, surrounded by sugar cane, stopping every six or seven hundred yards at a clearing. The *batey*. About a hundred and fifty Kongos got off at every stop. The train started up again brutally, jolting the rest of its human cargo.

Throughout the entire Dominican territory, an army of trains, but also of trucks: fifteen thousand Kongos for the *bateys* of the CEA.

The economy of the Dominican Republic is based principally upon the exportation of sugar to the United States, and therefore upon the cultivation of the cane on sixteen immense plantations divided into three main types of ownership. The National Sugar Council (the CEA), a nationalized enterprise depending directly on the Dominican state, owns more than 247,000 acres, distributed over twelve *ingenios* (the complex made up of the refinery, in which only Dominican laborers work, and the neighboring plantations which supply them, worked by 70 percent to 90 percent Haitians). The "Vicini" business, one of the ruling Dominican families whose office in New York was established in 1882: three *ingenios*. Gulf & Western, the gigantic North American multinational, is involved in multiple sectors of the Dominican economy, and controls with nearly absolute sovereignty all that goes on within its immense "kingdom": 308,875 acres of cane, 17,600 laborers grouped in 125 bateys, out of which comes 40 percent of the total Dominican sugar production.

The contract signed with Duvalier for the hiring of the 15,000 Kongos is (theoretically) to furnish the manpower for the CEA alone—that is, the state-owned enterprise.

Estimé Mondestin and his companions' groups arrived in a truck. From Barahona, they'd been driven to San Luis. From there, they were carted off once again.

The driver didn't slow down to negotiate the curve. The Kongos were thrown scrambling against the wooden rails of the pickup. They were standing up in the back of the truck, packed in on top of one another, continually bumping and banging into the packages on the floor and each other, rattling and reeling to the rhythm of the chaos.

They were exhausted, had no longer even the strength to speak, to comment on the scenery. Besides, there was nothing to comment upon, they could see nothing but cane, and if by chance it wasn't cane, it was again still more cane that they saw. The vehicle slowed down. It seemed to them that it was tackling an upgrade; the engine was struggling while the driver down-shifted.

Without a transition, without an intermediate zone, a cluster of habitations appeared. The truck braked, skidded in the dust and ground to a halt in a deserted spot, at a slight distance from the group of huts, the fog of dust raised by the wheels slowly settling. The Kongos were standing motionless, grey with the soot of many long miles of route, overcome by the sun and the voyage. At the moment, no one thought of budging.

"You can get out now," bellowed the driver, slamming his door, "*Rápido! Rápido!*"

He was in a hurry. They didn't pay him much for each trip, he only had one thought in mind and that was to finish up as fast as possible, get rid of these cursed Kongos and leave again, immediately.

"*Vámonos, vámonos! Rápido!*"

The first Kongos were getting ready to obey. A man was running toward them, a black like them, shouting at them all the way, and in Creole.

"Don't get out! Whatever you do, don't get out!"

Antoine the viejo slowed down, trying desperately to catch his breath, and walked the last few yards.

"Don't get out!"

The driver, with a threatening look, turned toward the newcomer. "Who the hell asked for this one's opinion anyway?"

"He's a *viejo*," said Dieudonné Labelle to Mondestin, "an old-timer. A veteran."

"Faster, goddammit. Get out! Get out!"

"No! Don't get out!"

"But why?"

For the first time, a Kongo intervened in what was happening.

"There's no one here to receive you. The authorities from the sugar factory aren't here. If you get down, you're going to set here and rot for two days!"

Antoine the viejo swore softly. Every year it was the same thing. Contrary to what is said in the contract, nothing is provided for the arriving Kongos. And since nothing is provided, no one starts to even think about getting organized until they arrive. The savanna, a livestock pen, no roof, nothing — as long as the responsibles aren't there. If it rains, they're out of luck; they stay outside and get wet. You have to wait for the bosses. But the bosses are in no hurry. Sometimes they arrive two days late.

"Don't get down unless they give you a roof."

The driver flew into a rage, started yelling at Antoine the viejo, and they launched into a long argument in a language unknown to the majority — Spanish. At every other phrase, every other interjection, the driver ranted and raved in the direction of the Kongos:

"*Vámonos*, Kongos! Get out!"

The Kongos didn't understand anything. The driver was screaming even louder, and they were understanding less and less.

A crowd started trickling out of the shacks, approached the truck, encircled it, expressed one opinion, then another, joined in the discussion, and by listening carefully to the ever-increasing buzz, one thing was evident. All these Haitians seemed to speak Creole and Spanish at the same time. But the driver didn't give a damn. It wasn't his problem, all he wanted was to get going.

In the end, it was the Kongos who got tired of it first. "Me, I'm getting out," said one, "stand up in the truck or on the ground, I don't see any difference." "Me too," said another, "you can't sleep in this crate anyway." "Besides," added a third, "we'll have to get off sooner or later. Better not attract any attention."

Antoine the viejo watched them descend with concern and disapproval.

"You're wrong, boys! You know, if I tell you something it's for your own good."

Others followed the first ones, the last ones followed the others, each one following another, each one followed by another one; soon the truck was empty.

In a certain sense, Estimé Mondestin was very satisfied.

This time, they had really arrived.

Article 2: The State Sugar Council (CEA) agrees:

e) To put at the disposal of the Haitian agricultural workers and their families, from the date of their entry in Dominican territory, during their sojourn in the different work centers, and up until the date of their departure from the Dominican Republic, dwelling units or communal apartments providing all the conditions of hygiene and sanitation required by law, as well as furnishings (tables, chairs, bed). The roof of these habitations must be covered in order that the workers not be exposed to inclement weather.

f) To permit the Supervisors and Inspectors of the Haitian Embassy in Santo Domingo to visit the premises of the latter in the Dominican Republic. Moreover, the dwelling units must be equipped with metal beds and mattresses, provided with drinking water and proper facilities for baths and other conveniences of the above-mentioned workers. The installation of proper, hygienic dining halls is compulsory, so that the workers will have at their disposal suitable places for their daily meal . . .

Article 23: The Haitian agricultural worker who, upon his arrival in the Dominican State sugar factories, is temporarily not given work, will receive an allotment of 0.75 pesos a day for his food.

They were idling about in the middle of Batey 7A. They would have liked to look around a bit, check out in detail this new place,

49

their new home. They had been forbidden to budge. Some Dominican had given them the order the night before. You stay right there, you'll be taken care of.

They were taking a look at the buildings from the spot where they'd been parked. The shacks appeared to be in a state of dilapidation, ancient, made of rotten boards. That was the first impression. When they arrived, the viejos had told them: "You are Kongos!" Big deal! As if they didn't know it. But nobody had really explained to them who were the viejos. Estimé Mondestin had observed them with surprise — there seemed to be a lot of them — and wondered for a moment if they were Haitians or Dominicans. "Those are the viejos," repeated Dieudonné Labelle, who seemed to know the goings-on of the place. From then on, Estimé Mondestin knew that those Negroes there, who seemed to speak Dominican and Haitian, were called the viejos. That was all he knew. The one he was watching, but all the others as well, moved about slowly, seemed to be in a very bad state. He tottered and tattered along at a snail's pace.

"They are Haitian," specified Dieudonné Labelle, by way of further enlightenment. "Haitians who live here permanently."

"How many are there?"

"No idea. Pretty many, I believe."

"But who exactly are they?" insisted Estimé Mondestin.

Dieudonné Labelle gestured scornfully.

"Well, my friend, all these Haitians in Santo Domingo are illegals, or ones who were sent but never went back to Haiti. They live like dogs. They don't get any respect. Anyhow, *yo pa bon.* It's no good. Since they don't need a helluva lot to live, a plate of rice, a little oil, they consider themselves happy. But if you've got kids to feed, that's not enough, is it?"

"If they are Haitians, they are going to be our companions!"

"No. We arrive, they look us over, but soon they won't even see us. Not even as Haitians. They take themselves for Dominicans and treat us like Kongos."

"You think?"

"Of course. Even us — who've been here before, they treat us like Kongos."

"But we are Kongos, as I understand."

"Yes, we are Kongos. But for them and for the Dominicans, it's the same thing as a beast of burden. They don't want anything to do with us."

Estimé Mondestin shook his head and took a few hesitant steps. He was surprised. If a Haitian meets another Haitian, they should shake hands!

"You'll see," cried Dieudonné Labelle. "It's with the Dominicans that they communicate, they think they're Dominicans."

For the moment, it did not appear so. They seemed very interested, hovering around the Kongos, asking them questions. "How's everything in Port-au-Prince? Has the country changed this year?" "And the women—still as beautiful in Jacmel?" "Does anyone know the Mirebois family?" Among the viejos there were some from the Cape, from Jacmel, sons of Léogane, survivors from the northeast, exiles from Ouanaminthe. They were inspecting the new arrivals to see if there wasn't, by chance, somebody they knew among these cane cutters.

"How is the *zafra* here?" Estimé Mondestin asked a viejo who had spoken a few words to him.

"It's no good," said the man, with a smile so pale that it didn't even resemble a smile.

"It's no good?"

"It's a disaster."

Estimé Mondestin gazed at him, astonished. A disaster in Dominicanie! "*M pa konprann.* But why?"

"It's bad, the *zafra.*"

"But why bad? Isn't there any cane?"

"There's plenty of cane. But it's got no weight and we're paid by the weight! Well, it's not the cane that's bad, it's that the scales are fixed."

"How much do we make?"

"A dollar thirty-five a ton."

"Is that good?"

"No, it's bad. Before they paid us less but we earned more. I could make myself thirty or forty dollars while now I can't even manage twenty."

"A day?" asked Mondestin, his eyes popping.

The viejo opened his mouth strangely, staring at him for a second in silence. Then he burst out laughing.

"A day?! Ha! Ha! Ha! No my friend, for two weeks!" This time it was Mondestin who was staggered, thought he hadn't heard right. He hesitated.

"But. . . but they told us in Haiti fifteen dollars a day! They told us. . ."

"Yes, you too, they told you too. . ." The man lowered his head, overwhelmed. "Poor, poor, poor people," he repeated softly. "If you only knew what you were getting into."

Estimé Mondestin was perfectly still, didn't know what to do, didn't know what to say, didn't know any more. The man closed his eyes, continued as if obsessed.

"The scale is fixed in cahoots with the *tornillos.* So they bring in a vehicle that weighs ten or twelve tons and it only shows four or five! That's the way it goes."

"But how long have you been here?"

The man thought for a second, his lips moved silently.

"Twelve years."

"Twelve years!"

"Yes, it's at least twelve years."

"And why do you stay?"

"I left my wife and my four children in Haiti," said the other, not responding to the question.

"Me, too," cut in Estimé Mondestin, "but I only have three." (Questioning look.) "Children that is, not wives." (Brief laugh.)

"I got into debt to leave."

"Me too, that's exactly it, me too," Estimé Mondestin heard himself exclaim.

"I've got nothing to go back with."

"Nothing!?"

"Nothing!"

"Nothing after twelve years?"

"Nothing. How can you go back when you've got debts?"

"You can't," said Mondestin.

"I'd go to jail."

"Yes, to jail." Mondestin thought of his usurer, felt the cold sweat on the back of his neck. "Any news?"

"I don't know how to write, and my family either."

"It's awful," pronounced Mondestin, who in listening to the old man, had for an instant the eerie feeling he heard himself talking. He dismissed this stupid idea with a brusque toss of his head. "But you are going back!"

"I've been here for twelve years. Hope of returning? No, it's hard to imagine." The man let a tear fall silently and ground it with his foot. "It's hard to imagine."

Estimé Mondestin shuddered violently.

But it is true that once the initial flurry of interest passed, the viejos welcomed them without too many smiles and with an enthusiasm at most lukewarm.

To tell the truth, it's a long story. It starts around 1915. The United States, taking advantage of the First World War, jealous of the remaining European presence in the Caribbean, enforces the famous Monroe Doctrine. America for the Americans. For the North Americans, it goes without saying. Armed with a big smile — for the propaganda, and with a big stick, for the rest. During the Spanish-

American War, the "*splendid little war*"* (1898), whose principal objective was to insure ample sugar provisions for the American People, Puerto Rico and Cuba had already been annexed. Next, Haiti, from 1915 to 1934, and the Dominican Republic, from 1916 to 1925, are occupied. There are undoubtedly American nationals to protect. Profound economic transformations are imposed on both countries.

In the Dominican Republic, the cultivation of sugar cane is intensively developed. In Haiti, sisal and coffee.

The introduction of big companies in Haiti accelerates the breakdown of the small traditional peasant economy. The peasants abandon their gardens, regroup in poverty-stricken agglomerations near the big plantations. The dispossessions multiply, and challenge — thanks to the machinations of a well-orchestrated judicial scenario — the peasants' right to occupy state-owned land without a title. In the absence of any records, the door is left wide open to the most flagrant and arbitrary expropriation. The occupier and his accomplices have a field day.

In 1918, under the direction of a former officer, Charlemagne Péralte, fifteen thousand Haitian peasants revolt against the Yankees, the reinstatement of the feudal system of obligatory work for the landlords, and forced labor on the roads. A veritable extermination campaign is engaged, led by the U.S. Marines, aided by their indigenous reinforcements, the Haitian gendarmes. This uprising will mark a turning point in the world history of repression. For the first time, the Marines establish an infantry-aviation liaison, and put into practice the techniques for sealing off, and search-and-destroy, that will be incorporated into the doctrines of counterguerrilla warfare. They will use the experience acquired shortly thereafter against Sandino, the "General of Free Men" in Nicaragua. Thousands of peasants on the side of the rebels are killed.

It is at this moment that the price of sugar cane, and its demand, augment dramatically, since the First World War had considerably diminished European sugar beet production. A fantastic expansion of the sugar industry immediately follows in the Caribbean, under American baton.

The *ingenios* (combination plantation-factory) devour the land in the Dominican Republic. In 1918, the *Central Romana*, one of the largest sugar complexes in the world, was firmly established and is still functioning today. In 1925, when the Marines left Santo Domingo, of the 21 existing ingenios, 11 belonged to two American consortiums, *The Central Romana Incorporated*, previously cited, which is a subsidiary of the *South Puerto Rico Sugar Co.*, and the *West India*

---

*In English in the original. — TRANS.

Finance Co. Five others maintain strong ties with one or the other of the two groups. These two corporations represent 80 percent of the total worth of the ingenios in the country and the same percentage of the total land surface dedicated to the sugar cane.

In Haiti, the effects of the unequal distribution of resources and of the demographic pressure which was forcing out the inhabitants even before the American occupation are aggravated by this foreign presence, the expropriations which ensue, and the repression which accompanies the whole situation. A vast propaganda campaign about the employment possibilities which exist in the ingenios in the vicinity is then orchestrated by the official press of Americanized Haiti. *"Sell your land if you still have any left, don't regret it if it's been taken over, it's not worth anything. Go and settle in Cuba or in the Dominican Republic. There is sugar cane to be cut, you will get rich!"*

From the Central Plateau, from the North and the Northeast, 20,000 Haitian peasants cross the border in thirteen months — direction, the Dominican Republic. These cunning tactics not only precipitate the departure of a multitude of peasants still hanging on to their land, but also deprive the revolt of its grass roots — the dispossessed.

In the Dominican Republic, opening the country to the Haitian labor force and that of the Virgin Islands permits the creation of a category of immigrant workers easily maneuvered into accepting wages on a level inferior to that of the most basic subsistence.

The occupier holds all the trumps.

If, in 1929, American agricultural investments reach 70 million dollars in the Dominican Republic, and 919 million in Cuba, they will not exceed 8.7 million in Haiti. The role of this country is already clearly marked: it will be a reservoir of cheap labor for the exploitation of the plantations in neighboring territories.

The years pass. The economic, social, and political situation of the Haitian peasantry continues to deteriorate. A new phenomenon appears regarding the small Haitian sugar industry. Up until World War II, the family-owned plantations relied upon sharecroppers, the *métayers*, the *dé mouatyé* (the two halves), to work the fields. The generation holding the power around 1947-48 decides, after numerous incidents with the peasants, to take back the total direction of the land. The Haitian peasant becomes an agricultural worker, hears the ongoing propaganda, and believes he will find better pay in the Dominican Republic than he receives in Haiti. Outside of the sugar activities, those who continue to live under the regime of the *dé mouatyé* produce on land which does not belong to them. They are obliged to pay all the production expenses. Knowing they must give up half the fruit of their labor, they are content to produce the minimum. They are not interested in improving, investing, or innovating. They don't even know if they will still be on the land the following year. Their reasoning is simple. *"I'm going to raise what I need to live, my family and me, and I will go and work in Dominicanie. I'll work the season there, and considering the high wages (!), this money will be all profit!"* What he doesn't know, is that he will earn practically nothing, that he will sink into debt, find himself in a trap, and, often, will not be able to come back.

The migration becomes institutionalized, an immediate solution to the deep-rooted problems the Haitian bourgeoisie does not care to resolve.

In 1960, Fidel Castro, leading his *barbudos*, takes power in Cuba. Like the Trujillo regime (Dominican dictatorship), Batista's Cuba stooped to the aid of smugglers and slave-traders, and signed on cheap labor in Haiti. With the arrival of the new regime and its reforms, the conditions of employment and of the existence in the plantations changed drastically. The Castro regime put an end to the slave trade, "cubanized" the Haitian labor force that remained, and gave it back its human dignity.

The United States, of course, organized a blockade, and boycotted Cuban sugar.

A shot in the arm for the Dominican plantations which take up the slack.

During this time, in Haiti, the situation becomes outright catastrophic. Under the heel of Francois "Papa Doc" Duvalier, racketeering runs rampant, and the people are systematically bled for all they've got. An entire country is taken hostage by a terrorist mafia. The Haitian government distributes the land to its accomplices, its favorites, its lackeys. One and one half percent of the population thus owns 66.2 percent of the arable land, and doesn't even make use of half of it. Three hundred thousand peasant families live without land. On 14 November 1966, an agreement is made between the government of Balaguer (ex-lieutenant of the dictator Trujillo, who in the meantime had been assassinated) and that of "Papa Doc," determining the financial arrangements for the employment operation of the Haitian agricultural workers immigrating to the Dominican Republic for each sugar season. An accord still in force today. The slave trade is made official. On 20 January 1967, the first annual contract is signed for the dispatch of 20,000 workers to the sugar fields. Besides the wages paid to the workers, the Haitian government received a prime of ten dollars a head, and of forty-nine dollars for the contract of each worker, a total of $1,380,000 which never appeared in the Haitian State official budget. *This contract is for the protection of our nationals*, the mafia in power in Haiti has claimed continuously. In fact, it allows them to get their cut of the action. Further, the 15,000 *braceros* sold presently, by contract each year, only constitute the visible part of the iceberg, an almost negligible augmentation, needed for the peak period. The bulk of the sugar industry's menial labor force is composed of the sons, grandsons, descendants of those who came, over the years, to irrigate the Dominican soil with their sweat, and who stayed, trapped in a machine that they make run and which methodically crushes them. In 1920, the official count listed 28,258 Haitians in the Dominican Republic. In 1970, the Dominican Planning Commission estimated more than 100,000. Today, there may be about 250,000.

The viejos.

The Dominicans did not, in fact, take care of them, and in a way, neither did the viejos. At nightfall, they were merely rounded up by a silent white man who distributed two rolls with a piece of sausage and a bottle of cola to each one. Thus they didn't starve. Estimé Mondestin, Petit Pierre Déroseaux, and Dieudonné Labelle, accompanied by a small group of the other Kongos, took refuge for the night in the semblance of a shelter they'd spotted at the edge of a long series of shacks. A few twisted wooden poles held up the main beams on which had been placed a now rusty corrugated metal roof. They'd moved a few rocks and small boulders out of the way, and lay down among their meager bundles. They groaned at the discomfort, and one of the Kongos got up, headed for an apparently empty shack facing them, just to check it out. It was a large, low-lying edifice, also covered with corrugated metal; punctuated every three or four yards by a closed green door, over the upper right hand corner of which were what appeared to be six tiny rectangular air holes. The Kongos stopped, surveyed its rather uninviting aspect, and pushed open a squeaky door.

"What is it?" cried Déroseaux.

From where he was sitting, the unveiling revealed nothing but a black hole.

"It's very dirty, my friend. It's a stable for the animals, I think." The Kongo stepped in, and emerged a few seconds later, visibly disgusted.

"It's mighty dirty, but until we get our lodgings that they promised, we could maybe. . ."

He didn't finish. A Dominican who was passing, a small man with a nasty look topped off by a white plastic safari hat, a *capataz*, they learned later — that is, a boss, in the sweat-soaked language of the batey — started bellowing at him in bad Creole. "What the hell

56

are you doing there, boy?" he snarled. "You've got no business there! You better wait for orders, and we're the ones who give the orders around here! Get back where you came from! *Y rápido, por favor!*"

The Kongo returned to the group grumbling, and the group grumbled also; if it were a question of something habitable, they could understand, but that was nothing but a pigsty. They grumbled and grumbled. Not only that, this capataz had insulted them in passing, had sworn at them in Spanish, but they understood that it was a curse because it's the tune that makes the song, and a curse, be it in Creole or Spanish, is a curse is a curse. So one of the Kongos yelled something at the capataz, backed up by a chorus of the other Kongos, and it was a viejo who happened to be passing who had calmed them, an old man with stooped shoulders. "If you answer him back, things will go badly for you," he told them.

They had accepted the situation, and once more went to bed on the ground. But it was the last time for sure, they'd sworn to themselves.

The next morning, from four o'clock until eight o'clock, the Dominicans ignored them, not the slightest attention until ten o'clock.

At eleven o'clock, the encroaching noise of vehicles moving about stirred the overwhelming dry heat, and they understood, by the activity that was triggered off in the batey, that those in charge had arrived.

They were all Dominicans, and all very important personages. There was the "*el señor administrador*," tall, dry, and curt; the "*el señor mayordomo*," very obsequious towards the administrator, and who left a trail of heady perfume in his wake; there were numerous capataces, a dozen or so at the moment, they, too, very obsequious toward *el señor mayordomo*. The entire party, with all the obsequiousness, from the bottom to the top, very busy.

The administrator is the commander-in-chief of the ingenio, the head of the factory and the plantations. Everything comes and goes through him. The sugar is extracted in his factory, under the still virgin smokestacks in this beginning of the season.

The majordomo is the chief administrator of the batey, and its most important personage.

The capataces, the foremen, assign and survey the work, and are in the plantation all day long.

When the season is in full swing, the administrator is rarely seen, and always accompanied by a great deal of fanfare. The majordomo makes his round in the fields in an automobile. The capataz on horseback. The Haitians on foot.

That's fine. That way you can see at first glance with whom you are dealing.

The administrators and the majordomos are always armed to the teeth, revolvers and tommy guns. They never have any discussions with the Haitians.

So, at 11:30 the bigwigs had appeared, and examined the Kongos from afar, as one would to buy a mule or a work animal at a livestock auction.

They'd been lined up, a straight line, *por favor*, and had remained standing in the dehydrating sun for not more than two hours. They were very hungry, but only one of them fainted, a farm worker from Léogane, a guy not very tough. A capataz kindly revived him with a few kicks. It appeared that you shouldn't waste water. It was true, they hadn't drunk anything, either; they would have preferred not to think about it.

Estimé Mondestin was very surprised when they led him and the rest of the line in front of the long, low building from the night before, the one where they'd gotten chewed out. Some capataces opened the doors, and the air was filled with a very unpleasant odor of mustiness and shit. It was thus a habitation, twenty feet wide and two hundred feet long, divided off every twenty feet by a partition. Each room so demarcated had a door with a number. Empty, windowless cells, practically devoid of aeration in this climate. A cot or two, a bunk bed here and there, none with mattresses, made up a vague semblance of furniture. And that was it. Really nothing else at all. They were herded in and assigned four to a cubicle. They entered, blinking, swung around, and around again. No use in searching for anything. Four walls. Not a table, not a chair, nothing in the way of hygienic facilities, not even a sink. Nothing. Nothing but the four walls.

"How are we going to sleep? It's empty here!"

They went out again, distraught, bewildered, amazed at the appearance of the cottages. They had never been maintained, were strewn with garbage and junk. It was not at all what they had hoped for.

Estimé Mondestin and Petit Pierre Déroseaux bailed out the sixth cubicle in the company of two peasants they didn't know, a certain Brutus, stalwart and silent, and one named Gérard André, of a more delicate build, wearing a superb flowered shirt, undoubtedly recently purchased. A slightly sad smile on a face without other visible distinguishing characteristics. Petit Pierre Déroseaux contemplated the one and only rusty tubular iron bunk bed, without a mattress, shoved in the corner of the obscenely naked room. Two beds — beds, huh! — for four people. He burst outside, furious, and hailed a capataz.

"And just where are we going to sleep, huh? Where?"

"*Aqui mismo, hombre!* Right here."

"That's impossible! That thing is no house!"

The capataz burst out laughing, moved his massive frame a few steps, and pushed back the wide-brimmed hat which shaded a good part of his face.

"Better get used to it, my boy."

"I've got a right to refuse, even."

"I'd recommend it," snickered the capataz. "These lodgings were built in 1940 by Trujillo to shelter animals! I wonder if it's not even too good!"

"We won't sleep there," stated Brutus, emerging from the vile chamber.

"You'll sleep where you're told to. If you don't want to sleep, do whatever you want; stay outside, the stars are beautiful at night."

"We're not going to sleep there!"

"Listen to me and listen good, *hombrecito.* The Dominican government bought you for *mucho cuarto, anpil lajan,* big bucks, *ou konprann?*" And he spoke Creole, this Dominican, like a real Haitian, except maybe for a touch of Spanish accent. "And now you are all going to calm down and shut up because if not I'm going to kick your ass! *Ou konprann?*"

"This is not what we expected," sighed Déroseaux, thumping his thighs with his fists. "Not at all."

"We're not prisoners," growled Brutus, with a dark look, as dark as his voice, as dark as his eternally deceived black skin.

"Sure, you're not . . . Listen, if you continue to piss me off, what you get is your business, because you are all dogs!"

Another capataz, small and dry, with a nasty smile, was approaching, rifle in hand.

"*Qué pasa aqui?* What's going on here?"

"These full-of-shit Haitians think they're American tourists and want to sleep in satin!"

The man grunted, placed the butt of the gun against his thigh, in the hollow of his groin, the barrel on his forearm. In front of him he scornfully eyed the little group filled with rage and disillusionment.

"Here, you better take what comes along. They sold you for a bundle of dollars. They sold you like dogs!"

Estimé Mondestin didn't like this at all. But what could he do? He hadn't the slightest idea.

When they had been piled in the two long *barracones* like captives, those who remained were led to wooden shacks, which didn't even have a cement slab.

Devoid of mattresses, the few available beds turned out to be unusable. Déroseaux tried his. The taut metal wires that served as springs stuck him in his flesh. "Yeah, yeah, yeah, mattresses you'll get soon," snapped the capataz, impatient. As if that were all he had to do! "Some what? Some sheets! Hah hah hah! And then what else? Breakfast in bed?"

Around four o'clock they were rounded up and told to report to the *bodega*, the batey's grocery store. It was the first time they had a chance to get a look at the camp in its entirety.

A batey is comprised of about three hundred persons, two hundred Haitians and one hundred Dominicans. The Dominicans gravitate around the cane, but do not cut it. They are painters, pruners, drivers, chauffeurs, merchants, *pesadores* (who do the weighing), *wagoneros* (who maintain and operate the railroad), *grueros* (who load the cane on the wagons), mechanics, those in charge of the water supply, cultivators — all kinds of jobs.

But the cutting of the cane, one of the hardest occupations in the world, is the work of the Haitians.

The houses of these Dominicans, who they had not yet had a chance to meet, constructed in wood, situated on the periphery of the batey, appeared very beautiful to Estimé Mondestin. They were nevertheless dreadfully modest. But in the kingdom of the Kongos...
On the other hand, those belonging to the well-to-do Dominicans, the majordomo, the capataces, were permanent structures, complete with little gardens. Mondestin caught a quick glimpse through a few open doors in passing, and was keenly impressed. "You'd never dare to spit in one of these houses, as comfortable as they are," he said to himself. They were very beautiful homes.

In the center of the batey, already much more run down, stood the barracks of the viejos. As far as he could tell, it seemed to Estimé Mondestin that some of them had wives and children. What's more, viejos and Dominicans seemed to be on good terms. Because of their seniority, probably.

Finally, furthest back in the camp, a few yards from the first rows of cane, were the *barracones*. Six long parallel buildings where they put the Kongos. Two on one side abutted a long precarious shelter; then a wide empty lot extended as far as the other four, then a few more wooden shacks. Some of them were still empty.

The store stood slightly apart from the facades of the Dominican houses, right on the edge of the dirt road. On the other side of the ochre yellow strip, the rutted and pot-holed result of last year's rainy season, the railroad tracks glinted in the sun. Just beyond, a sea of sugar cane.

The *bodega* — a shack constructed of wide, dark green planks erected vertically on a raised cement slab, the access to which was assured by two steps—its wide facade presented a long opening equipped with a counter on the inside and an awning on the outside.

On the shelves, behind Scorza, the *bodeguero*, were a long succession of rows of bottles of rum, condensed milk, cans and soap, belts and lamps, piles of stuff, but mostly rum. On the floor, there were sacks of rice, beans, flour, all sorts of basic foodstuffs.

This time, the Kongos didn't have a choice. They received a pound of rice for each two persons, a piece of sausage and a little bit of oil. "Don't waste it," they were advised, "it's for several days."

They had nothing with which to prepare their food. They didn't speak the language, couldn't make themselves understood to explain. A truck arrived, full of pots and pans, the kind ordinarily found in a trash heap. Those who still had a bit of pocket money chipped in together to buy the least dented ones. Estimé Mondestin and Petit Pierre Déroseaux spent their last pennies and paid for their two companions.

Their next door neighbors, but others too, wandered through the batey, hoping to find some kind of aid, but from whom? The viejos maybe, these Haitians who seemed to live more comfortably, you never know.

A number of them had returned a little while before from the *desavero*, the weeding of the three or four feet adjacent to the cane fields that's done before the cutting begins. The welcome was on the cool side.

"Oh, you Kongos, you are a pain in the ass."

"But we are brothers, Haitians like you!"

"Haiti, Haiti," said one of the viejos. Then, haughtily: "I will never go back to Haiti."

"It's our country!"

"It's a cursed old country!"

"A cursed country!"

"Yes! A cursed country!"

"But it's not my fault! You can't help us a little? We're here, we've got nothing..."

"Help you!" spat the viejo. "Do I see you helping me?"

"But I just got here and..."

"I know very well you just got here! You know what you are doing in this country? You come here and cause a type of unemployment, that's what you do when you get here!"

The Kongo was silent, taken aback.

"It's true," spoke up another viejo, dressed in rags. "If the Kongos didn't come, we'd cut according to the prices fixed for the Dominicans, but you, you come and slash the rates!"

"You know very well it's not us who . . ."

"We're more experienced, without you we could earn more. You are one big pain in the ass and that's it! You and your Jean-Claude Duvalier!"

Another continued, aggressive and bitter, showing his bare feet and his torn shirt.

"Jean-Claude keeps on raising his prices, he sells you to the Dominicans for more and more, and so they pay us less and less to make up the difference, and abuse us for their revenge! We'd rather not see you!"

The Kongo left, hanging his head in despair.

"The viejos don't speak to us, don't help us. It's the Dominicans they talk to. They have the same language, they speak Spanish, yes, *y ap palé pangnol!* They don't have any problems. Their houses are the same as those of the Dominicans. They are not Haitian any more, but Dominican, they speak ill of Haiti. No one wants to see us, the Kongos, I don't know how these viejos got to Dominicanie, but they've forgotten that one fine day they arrived."

Then a viejo shouted, told him to stop and wait, entered his shack, where he called a woman, came out again holding an old bowl the worse for wear, and approaching a bit sheepishly, offered it to the Kongo. "Here, you can give it back to me after your first pay. Haiti, you see," he said, "it's not that I don't want to go back there, but as long as Duvalier is there I will never return. If I went back, I would starve to death while he would continue to get rich off of my misery. I'm not happy here, but I have a little to eat. Don't lose my bowl." Then he turned on his heels, went back into the two rooms where he'd lived for fourteen years. In one of them there were four beds. The nine other people who were living with him piled in.

It's not that the viejos were bad people. It's just that misery had hardened them.

There were no toilets. The detail might seem trivial—it's not. "The plantation is big," mocked Antoine the viejo, "that makes fertilizer and it's very good. The odor of Negroes makes the cane grow!"

Or rather, it would be honest to clarify that there was exactly one latrine. Without counting those of the Dominicans, out-of-bounds, of course, to the Haitians. One latrine for two hundred people, you'd have to see it, it was already unusable. Especially since there wasn't any water either. No water in the latrines, no water anywhere. Petit Pierre Déroseaux realized it when he went to wash up. "Where are the showers?" he'd asked. Someone indicated them to him, on the other side of the camp. A dirty, light grey hut with three openings; in front of each hung a shredded piece of plastic, and at the back of each one of the thusly fitted-out cubicles were three pipes going up to the ceiling and then stopping there, permanently dried up. He left again, his mouth bitter. "Isn't there even a sink somewhere?" he'd asked a viejo. "Sink...," murmured the other. "Oh, yeah, over there, in back! But all it is is the pipes, no faucet and no water!" "There's damn well got to be some water somewhere," swore Déroseaux. "Sure, my friend, over there, in those barrels!" In each string of barracks there were installed two big rusty drums; Déroseaux had noticed them, but had also discovered that they were empty.

"But they're empty!"

"Yeah, that's a big problem. It's brought in in barrels, on donkeys. Sometimes two days go by with no water."

"What if you're thirsty, then what?"

"There's the river, but it's kind of far."

It was kind of far. The closest river, gushing muddy yellow broth, where the women went very early each morning to wash the clothes, and where he, later, would get used to bathing, once a week, was 600 yards away.

Batey 7A, however, proved to be a rather privileged spot. Just before nightfall, the majordomo gave the capataz some sacks to distribute. They were burlap sacks, a little dirty and rather full of holes, for those who didn't have a bed. They received one for every four Kongos.

In the evening, a fight broke out in the barracks, precisely over the matter of beds. They heard cries, then two men burst violently out of their cell, and one of them was beating on the other.

Antoine the viejo, who was on his way home, retraced his steps and joined the small group that had formed and was commenting on the altercation, divided between disapproval and excitement.

"It's a fight," shot Dieudonné Labelle, seeing him arrive. "A fight between Kongos."

"Yes, I see."

"In our situation we shouldn't fight like that," began Estimé Mondestin, horrified by so much violence.

The two guys were really going at it. "I've got a bed and I'm keeping it!" screamed one of them, out of breath. "*Ou konprann?* I'm keeping it!"

"There are many Kongos but not many beds," noted Dieudonné Labelle.

Still seated with his back against the wall of his shack, he got up to get a better look at what was happening.

"Every year it's the same story," said Antoine the viejo. "Mutual aid, no way. Here, it's every man for himself."

"It's no good," frowned Estimé Mondestin. "We shouldn't."

Antoine the viejo raised his arm, a fatalistic gesture, and smiled sadly. "No, of course not, we shouldn't."

"The Haitians act like animals in the bateys," he went on. "There are constantly quarrels, arguments, serious disputes; which sometimes end in a death. Sometimes people who were friends in Haiti don't even want to know each other any more once they get here in Dominicanie."

Estimé Mondestin, aghast, said nothing. Antoine the viejo continued. "It's survival."

Later, when one of the two protagonists collapsed and had quieted down, the Kongos went to bed. Some had succeeded in heating up a little rice on a few planks pulled out of what looked like the beginnings of a trash heap.

Those who didn't have a bed stretched out on the hard ground. Estimé Mondestin found some old cardboard cartons and spread them out to make himself a bed and tied himself up like a sausage in the sack they'd given him.

The night loomed, silent and livid. Not even a radio to be heard. In the adjoining room, four disillusioned Kongos spread out the one and only sack that they had been able to recover on the cement slab. They lay down side by side, each with his back on the canvas and with the rest of his body and head sticking out on the cement. They didn't have to turn off the light — there wasn't one.

At two o'clock in the morning, Petit Pierre Déroseaux, wracked with insomnia, got out of his bed, whose naked springs without a mattress were torturing his skin.

The sun had barely begun assailing the sky. It was already hot. The Dominican sniffed violently and stomped his unpolished boots in front of the open counter in the bodega.

"*Hola, hombre*," he brayed, for the benefit of the bodeguero who must be fooling around in his back room, the bastard, "*deme mi amanecer!* Give me my morning 'wake-up'!"

Scorza appeared dragging his feet, recognized that old swine Gustavo Perez, grunted an offhand greeting, and served him the desired glass of rum. Gustavo grabbed the glass, held it up to the light, admired it with half-closed eyes, and downed it in one gulp. His wandering glance fell on a couple of the sheet metal advertisements nailed to the wall of the bodega since the beginning of time. A *mi lo mio, Montecarlo*, for the cigarettes. *Bermudez, tradición de calidad*. He disregarded the others which didn't interest him.

"Ay, *Bermudez, qué bueno,*" said he. "*Bermudez,* I like that. *Dame otro trago!* Give me another one!"

The bodeguero took the bottle of Bermudan rum, and expertly poured a shot without spilling a drop—second nature for him. "*Salud, hombre,* here's to you, to us, and bottom's up once again."

The Kongos were slowly arriving, heading towards the bodega on the steeply cambered dirt road that traversed the batey. Gustavo Perez leaned towards Scorza, snickering softly.

"How are our turkeys coming along?"

"About well done, I'd say."

"*Bueno. Vamos a ver lo que pasa.*"

The Kongos were done just about right. Their few remaining dollars had hit the road long ago. They had already been there for a week and still were not working. You have to wait for orders from the administrator, *el señor administrador,* was the word from the major-domo. They were awaiting their orders. But one has to eat and they were crying hunger.

They ascended the two steps, stopped timidly in front of the counter. The boldest approached.

"*Eské ou gin arro'?*"

The bodeguero put his hand behind his right ear, feigning a frown and leaned towards the man. "*No entiendo.* I don't understand." He understood perfectly well.

The Kongo grimaced, bit his lip, concentrating on his request.

"Arro'," he said, "arro' " and he pointed at the sack whose surface was white with grain. He wanted to buy some rice, which in Spanish is arro' (arroz), and also some sugar, which is called azuca' (azucar), at the store which is called the bodeg' (bodega). He had already learned that for vocabulary, he'd already learned all that.

"*Arro' and azuca' po' favo'!*"

"Ohhh, some rice," exclaimed Scorza, and he banged on the counter. "*Tienes dinero?* Got any money?" Then, in response to the puzzled look: "*ou gin lajan?*"

In such circumstances he easily forgot that he neither spoke nor understood Creole.

The Kongo had no more money but he was hungry. He attempted to explain with sign language, and he explained well. That's not Scorza the bodeguero's problem. He was categorical. No money, no rice, no nothing. The news reverberated among the desperate Kongos. Noël Dessources—the spokesman for the little group was named Noël Dessources and spokesman he was, because he spoke the best Spanish—seemed to suddenly have an inspiration. He bent over, disappeared under the counter, surfaced, and placed on the wooden plank a considerably worn pair of shoes which nevertheless still slightly resembled shoes. Scorza picked up the shoes, looked at them, whistled in disgust, then placed them, without a word, on the counter. He only opened his mouth to conclude the deal. "All right, hombre, but your shit-kickers aren't worth a pin."

When the Kongos had retreated with a little rice, a little oil, and a little of nothing else, Scorza had taken two pair of shoes still in walking order, and a dirty but still-in-one-piece t-shirt. He leaned once again toward Gustavo Perez.

"Yes, I do believe they're ready."

First, they stayed three days without anyone having given them a cent. Then, the responsibles remembered the existence of a contract. Especially since a few Kongos who had participated in previous zafras had reminded them of it. In the interim period before the work actually starts, they are supposed to be given 75 centavos.* It was written; just because they didn't know how to read didn't mean it wasn't written. They knew, and that was it. It was thus envisaged that this should be done. From daybreak onward, they stood in line in front of the *oficina* to receive their 75 kobs. Sometimes they were put off until three o'clock in the afternoon, by then hunger was already long since gnawing at them. They chipped together, each "roommate" putting in 50 centavos, and one of them going to buy some rice, a few bananas, some dried peas, or some *picantines* (canned sardines). They saved the remaining 25 centavos to pay back what they had already had to borrow, in order to survive the first days, from the few Kongos who still had some money, in other words, practically nobody; or, from those who had received some, in other words, a few of them. Received by trading everything in their possession. At the bodega, there was no credit for Haitians. They had liquidated their meager assets. This one his shoes. That one his extra pair of pants. A transistor radio without batteries. A new shirt. A used shirt. The remains of a shirt. The Dominicans in the batey liked the things that came from Haiti, but claimed that they were not very good quality. They bought them for a mouthful — not of bread, too prohibitive — but of beans or rice. And the Kongos considered themselves truly fortunate; it was a favor that had been done for them.

It was misery and it was hunger, and the more the time passed, the more they had nothing.

What's more, on this particular day, the money not having arrived at the *oficina*, they had not been paid.

Plain and simple.

Estimé Mondestin was roaming about the batey, distraught. If you don't have anything to pawn, they won't sell you anything. That

---

*In 1981, one peso = one dollar, thus 75 centavos = 75 cents. — TRANS.

doesn't make you any less hungry. He heard a group of Dominicans laughing. Elbows on the bar, they were drinking rum. He was wandering aimlessly, raking the dust with his bare feet. Lost in his thoughts, he bumped into a white. All the Dominicans were white, not really white, but still good and white, a white a bit darkened, of mixed blood. In any case, white compared to the total black of the Haitians, *nègre* from head to foot. The man insulted him nastily— *"hijueputa de haitiano*, can't you look where you're going?" then continued on his way in the direction of the amused drinkers, already smiling at the incident, rum in abeyance, glasses suspended in the air.

"How damned stupid can they get, these Haitians!"

"What a bunch of stupid assholes!"

A small wrinkled man stopped laughing and put down his glass.

"Knock it off," he said, obviously vexed. "These are men, like you, they should get some respect."

"And my ass, it should be respected?"

"I don't know where your ass is, it looks like your trap—ha, ha, ha!"

"Any idea what it says to you, my trap?"

"It doesn't say anything, it runs like diarrhea and it farts!"

"Ay qué vaina!"

They served themselves some more rum to lubricate the laughter.

"You have to respect them," continued the little man. "They are men like us."

"Men like us? But *we* don't cut no cane. We're not slaves."

"They are also human beings."

"Cane cutters ain't human beings."

"And us, who are we, imbecile?"

"Certainly not cane cutters. We've fallen pretty low, but not that low."

The man turned towards the others, pointing at them one after another.

"He's a *cadenero*, he's a *gruero*, he's an *agutero*, and he's *capataz de corte*! Do you see any cane cutters in there?"

"It's a job like any other."

"Oh no. It's a job for slaves. A job for Haitians. The proof is that not one Dominican does it."

"Listen, *hombre*, they left their country and came here to make a living. They are workers like us. You have to give them some respect."

The big Dominican looked at the small wrinkled one, and shaking his head, let out a long whistle, then grabbed the glass of rum Scorza had just poured him. "Get off it, Manuel Galéano. You give us a pain in the ass. You're not at one of your union meetings!"

They continued to talk. And then there were bursts of laughter. And then life went on. But Galéano, the small wrinkled one, was steadfast in his opinions. He knew that many Dominican workers thought as he did. But he knew also that an even larger number thought the opposite. Life was hard for everybody. It was easier to take it out on these *nègres* than to take on the huge machine with its rich, its police, and its dogs, that was eating all of them up. He understood.

Estimé Mondestin, of course, had understood nothing of all this. This language was totally foreign to him. He simply noticed that one of the Dominicans had insulted him, and that another, a stocky little guy, had thrown him a look full of understanding. Maybe the Dominicans weren't all so bad after all! He took off slowly toward his barracks, his stomach fatigued from having struggled so against the insidious emptiness. He was accosted by a man, someone he didn't know but who spoke good Creole.

"Well, my dear friend, how's life?"

"It's not too good at all."

"What's the matter? Do you have some troubles?"

"I'm very hungry, my friend."

"You're hungry . . ."

"Yes, I'm very hungry."

"I know this problem. I've been through it."

The man put his hand — a long and not very damaged hand, not the hand of a sugar cane cutter, those are all cracked, not really the hand of a manual worker — on Estimé Mondestin's shoulder.

"I suppose you must be out of money."

"Nothing at all left."

"You are a serious kind of guy?" the unknown Dominican questioned suddenly. "You are going to work?"

Mondestin looked at this guy out of the corner of his eye and wondered what he was getting at.

"I'm going to work a lot. When a Haitian comes here it's to work hard. But at the moment, they don't give us any work, that's the whole problem."

"It's nothing. Your problems will be over in a few days."

"But you have to hang on until then! Especially since they forget to pay us sometimes!"

"They forget," echoed the Dominican, with a disgusted look. "They forget, these jackals!"

"Ah, yes, they forget."

"That won't last." The man threw his hand to the Kongo. "My name is Gustavo Perez."

"Estimé Mondestin, Haitian Kongo."

"That I know. You know what we're going to do? We're going to open you an account. You look like a good guy to me."

"An account..."

"An account at the bodega."

Estimé Mondestin smiled bitterly, caught a glimpse out of the corner of his eye of two passing women, baskets on their heads; his eye followed them for an instant. They were Haitian to be sure, but were not laughing as the women in Haiti laugh. He shrugged with fatality.

"They don't sell to Haitians on credit in that store. If they give you any credit at all, you have to put up something as security, like a pair of pants. I don't have any more. I'm not going to go around bare-ass."

Gustavo Perez laughed, revealing rotting yellow teeth. He led Estimé Mondestin toward the bodega.

"Let me take care of it and don't say anything. I know the bodeguero well. You're going to be able to eat."

Mondestin's stomach jumped several times somewhere in the painful zone, above the belt.

Estimé greeted the bodeguero with a nod of his head. Gustavo Perez slammed his open palm on the counter. A discussion began, of which Mondestin understood nothing. He had a closer look at the store to pass the time. Four rows of bottles, no less. The Dominicans drink a lot of alcohol. Belts, matches, candles, caps with long visors, pots that shone, plastic bags, stacks of batteries and piles of whatever, and the scale, whose round dial hung from the ceiling by a chain, held the large empty tray with a hook.

A nudge brought him out of his reverie.

"It's gonna work."

"What did you tell him?"

"I told him that you are a personal friend. An old friend from...."

"But we just met!"

"That's all right, he doesn't know. I told him you are a dependable guy, that he can give you credit."

"And he accepted?"

Gustavo Perez leaned towards Estimé Mondestin, who discreetly recoiled, offended by an unhealthy odor of rotten rum.

"I happen to be someone rather important, he can't refuse me anything."

Mondestin shook his head, happy and impressed. He bought some matches, some gas to make a lamp, sardines, some oil, dried peas, and rice. The bodeguero weighed it out, not very generously, either, and sold him his pound for thirty centavos instead of twenty-three, but naturally, eh, because of the credit! Gustavo Perez made the merest suggestion of a gesture in the direction of the bodeguero, rattled off a few words which ended with Bermudez. "If you don't mind," he said to Mondestin, "I don't have any money on me, I'm taking a pack of cigarettes and a small bottle of rum on your account, we'll settle it a little later." "Take it, go ahead," commanded the Kongo, "I certainly owe you that much!" Then he continued.

"No problem. In a few days, we're going to work, I'll be making a good living."

"Thanks again, *mucha' gracia'*." He left, headed for the barracks, the *barracon*, his arms loaded. He was whistling.

"As far as ripe goes, they are plenty ripe," breathed Scorza the bodeguero, making out the tab of Kongo Mondestin. "Plenty ripe."

Gustavo Perez smiled silently, putting his hands on the back of his hips.

"*Bueno hombre*, I'm off to the fishing grounds! See you later, I'll introduce you to a friend!"

They broke out laughing. His heavy step resounded in front of the bodega, then grew fainter, muffled by the dust, as it penetrated deeper into the batey.

Having arrived at the corner of a shack no more dilapidated than any other — you could see inside through some rotten boards — Gustavo Perez spotted a Kongo who, eyes lowered, mumbling to himself, took ten steps forward, stopped, then turned around and retraced his steps, very indecisive. He watched him for a moment, then started walking to meet him, as if by coincidence. "Well, my dear friend, how goes your life?" "It's no good at all," replied the Kongo, once over the initial moment of surprise.

They were there, sitting, didn't have five cents to eat, hunger plaguing their bellies, all huddled in the few shady spots, tracing vague designs in the dust, exchanging a few desultory words, black blotches drying out on the yellow ground. And the time was oozing by like a river of boredom. They weren't at all satisfied by the lack of activity, but when they protested the capataz sent them to the major-domo, who in turn very kindly put them off indefinitely. "Patience, my friends. The zafra will start in a few days." They didn't say anything and, resigned to their fate, thought of their children, their wives, their families without support in Haiti. They weren't used to this form of misery, didn't know what to do. So they did nothing.

Until a big Kongo with *gro djol é nin krasé* (thick lips and a squashed flat nose) got up, exasperated. "We can't stay here like this," he said. And other voices echoed his. "We can't just stay here like this!"

They all got up.

They went to complain because they were hungry, and that is what caused the fracas. They were very badly received by the majordomo. He was late and expected by a certain Manuela Garcia y Garcia. It was not the right moment. Really not the right moment. "You'll have to manage," he said, "the work will start when it starts." That was no answer. The tone rose. "We left our country ten days ago," shouted an angry voice, "and we still haven't earned anything! How long is that going to last?"

The majordomo clenched his jaws and his eyes flashed angry sparks. Then he relaxed. The capataces were coming running, and they had their rifles.

"Break it up immediately, you lousy pack of Kongos!"

"We came here to find a better life."

"You're going to find it sooner than you think if you continue to piss us off. A better life for eternity!"

"We came for our wives, our little ones, our families, we want to accomplish something!"

"You are going to work, if that's what you're missing! Don't worry, you're going to work! Work, hah, we'll give you some work!"

And voices from every direction collided and clashed, exclamations, indignation, and the feverish heads became all the more inflamed. "We're not dogs, we want to work!".

"Break it up, get back to your barracones."

"We have nothing to do there."

"Save your strength, you'll need it soon!"

"We have nothing to eat!!!"

"Well, sleep then."

"There's no beds! We can't sleep, we can't eat, we have to sell everything to survive! We want to work right now!"

"It's coming, it's coming, wait."

"Wait, wait, that's all we've done since we got here. We'd rather stay home and do nothing than to do nothing here. Or, let us leave!"

And the big Negro with *gro djol é nin krasé* rallied the others with an upraised arm.

"Since there's no work here, we're leaving!"

"We're leaving, we're leaving," they shouted, they cried, "we're leaving!"

The majordomo, white with rage, leaned towards the small capataz with the malicious look, said something in his ear, and left, striding toward his lovely house. The capataz got up on a wooden box to dominate the assembly, and began screaming. The other capataces had come closer, encircling him, squared off, glued to their guns.

"You are forbidden to leave this batey."

"We're leaving, we're leaving!"

"We're leaving!"

"No one leaves here without permission," screamed the small capataz, to drown out the chaos of cries, "and let one thing be clear, there will be no permission."

"Give us some food, we're leaving!"

The tall Black with *gro djol é nin krasé* had had it, didn't want to hear it any more. The capataz jumped down from his crate, headed nervously towards him.

"You will not leave. You are here by order of your President."

"The President, we don't give a shit," cried a voice, and they all froze. (They weren't used to that. In Haiti, they throw you in prison for less than that, they mutilate you, they kill you. The President is sacred.) "The President, we don't give a shit, we're leaving!"

"You can't leave! If you're caught, we kill you!"

"You don't have the right. There are laws in Dominicanie."

"Those laws aren't for you, they're for the Dominicans! The first one caught outside of the batey will be shot, you understand?"

"Our President will intervene," cried a more cautious protester.

"Your President is a poor devil. He needs money."

Other Dominicans had drawn closer, as well as a few viejos who were buzzing in lowered voices among themselves, and also some women who were watching from afar, frightened.

"We're not dogs!"

Diverse reactions, a cry of protest, momentary impasse; the Kongos held up their heads, caught a glimpse of the sun's disc, tightened their ranks. "The sun shines on everyone, we believe."

"Your President Jean-Claude doesn't have any factories and he knows that Guzman has got fields of sugar cane, coffee, avocado trees, all that! That's why he sends his little dogs to eat at our door!"

"We come from Jean Rabel, from Gonaïves," hurled a voice on the verge of tears, "we..."

"You don't have any land...you don't have anything!"

We do have a country, and the heat beating down on their heads, on the roofs, this is a bad man, my friend, a bum. Me, I thought I'd make a living here, where's the majordomo? Road deserted here, but in the distance, a cloud of dust. So, we accept the situation—we use our clothes for a bed, they're going too far, you bet, it's really too much, how long can you keep on taking it? Abuse, exhortations, we're up against the wall, my friend, the time that goes by and still no work, but we are so hungry, really.

"We're not going to let ourselves be had!"

"*Puerco!* Dirty pig! If you had any decent land, you wouldn't have to come and eat elsewhere!" That was too much. The tall Negro with *gro djol é nin krasé* clenched his fists, advanced on the capataz. It was chaos. Punches, blows, rifle butts—a fight broke out. All hell broke loose, and the rising cloud of dust traversed the plain to the gates of the batey.

Alerted by the majordomo's telephone call, two charging jeeps of police armed to the teeth arrived, engines racing. Braking, skidding, braking. They jumped on the Kongos, rifles raised.

The Haitians fled in every direction. Rifle shots cracked; it was incredible. One Haitian, hit by a police bullet, died on the spot. Others in headlong flight elsewhere and in the fields. They arrested one in the crowd saying that he'd just been making speeches in front of the bosses' door. It seemed that that was the tall *nègre* with *gro djol é nin krasé*. They proceeded to arrest large numbers of Kongos. The Haitians had to hide in the plantation until the police were no longer able to locate them.

Estimé Mondestin escaped the forces of order. Lying in a cane field near another Kongo from the barracks next door, he panted, eyes closed. "There was a Haitian hit by a bullet in the brawl." "Really? You saw it?" "Yes, I'm sure of it, and... Shhhhh! Quiet!"

It was a long night. Estimé Mondestin stayed hidden until the next morning.

Now they knew fear. There were a large number of Kongos missing. Dieudonné Labelle, among others, had disappeared, and the tall *nègre* with *gro djol é nin krasé* but that was no surprise. No one knew anything about them. Petit Pierre Déroseaux spoke slowly, and his voice vibrated with choked-back anger. "There is one dead," he was saying, "and there are some wounded. They put plenty in prison. The dead one—they didn't even take care of his body. They beat up one of my friends and arrested him. His name is Aristide. There was no lack of shots. My friend went to prison, no one knows what they did with him, maybe they killed him."

He observed a short silence, gazed out at the row of doors growing smaller toward the extremity of the barracks.

"In fact, I don't know how many Haitians they treated like that."

Antoine the viejo nodded his head. He knew the truth. He'd been there for such a long time.

"It's almost every day," said he, "some are taken, some are beaten."

He stopped talking. All eyes followed his gaze. Emerging from all the habitations, Kongos, viejos, capataces, a few other Dominicans were converging on the road in front of the bodega. A truck had just stopped, full of new Kongos, their eyes bulging with fatigue.

"They are replacing those who've been arrested," Antoine the viejo said calmly, "and filling up the barracks that are empty. Work is going to start soon."

Estimé Mondestin breathed a sigh. He didn't want to say anything about it, but now he regretted having been hired. The viejo looked at him, wrinkled his old face as if he had read his thoughts, "Ah, yes my friend," he muttered, "here, that's the way it is. That's the way it is in all the bateys."

Kon sa bagay la yé.

*If some succeeded in getting back home, I don't know.
But in my batey, no one managed to. After a while everyone
asked to leave, but when the Dominicans found out, they
treated us real bad. They hassled us and they hassled us.
We were like prisoners. (Interview)*

Sé tout nèg ki kanpé! Everyone was on his feet, demanding the
return to Haiti. They said, "enough misery, we can't stay here like
this." They realized that grangou (hunger) was going to get them and
kill them. They gathered up their old clothes, and when the bosses
saw that, they got really rough and locked them up.

That did not happen in Batey 7A, but in Batey Otonsi.

Jean-René had left Croix-des-Bouquets full of illusions. He still
hurt in the spot where they had given him that shot in Barahona. For
that, if nothing else, he knew he would never return to Dominicanie.
For the shot and for the rest, he would never come back.

They had passed through the capital, Santo Domingo, without
seeing anything other than that it was big and beautiful, much bigger
and much more beautiful than Port-au-Prince, which had given
them hope for the future. Having arrived at night, they had been
parked in a corral for animals, and had eaten nothing up until four
o'clock the next day. But there's nothing to tell, it was the same in all
the bateys. Finally they consented to lodge them. Six rooms for seventy persons. For seven days they slept on the ground, on cement, and
in a fever. They had said, "we don't like this, we're going back." Had
stormed a truck. All at once, they were given a working over and a
few beds.

For nineteen days they remained without working. Each day
they received a card for a little rice and corn. Sometimes the
Dominicans maneuvered to seize their cards and thus steal their day's

food. They weren't given any money. But that day it was *sé tout nèg ki té kanpé!*

Forty Kongos out of seventy had decided to leave.

The others were staying because they were afraid, because they were hungry, because they felt too weak to walk, because they still hoped to accomplish something.

"They are going to kill you!" said the viejos. "Who cares, we're dying anyway. We aren't allowed to escape. We'll see about that, we're not staying. We came here to eat and it's hunger that is devouring us. We won't stay."

In spite of the rain, in spite of the night, they were leaving, and they had their machetes in hand. A wet tramping of feet was moving through the batey, first slowly, hesitantly, then faster, more consistant. Ricoeur was at the head, or Roger, or another. Jean-René was immediately behind. The little troupe was following.

Who had alerted them, no one ever knew. Just outside the batey, where the road sinks into obscurity and plunges into the cane, three gendarmes stood out sharply from the shadows, and three rifles against the sky. Two words cracked, well articulated.

"Adonde van?"

"Where are you going?" The responses were as varied as they were numerous, but essentially all were alike. "To the capital." "We're going home." "To Haiti." "We're going back. We've had enough. We're leaving."

Marcellin, a Kongo who spoke a few words of Spanish, conducted the interpreting.

"Nos vamos. We're leaving."

"Where do you want to go?"

"We're leaving for Haiti."

"You've been sold."

"We don't give a damn. We're leaving."

"You have all been sold for more than eighty pesos each."

"We didn't get any of it!"

These three particular gendarmes were not too bad. Especially since they had facing them forty determined-looking Kongos armed with machetes, whose eyes were gleaming brightly in the black of the night. The majordomo was away at the moment, no means of telephoning for reinforcements. And besides, shit! Forty lost, two hundred gained! They weren't going to get themselves carved up for so little.

This was the first of a long series of miracles. The Kongos went on.

They walked. The houses, when there were any, were nicer than the ones in Haiti. The land greener, richer, deeper, more luxuriant. Evidently, it produced. However, no abundance whatsoever, and often, just beyond the cane plantations, no more than a few steps out of the way, a third-worldish vision awaited them. A truck thundered past, cleaving the morning heat with a long trail of dust that fell down again in a dry pulverulent rain. The incandescent sky gripped the horizon. Blisters of heat bursting from the depths of desolation, a pueblo of pariahs carried its cross on the avenue of disillusion.

There is not an enormous difference between the standard of living of Haitian peasants and that of a large number of Dominican peasants. Sixty-four percent of the Dominican peasant families receive a salary of 50 pesos a month, that is, 44 percent of the total agricultural revenue. Eight percent obtain an income of between 100 and 300 pesos, which represents 22 percent of the national agricultural revenue. Dark figures against light hammocks, two hundred days of work a year and then nothing. Sit and wait. Dominican campesino.

"What in the hell is that?" wondered a shadow with an acrid voice.

"Looks to me like some cane cutters. Haitians."

"What are they doing here?"

"Who knows... They're passing by."

"Cane cutters... Ay, *puta!*"

In a society whose largest socioeconomic stratum is made up of the unemployed and the underemployed, a foreign labor force, upon whom depended the bulk of the country's economy, was passing by.

"Cane cutters..."

A man was watching them, scraping the ground with his holey shoe. He really didn't know how he was managing to live. He was watching the Kongos and he was thinking. "No work, all right, it's rough. But cut cane? No thanks! Sooner beg!"

In all the countries of Spanish tradition, working the cane, particularly cutting it, is discredited. Too associated with the image of the Negro slave of old. The old days? "Ah, no," he mused, "a Dominican is not used to life in the bateys, the absence of hygiene, the lack of privacy and crowded conditions. I'd miss the warmth of home, be it the wretched home that it is. I'll go there the day the conditions have changed. If I can live there with my family in the plantations, educate my children, all that... There are not even any schools in the bateys. No doctors. Nothing. I'm not a slave, let them get that through their heads. I'm no Haitian!"

The Kongos were walking, running, fleeing, about to enter a pueblo.

Some more gendarmes were there, very violent, but insufficient in number.

"You will not get by. Go back to the plantation."

"We will get by." Then in a determined tone: "no more plantations, *pa'a nosot'os!*"

"Very well, Gentlemen, we're going to lock you up."

The bell tower of a white church jutted out above the disorderly line of roof-tops. The gendarmes withdrew, you don't lose anything for waiting, we'll go and get some help. (Difficult to go ahead and shoot in plain view of everyone, they weren't, after all, in a batey.)

They turned into one street, surged headlong into another, emerged at a square, a few palm trees, a few scraggly flower beds; exhausted, they sat down on cement benches made out of the same cement as the paths. "And now what do we do? The police are going to come back—and in force." Jean-René, Ricoeur, Roger, and a few others put their heads together. "What do we do, what do we do? They are going to arrest us, we need some weapons." "Weapons?" "Yes." "No." "Yes." "Not even." "*Véritab zam sé lajan.* The most effective weapon is money." "I know, but we don't have any."

"No, my friend, we don't have any!"

Marcellin and Roger were watching four guys arrive with the rapid and muffled tread of conspirators. They were four; three Dominicans of more or less dark complexion, and one good and black, as black as a Haitian. He was one.

"We're going back to Haiti. First we're going to the capital."

"Better not stay here, you've been spotted, everyone saw you pass by. The police are going to come."

"We don't have any place to go."

"*Qué dicen?*" demanded one of the Dominicans, a big guy, not very well dressed, addressing the Haitian among them.

They launched into a short discussion. Four of them had come looking for them, and Jean-René noticed that their eyes were gleaming. The black turned to them again.

"We can help you find some work elsewhere."

"Really? Paid work?"

A wave of hope swept through the group and even those the most reclined were whipped to their feet. "Really?"

"There is work in this region, we're going to help you."

"Cutting cane?" piped up a worried voice, "in a batey?"

"No, no! There is all kinds of work here in Dominicanie. Fruit, coffee..."

"Let's hurry it up," ordered one of the individuals, peevish and sharp, "*No hay que perder el tiempo! Vámonos!*" He was surreptitiously casting quick looks towards the far end of the square, as if he feared the approach of a vague danger.

"*No vamos a perder el negocio,*" he snapped to his companions. "Let's not botch up this deal!" But no one in the little troupe understood that. Stretching it, maybe Marcellin, but still . . . but yes, maybe Marcellin. He moved nearer to Jean-René, grimaced and ran a dirty hand through his bushy hair.

"I don't like the way he talks."

"What's the matter?"

"I don't know. I can't catch all of it, but they are talking about *negocio*, about doing some business. . ."

"What I don't like is their eyes. They shine too much."

The four men were leading them along, posthaste. "They say we're going to work. They even know of some possibilities. Me, I'll go for it. Even hard work. *Si Aisyin nan misé, sa plis intérésé 'l travay du.* When a Haitian is starving he is ready and willing to accept hard labor. It's true, really. Where are they taking us?" "To some Dominicans." "Ah, that, my friend, is inevitable. I tell you: except for in the batey, I'd rather work for a Dominican than a Haitian. That's right. *M pito travay kay mulat, nèg noua sé mové moun!* I prefer to work for the mulatto, the black is rough and mean." "But not in the batey. Hah, not that, never in the batey! Me, my friend, I'd just as soon die, but not in the batey. Or then, I go back to Haiti." "But what would we do in Haiti?" "Starve to death, as usual." "Yes, but at home. It's hard, really. You can't spend your life dying!" "But in the batey we were dying." "Ah, yes, really we were dying. We were lucky to meet these guys."

Forty Kongos in the alleys of a small town all huddled around its town square, and a bandstand with a band did not go unnoticed. "Too little noticed for this business to be honest," thought Jean-René, suddenly.

"Vámonos! Vámonos!" They followed.

The four guys had stopped for an instant, were holding counsel on the temporary destination of the escape party. Women were passing, passing and turning around, kids were running by, and stopped running, some hawkers were approaching, interested, then fell back quickly, continuing their perambulations. "These nègres didn't have a peso to their name! Bums, these Kongos! *Ay hombre,* the Kongos, *qué miséria!*"

Garage, maybe, or warehouse. They didn't know. They were led into a dark room, the windows closed with massive shutters. The men told them, "Stay here, we're going to contact who we have to contact, we'll come and get you." The Kongos complied without batting an eyelash. They all jumped when they heard a heavy bar fall into place on the outside of the door, and the dry click of a lock snapping shut in the semidarkness.

Jean-René hurled himself on the door, pushed and pushed.

In vain. They were locked in. They were prisoners.

In the Dominican Republic, due to the appalling working conditions, numerous plantations, coffee plantations, *fincas*, vast agricultural concerns, permanently lack manpower. They are ready to pay to obtain it, whether it be provided by force or by free will. And they pay.

Eleven pesos a head for Haitians.

They roared, they pounded and paced, but not for very long; it was not in their best interest to attract attention. They were frothing with rage and despair. They had no idea just exactly what the others wanted to do with them, but they were locked up, which was enough to understand that once again they had been hoodwinked. Someone was weeping. That did not prevent the night from falling on a seriously compromised fate.

However, they did not give up.

During the night, as far as anyone knew, they broke open a small door that had been initially hidden in the rear of the large room by a pile of old boards.

They were still forty, and still running.

It is relatively easy to write it: they walked three days without eating. Three dawns, three mornings, three noons, three afternoons, three twilights, without ingesting one single thing on the road, on the impassively long route, one can succeed in imagining. But to walk them? Could one walk them?

They trudged them. Everyone agreed and determined. And with the machetes. And without money. They asked for food. A few Dominicans gave ten centavos, but they couldn't do anything for forty, those poor Kongos.

An occasional question, no reason, just to say something, to prove one's existence, and a response always the same, very measured, very dignified.

"*M grangou anpil monchè.* I'm very hungry."

What else was there to say? The sun was pouring down on the ground, asphalt burning under the dry waves of heat.

Jean-René, suffering from a pain in his right calf, had decided to go on at whatever the cost. He knew that he would make it. *Nèg noua toujou gin plis fyèl pasé lot yo*, he repeated to himself regularly to give himself courage. The blacks are always more resistant than any other. Anyone else would have stopped, but they already perceived high, light spots in the distance, a confused mass in the fog of heat, the beginning of the grey suburbs of Santo Domingo, the capital. Jean-René was silently singing a hymn to Legba, the god of the crossroads and long journeys. He smiled in spite of the weakness, the pain, all the pains, accelerated a little, caught up with Roger.

"Do you know who we are?"

Then, without awaiting a reply, which in any case was not forthcoming: "We are *nègres marrons!*"

He laughed feebly. Roger also. Then they straightened up proudly. *Nègres marrons.* Negres in flight.

The word, from the Spanish word *cimarron*, originally designated domestic animals like the pig, returning to the wild. In colonial times, that is, in the days of the French masters, the slaves' lot was so bad that they had only the choice between submission, revolt, or flight. Many fled. The "marrons." And this word, at first ignominious, had acquired the mark of honor in struggle and in courage; that which had been pejorative became a title of pride. *Nègre marron.*

Roger was trundling along, slightly hunched over, a violent pain in his kidneys. You can be a Haitian, illiterate, and you know very well what being a marron means. The oral traditions are strong. He grimaced.

"Marrons, OK, but better not get caught."

The Black Code of Colbert (1685) provided heavy punishments for the apprehended runaway, especially in the case of a second offense. A month's absence was punished by the mark of a branding iron on one shoulder, and the cutting off of the ears. The second time, they cut the buttocks or hamstrings, and branded the second shoulder. The next time, that was it, death for the rebel.

"We're going to make it! And besides, they don't kill the *marrons* any more."

"What do they do to them?" asked René.

"What do they do to them?"

"Yes, what *do* they do to them?"

Jean-René, not knowing what to answer, let his eyes wander off, over the road which, before disappearing on the horizon, widened, traced an asphalt furrow — clear, neat and well-outlined.

"I don't know," he answered, "but we are Haitian, we are not slaves any more." His eyes closed with fatigue; one step, two steps, three steps, four steps, he opened them in a dizzy, burning haze, heard his stomach screaming. He gritted his teeth and turned toward his companions.

"We will never again be slaves! What Haiti did, few others have done!"

Few others.

The Haitians carried to the finish the first triumphant Anti-slavery Revolution in history. An enormous influence, a fantastic legacy, for the enslaved or colonized peoples of the Americas.

The Arawak Indians, the first occupants of the island, called it *Ayti*, the high and wild land. They practically disappeared during the sixteenth century and the coming of the Spanish. There were less than three hundred left in 1687. The Indians had found the Spanish more savage than themselves.

During this time, in 1629, the first French settlements were established in Tortola, a close dependent of the island. These pirates and buccaneers left their imprint in the adventurous legends of the Caribbean, pursued the Spanish galleons in the Caribbean, and, like the Indians, hunted the wild oxen whose flesh they smoked on grills called "boucans"; (hence, *boucanier*: buccaneer). They took the opportunity in passing to rename Hispaniola — from the name initially given by the Spanish — which became Santo Domingo; the name of the capital, and eventually to Saint-Domingue in good French. They then degenerated and disappeared. The colonization was carried out by "serious" people.

The Treaty of Ryswick (1697) officially recognized French sovereignty of the western third of the island, what is now the Republic of Haiti. The rest remained under Spanish domination.

The exploitation of the colony commenced. Black slavery, inaugurated at the beginning of the French colonization, is provisioned for about thirty years by purchases from the neighboring islands. They then moved on to a more direct importation.

With the advent of the great seafaring discoveries, the black African kings, who were already trading with the Arabs, became aware of the significance and extent of the market. It is not really anything new. The slave was already, and had been for a long time, a medium of exchange in circulation throughout Africa. But from one day to the next, the scale of the traffic was to change. The majority of the slaves came from the region of the Gulf of Bénin, principally from Dahomey and Nigeria. The economy of the Dahomean kingdom would, for a long time, be based on slave trade, promoted to the rank of a national industry. Annual expeditions against bordering territories permitted the king — what was the name of the dynasty? — Mobutu, Bokassa, Amin Dada, Duvalier? — to assure himself the monopoly on the thousands of captives sold to the Whites. The Congo, Angola, Senegal, and Guinea were also made use of by the French slave traders. The ships coming from Nantes, France alone transported one-half million African slaves to the Caribbean and the American continent; but during the entire colonial period, there were more than fifteen million Blacks transplanted. And for each one arriving on the coasts of the New World, about five died in Africa or during the crossing.

The misfortune of some is the fortune and the infamy of others. In the last quarter of the eighteenth century, Saint-Domingue, which produced sugar, coffee, indigo, and cotton on a large scale, was considered to be the richest colony in the world. At the time of the French Revolution, it boasted 800 sugar plantations, 3,000 of coffee, 2,950 of indigo, and nearly 800 of cotton. It had as well, 600,000 slaves, 30,000 free (or emancipated) mulattos, 16,000 poor Whites, 5,000 rich Whites, and a few thousand each of marrons, soldiers, and civil servants. In that epoch, the freed mulattos, fruit of forbidden love between black slaves and white masters — which earned them a relatively privileged treatment — owned 30 percent of the land and riches of the colony, including 2,000 plantations and a few small sugar ingenios. They possessed 25 percent of the slaves as well.

Up until the great uprising of August 1791, this mulatto middle class, isolated between the masses of slaves, the colonial bourgeoisie, and the white middle class, constituted the revolutionary core of the colony. It considered the French National Assembly its most solid ally in the struggle for political and social rights.

This mulatto middle class was able to disperse the "Grand Planters" Assembly in April 1790, in close alliance with representatives of the metropolitan bourgeoisie and the colonial bureaucracy. Shortly thereafter, the French National Assembly legislated new laws, maintaining slavery, but establishing equal civil rights for all free individuals in the colony. The colonial bureaucracy refused to enforce the decrees.

A first rebellion, led by Vincent Ogé and Jean-Baptiste Chavannes, was drowned in a bloodbath by the colonial troops.

Seeing this, the mulattos armed the slaves in the southern part of the country. This was a big first. The slaves, under the direction of Beauvais and Lambert, veterans of the War of Independence of the U.S., fought and defeated the slave owners.

It was but the beginning.

On 14 August 1791, at Morne Rouge, in the Caïman Bois forest in the northern plain, the Negro Boukman, powerful in his prophetic eloquence, took, together with his partisans, a solemn oath to "Live free or die." The call to revolt was sealed with the blood of a pig in a sacrificial ceremony. All these Negroes brought from Africa — Peuhl warriors, Mondongues, the mighty Mandingues, tall Yoloffs, Ibos, Bambaras, Aradas, Dahomeans — eliminated little by little their intertribal differences and were able to form a fighting unity through the medium of voodoo, an ensemble of beliefs and rites of African origin, subsequently becoming closely mingled with Catholic practices.

The uprising. The plantations are set ablaze from one morne to another. The frightened planters recognize the political and social equality of the Freeman, which was ratified by the decree of the National French Convention on 4 April 1792,* and in so doing, win the support of the mulatto slave-owning middle class.

Spain had declared war on France after the execution of Louis XVI in 1791. The Army of the Republic, backed by the men of Toussaint Louverture, the "Centaur of the Savannah," launched into a fierce struggle against the Spanish, the English, the Royalists, and the large plantation owners who were under the protection of England.

Spain withdrew from the war in July 1795, while in 1794 the Convention had abolished "the enslavement of Negroes in all the colonies."

The English troops, allied with the big white planters, and the slave-owning Freemen were crushed. Their losses amounted to 45,000 men and 20 million pounds sterling.

Thus a double power sprang forth, based on the two principal classes: the former slaves and the mulatto middle class. A civil war broke out, fanned by the colonial powers which exploited the antagonism between the blacks and the mulattos in order to weaken the Revolution. The former black slaves emerged victorious from the conflict.

"The power that I hold I acquired legitimately, and only the will of the Peoples of Saint-Domingue will force me to renounce it." The Constitution drawn up under the direction of Toussaint Louverture named him Governor for Life of the French colony of Saint-Domingue and its inhabitants, but also proclaimed the internal autonomy of the colony.

Napoleon Bonaparte, who had just seized power with the coup d'etat of 18 Brumaire,† took it rather badly. This unilateral constitution of Toussaint constituted an act of rebellion against France!

The fleet commanded by Admiral Villeret-Joyeuse, composed of 86 ships, set sail for the West and arrived on 29 January 1802 in the Bay of Samana. On board was General Victor Emmanuel Leclerc, Napoleon's brother-in-law, commanding 21,900 veterans of the Rhine, Italian, and Egyptian campaigns. The fine flower of the French Army. The best cadres in Toussaint's army were eliminated after long and violent combat. The French occupied the strategic

---

*Having just done away with all noble privilege in France. — TRANS.

†18 Brumaire: The day, according to the French calendar, when Napoleon Bonaparte took power. — TRANS.

spots on the island. On the night of 10 June 1802, Toussaint Louverture was arrested, betrayed by Leclerc, to whom he had submitted and given up 30,000 guns, in exchange for the latter's promise to free the Negroes. He was embarked on the frigate "Créole" and deported to France. There he died on 7 April 1803, in the Jura mountains at the Joux fortress.

The peasant masses had already thrown themselves into the struggle. Besides the deportation of Toussaint, they had learned of the reestablishment of slavery in the other French possessions in the Antilles, Martinique, and Guadeloupe. Their spontaneous uprising was joined late but then taken in hand by the majority of the Black and Mulatto generals, Belair, Dessalines, Christophe, Maurepas.

In twenty months of insane battle, 58,545 white men debarked on the island in an attempt to bring her back in line.

Of the entire expedition, decimated by yellow fever and the black rebels, only 150 officers and 320 ordinary soldiers left Saint-Domingue alive.

The French capitulated on 19 November 1803.

On 1 January 1804, at the central square in the city of Gonaïves, all the leaders of the victorious army, with Dessalines at the head, solemnly proclaimed Independence. Slavery was abolished forever.

More than 103,000 men, French and English, troops of the most seasoned and best-equipped armies of the era, had just perished in the face of battalions of ragged Negroes.

Saint-Domingue became Haiti again.

Haiti, the first Black Republic in the world. An example for Eternity.

They had never seen anything like it, didn't even think it could exist. Santo Domingo hummed in their heads and everywhere all around them. An enormous city, no end in sight, houses superimposed upon houses, large avenues, automobiles that honked at every corner, and stores, especially stores. An insane array of shop windows full of shoes, records, fabric, records, shoes, household appliances, shoes, and records. Plus the *tiendas* with even more shoes. And others with records. Hawkers and peddlers. Dealers in used objects. Shoe-shiners, barefoot, bottle in hand. Mulatto women with wide derrieres and curlers on their heads. Some *guapas*, curvaceous, arching backs, *ay hombre!* And the omnipresent music, blaring forth from the toothless traps of all the booths and stalls. Bars and cafes, the crowd, going downtown or coming back, coming down or going back, turning, yelling, hustling and bustling, coming and going. "I want to love you one more time," shrieked a tearful singer, opening her heart and her thighs over a crackling loud speaker (raising the scorching air three more degrees). *Cerveza Presidente, Ron Bermudez*; beer and rum; rum and beer. Never saw anything like it, a veritable capital spread out under the sun.

And they didn't know where to find the Embassy. They took off down an avenue they had flushed out by chance, *Avenida Duarte*, it seemed. In passing, Jean-René's glance penetrated through an open door into what must have been a restaurant. His stomach. To the left of the opening, a very long counter, and behind a cash register, a Chinaman's head. Then nothing. His shaky legs had already carried him a little further. As far as a square, a wide expanse of more or less scrubby patches of grass cluttered with benches and a bandstand, surrounded by bus stops, crowds of passengers, newspaper stands. *El Sol, El Sol! La Noticia!*

They stopped, exhausted. Now what? Jean-René was gazing at the horde of vehicles surging past, unleashed by the last green light, in a blast of horns. Unable to focus his thoughts, he daydreamed for a brief moment. He was brought back to reality by the tribulations of an old man whom the motorists, seemingly in league, could not, despite their efforts, manage to run over. The old-timer had unwisely started advancing into the street, probably in the insane hope of crossing. He was holding in his outstretched hand a more and more trembling cane, which seemed to have the same effect on the excited drivers as a cape before a furious bull. Jean-René sensed an imminent death. That of the toreador, not of the bull. A small group of Dominicans were breaking up laughing.

"I'll bet a peso on the autos!"

That was a tidy sum. The others took the challenge. The verdict came quickly. Contrary to all expectations, the first one lost. His name was Manuel. The old man reached the other sidewalk choking, made a rapid sign of the cross, and disappeared in the crowd.

"*Esos conductores no tienen cojones!*" hissed Manuel, pretending to be greatly vexed. "These drivers've got no balls!"

They burst out laughing. It was at that moment that their eyes caught the group of Kongos who were wandering in bewilderment through the square. They looked completely lost. They were.

"What is *that*?"

Dilcia turned away; a pretty woman, her very suntanned face seemed to show a keen irritation.

"Haitians!"

"Filthy as they are, it's not hard to guess."

"What are they doing here?"

"Who knows? They're all over the place!"

They were four, three men and a woman, four Dominicans

among a multitude of other Dominicans, neither better nor worse; besides, why would the Dominicans be bad? They're not. People among the Peoples, they have enormous qualities, big faults, are divided into decent folks, poor folks, bastards, dirty bastards, the rich and the underprivileged, few rich — in power — many under-privileged — always swindled. Where is the infamy? The originality?

"It's a horde arriving from the west with all kinds of diseases," declared Dilcia in her shrill voice.

"All kinds of diseases? What kind of a story is that? These diseases you are talking about wouldn't be, by any chance, having black skin?"

"Venereal diseases! It's disgusting!"

"They don't have them any more than you and me."

"Oh yes they do! With them, you're sure to catch some kind of filthy plague you pass on to everybody!"

Ruben smiled, his eyes sparkling uncontained mirth.

"Eh bravo, my dear. I see you keep pretty busy!"

Manuel was slapping his thighs, and Fernando also. They were going to get on the waiting list. Dilcia shrugged, what idiots! Manuel got serious again and his face hardened.

"I don't know anything about diseases, I don't sleep with them myself. . .although it wouldn't surprise me. But they are savages! They pillaged, they raped, they killed!"

Ruben shook his head in anger.

"That's for sure. And in the back country of Haiti they still live as savages."

"*Mierda!* You still believe that?"

"But it's true," shrilled Dilcia, indignant. "Me, I don't want anything to do with those people. They steal children and eat them."

"That's just what I was saying," Ruben cracked up laughing. "They are cannibals."

"Nègres!"

Ruben stared at Dilcia in surprise and his eyes rounded to match his stupefaction.

"They're nègres!"

"Well, yeah, they're nègres!"

"And you, what are you?"

The mulatto woman nearly fell on her ass. Ruben sure asks some questions at times!

"Me, I'm Dominican."

Ruben nodded in agreement, examined Dilcia's rather warm, brown complexion, her frizzy hair, and her pretty, very full lips. The result was not at all disagreeable, that was not the problem.

"And Dominican of what race, *por favor*?"

"Don't be a complete moron, it's obvious. I'm *India; India obscura*, dark Indian.

Ruben let out a short laugh, long in significance, tapped his forehead with his index finger. "Oh really? You are Indian! Well then, let me introduce myself, I'm Jimmy Carter, President of the United States!" Then he burst out laughing, for he didn't feel like crying.

No one has ever wanted to consider himself black in Santo Domingo. Even at the time of Spanish colonization, blacks and mulattos have always embarked upon a frenzied race towards whitening, the free blacks more than the others, such was their fear of being mistaken for a black, in other words, slave. In order to break all ties with the former past of servitude, Dominican blacks and their descendants, Negroes, mulattos, light mulattos, simply created a new color, new in name only: Indian, India, Indio, but which integrates itself much more harmoniously in the White, Hispanic, and Christian Republic, an artificial creation of the Dominican oligarchy in the face of Negro, Savage and Voodooistic Haiti, which menaces, of course, the purity of the Dominican race, i.e., this same oligarchy.

"Yes, I'm President Carter," continued Ruben, furious. Not only does Dilcia, a descendant of the blacks, stupidly claim to be a dark Indian, but she gives herself the luxury of holding the Haitians in contempt, as Negroes! "I'm going to tell you something! We are all White, Black, or Mulatto, but in Santo Domingo, there aren't any Indians! Whether you like it or not, you are a descendant of the blacks!"

She closed her mouth with scorn, gazing upon the noisy bustle of the busy, commercial main street. Couldn't prevent her eyes from falling on the Kongos, this herd of Kongos, there were at least forty of them, and what an appearance. . . A guttural sound escaped from her throat. She, descendant of. . . He didn't know it yet, but Ruben just lost a friend. She spat more than she spoke:

"I'm not interested in those people."

"So Haitians are people?"

She smiled at Manuel, who had come to her rescue, sarcastic and scornful. "They pillaged, they killed, they raped," he repeated another time, with force.

"Raped," emphasized Dilcia, with disgust. "Raped!"

Ruben absently scratched his neck. We Dominicans are always suspicious of our neighbors, these foreigners who come from the other side of the island. We have different languages and customs. There have been wars between us. You can't deny that the Haitians have committed certain acts of cruelty in the past. But we don't go down in history pure white, contrary to what they try to make us believe. The responsibilities are shared... The Haitian People nothing but a tribe of savage Africans... their Revolution, a barbaric war of sadistic Negroes assassinating Whites... What bullshit!

The tension does not date from yesterday. On 4 April 1792, when the National French Convention recognized the political and social equality of the "Freemen," it was careful not to abolish slavery. The black leaders, Jean-François and Biassou, as well as their lieutenants, Dessalines, Christophe, and Toussaint Louverture, were disappointed and packed up and moved to the western side of the island. They were promised arms, ammunition, the protection of the King of Spain, and most of all, the liberation of the slaves. They fought in cooperation with the Royalists and the English against the French Republic. But when, on 4 April 1794, the National French Assembly finally proclaimed the liberation of the slaves, Toussaint Louverture returned to the Republic with his army. His principal objective, the liberation of his People, was attained. Defending this essential acquisition against the enemies of France remained. His engagement permitted the French troops to defeat the English and the Spanish.

He was a traitor, the Dominican nationalist historians would hammer for a long time, practically up until today. They never forgave him this episode.

Ups and downs. What proved to be more serious was the invasion of the eastern side of the island by Haitian troops shortly after their declaration of Independence. One thousand French officers and troops were installed there, which constituted a potential base of departure for a possible reconquest of the island. What is more, on 6 January 1805, General Ferrand, the commander of this detachment, established a decree which explictly ordered attacks on the young Haitian nation, authorizing the "hunt for Haitians," who, once captured, would be sold in neighboring islands as slaves. Dessalines, Pétion, and Christophe no longer had any choice. To defend their recent independence they invaded the eastern part of the island to expel the French.

On 7 March 1805, the regrouped forces of Christophe and Dessalines camped in front of Santo Domingo.

On 28 March, the French warships, reported in the vicinity for two days, brusquely set sail to the west, in the direction of Haiti, stripped of her troops.

The panic-stricken Haitian leaders broke camp, and launched a forced march backwards to go and defend their young Republic. Provoked by an indescribable fury, they indulged in appalling and inexcusable carnage all along the way. This long wake of blood was never to be forgotten by the Dominican People.

It was nevertheless in the first third of the nineteenth century, during the occupation of the eastern part of the island, that the anti-Haitian racism appeared and spread, as the most evident expression of a nationalist ideology.

Hispaniola, the Spanish part, declared its independence in 1821, only to be annexed by Haiti the following year. Indeed, when Boyer arrived in Santo Domingo on 9 February 1822, putting a definitive end to the European colonial domination, his first decree was to abolish slavery in all the Dominican territory; but the latter stayed under Haitian domination for twenty-two years.

The fall of General Boyer marked the permanent separation between the two parts of the island.

This long history, to which one must also add the dictator Trujillo's massacre of 40,000 Haitians in 1937 — to which we'll return — left its traces.

The current situation of the Haitian "bracero" in the plantations only reinforces the existing racism, carefully maintained by the most conservative elements of the Dominican oligarchy. They live in these conditions because they are nègres. They are nègres because they live in these conditions.

"They are dirty," puked Dilcia, with a disgusted grimace. Then stiffly, observing their remains of clothing, "I never saw a well-dressed Haitian."

"You never went any further than your own backyard," remarked Ruben, unsympathetically.

"Yes, better not exaggerate," agreed Fernando, suddenly very earnest. "All the same, the Haitian has enormous qualities. Don't forget that it's the bird that resembles man the most." (A moment's silence to enjoy the produced effect.) In fact, he thought the complete opposite.

The Kongos had arrived at one of the far ends of the square. A few were sitting on the ground, heads thrown back in the pursuit of impossible relaxation, stretching the muscles of their legs with pained grimaces. Others were coming slowly. *Ki sa nou fé?*

"Better watch out!" declared Ruben, who was observing them attentively. "The day they don't come and work in this country any more, either we decide to cut the cane ourselves, or else we'll have to tear down the factories, pull out the cane and plant bananas and manioc in its place."

Fernando got serious again, took a few steps. "I'm not worried, we'll buy some machines."

"Machines," snorted Manuel, not at all convinced. "Machines... the best machine for cutting the cane is a Haitian!"

"You look down on them for their misery and their dirtiness!"

Ruben was tapping his foot nervously. "You don't even realize that it's you and your society that makes them live that way."

He sighed, sensed the bustle of the big city. A bus roared off toward the beaches of Boca Chica. A sugar ice vendor was squawking his wares. Three grinning and grimy urchins were racing around. All around, far and wide, in a vast expanse, sprawled Santo Domingo — rich, poor, colonial. One of the most beautiful capitals in the Caribbean and Central American region, according to travellers. Ruben slowly lost himself in his thoughts. In 1975, the price of sugar on the world market almost tripled. It went from 90 to 220 dollars a ton. The state budget was blown up by this economic boom. Balaguer, then in power, utilized this money; wasted it, but also built up many new areas of the city in the process. A great number of government civil servants, avowed as well as potential electors, received their house as a gift. Balaguer was of great "assistance" to his supporters at this time. The money was used for an urbanization program for the benefit of the middle classes; a program that was all flash, but which transformed the capital into what it is today — a very beautiful city. If, of course, you don't wander into the working class neighborhoods. It is thus that we possess an esplanade almost eighteen miles long of which any country would be proud. It starts in Haina, to the west of Santo Domingo, and ends to the east, after the airport. It's a marvel, with nooks and a public garden *el paseo de los Indios*, it's a marvel. And all that, thanks to sugar. But the sugar, who is at the root of it? The Haitians!

"This capital is built partly on their sweat."

"And the sweat of the Dominicans, maybe you better not forget about that."

"I'm not forgetting it."

"We work too, you know."

"Exactly! You should be able to understand."

"I live in the 'barrios,' the suburbs, the shit of Santo Domingo, and I earn a hundred and twenty pesos a month! You know very well!"

"Those who exploit them are the same ones who exploit us," explained Ruben. "It's a whole system."

"But we are Dominicans."

"You can be really dumb when you want to. You haven't understood yet that those who exploit them need to depreciate them to be able to do it even more? And for that, they need your complicity? If one day the Haitians refuse to continue living in the bateys, and if you aren't smart enough between now and then to establish a balance of strength in your favor, don't kid yourself; it's you that they'll send there. If you're not fighting to better the lot of the Haitians, you're digging your own grave."

"Those guys will always work the cane. They are good-for-nothings!"

A sad irony was apparent as Ruben's bitter eyes stared at him.

"Good-for-nothings...If you knew how the North Americans talk about the Dominicans who are in New York, you would have more consideration for the Haitians."

Then he said nothing more, wondering angrily how such an unthinking racism could develop in the minds of so many individuals not really bad at heart.

A woman passed, dragging a little girl by the hand. He didn't see them. The kid was crying and sniffling, dragging her feet with obvious unwillingness. The mother turned around, exasperated. "You are going to immediately stop your shenanigans or I'm going to smack you!" And more tears and louder howls. The mother stopped and looked around, completely at a loss. A spark flashed somewhere in her head; she turned to the puffy-eyed little girl.

"All right, now I'm warning you! If you continue your whining I'm going to give you to one of those Haitians over there and he'll take you away in his big sack!"

The child opened two big terror-stricken eyes and, in a desperate effort, choked back her sobs.

They still didn't know where to find the Embassy. A Haitian who was passing by had heard them and recognized the flavor of a few Creole words. He was amazed at their ungainly sight and at their number, especially at the sight of them, and had come over to see what he could find out, and helped them out of their predicament. He lived in Santo Domingo. "In Santo Domingo?" "In Santo Domingo. There are a lot of Haitians in Santo Domingo, my friend!" How do they live? The man made a vague gesture that meant nothing. Back to the pressing matters at hand. He agreed to buy two pairs of pants and a shirt, a meager baggage, from three Kongos, for the derisory sum of a dollar and half each. He wasn't rich, my friend. "Now, get a taxi," advised he, "ask him for the Haitian Embassy." It wasn't a bad idea. Five of them, including Jean-René and Marcellin, jumped into the cab the Haitian hailed, a great big old battered car. The others stayed put in the midst of a colorful stir of curiosity. "Don't move, we'll be back as soon as there's anything new." The taxi was very efficient, showed them all over town. They passed in front of the cathedral without knowing that under the dome, in a marble and bronze tomb, was an illustrious unknown. A certain Christopher Columbus. A little further to the west, they passed Las Mercedes

Church, built in 1555, sacked by the pirate Francis Drake in 1586. Big deal. They emerged at the Altar of the Homeland by way of El Conde street — busy, swarming, commercial, very cosmopolitan. The animated and colonial city became calm and modern on each side of Bolivar Avenue, the principal artery of the residential neighborhoods to the west. The seacoast, the big hotels, the streets of a discreetly luxurious smoothness. Involuntary tourists, they were going for a ride. The taxi driver stopped, asked a question, always the same one, started up again. He had no idea where this damn embassy was located.

He drove around for two hours for four and a half dollars, then brought them back to the square from which they had started.

"There you are," he said, stopping, "I don't know the way."

The others were still there, hadn't budged, hoping. They were still determined, but all were very hungry. So hungry that they couldn't even talk about it. Hungry, hungry, hungry, *ou konprann?* The five from the taxi were probably the most determined.

"To eat, the best thing we can do is to go to jail." That provoked an outcry.

"We didn't just get out of a batey to go to prison!"

"Besides, nothing says that in prison we'll get anything to eat!"

"We'll be sheltered."

"Sheltered from what? Not sheltered from beatings!"

"It's the risk you have to take."

"I'm not taking it. We better stay right here."

"Until next year?"

"Until we find a solution."

"The solution will be our deaths!"

"We have to stay right here."

The discussion was heated, to say the least. The five from the taxi left the group since quite obviously their idea was disputed. They took off on foot. A little before, they had noticed, on the far end of the square, a nicely painted green casern. They immediately introduced themselves and, to their great surprise, were summarily ushered out. They didn't need any prisoners. They felt their forces abandoning them. Marcellin had spotted a police station on Bolivar Avenue. They were sweating; looking, walking, they finally found it. They kindly laughed in their faces. Sorry, no cells. They took off, heads lowered and full of bad ideas, finally found another station, at the end of their strength, at the end of their rope. They were literally thrown out. They had already given. They wandered in every direction, completely distraught. Everywhere, they were sent away.

The city spread out under the sun, so beautiful, so unknown, so mysterious, so Dominican. An understanding passerby who knew—that man there knows! He knows? He knows! He really knows? He says he knows—wrote something on a slip of paper to give to a traffic policeman for directions to the Embassy. "*Muchas gracias*," said Marcellin. The man smiled amiably and disappeared. They looked at one another with joy, then consternation. Traffic, there surely was, but traffic cops, nowhere to be seen. And they were completely starved, more and more without strength, and more and more starved.

They walked round and round.

The building that suddenly loomed before them was massive, rectangular, and enclosed behind a large no man's land and high railings. It was the National Palace. "There are guards," said someone. They approached, determined to cry out, make a scene, to die if they had to, for they wanted to wander no further, like this, in the clutches of *Grangou*. The sentry proved to be very obliging with Marcellin. He mechanically tipped his peaked cap, gave them directions which turned out to be very good directions. Shortly after, they perceived a red and black flag, and recognized the coat of arms of their country.

Having been five leaving the square, they were sixteen to arrive; other companions in misfortune having caught up with them in the course of their respective wanderings. They planted themselves in front of the Embassy, stretching their emaciated arms toward their flag. Beloved Haiti!

The Dominican soldier on sentry in front of the diplomatic representation stopped them from entering. He had a gun and a no-nonsense air about him. All around were silent and elegant homes. "It's Sunday," he said to them, "you can't go in." "We are Haitian even on Sunday." "Don't want to hear it!" They protested very strongly, as strongly as their strength would permit.

The gate of the adjacent house, a lovely, discreetly residential dwelling, had been left open. They entered and stretched out on the lawn which was soft, ever so nice. When they realized that a furious, enraged individual, hands on his hips, was watching them from a now open door in the facade of the house, they didn't understand right away that it was in fact the owner. The man acted quickly. He mobilized a long hose, turned on a faucet energetically. The water hit them full blast, and once past the first blissful moment under the cool, powerful spray, they understood that they had to get up. They dashed out in all haste and some of them even had the strength to laugh. They sat down on the sidewalk in front of the embassy. *Grangou, grangou.* Then they lay down on their backs and watched the Dominicans who were passing with stiff-lipped airs. One of the Haitians at the end of the row held out his hand, a last desperate hope. Two Dominicans gave 65 centavos, the others who passed after gave nothing.

Marcellin and Jean-René were dispatched. They roamed the streets, parched with heat, between thick carpets of lawns and shady terraces. They had never seen at one time so many houses constructed of something other than rusty sheet metal or rotten boards. They finally found what they were looking for at the corner of a street. On a delivery tricycle with badly inflated tires was placed an enormous pot of boiling water covered with a large lid. The bored vendor was alongside. Marcellin approached him.

"Tenemos sesenta y cinco centavos. Qué podemos comprar?"

For sixty-five centavos they could buy one ear of boiled corn. The Dominican was understanding, poured them a good amount of salty water in a can recovered from the gutter nearby. He also gave them a lemon. They took off with their loot.

It was dinner for sixteen. Each one took a few kernels of corn in his hand, contemplated them at length, put them to his mouth, tried to imagine the taste, swallowed them without even realizing it, drank a little of the salty water. It was finished. Next, they went to quench their thirst at a faucet spotted near the garage of a superb villa. They were sixteen, and didn't have a whole lot to digest.

Dominicanie is a strange country. Imagine, over there, no one sleeps in the street. Around six o'clock, when the night was settling in silently over the whiteness of the residences, the soldier slowly came towards them. *"Que regresen a casa!"* "What is he saying?" "He says we have to go home." A volley of weak laughter greeted this incongruity. "We'd certainly like to! That's why we're here!" The soldier motioned again for them to leave. They lay down on the sidewalk anyway, and the guard undertook dislodging them, one by one, with half-hearted blows of his rifle butt. "Shit," said a Kongo, "you're not even allowed to sleep in the street."

In Port-au-Prince, in these conditions, there would be 30,000 walking in circles all night long.

The soldier had to give up.

The Ambassador, François Guillaume, arrived around six o'clock the next morning. Seeing them, he paled noticeably. "What's going on here? What the hell are you doing here?" "We are Kongos, we want to go back to Haiti." "That is completely out of the question." "We want to go back to Haiti, the Dominicans mistreated us." "You are going to return to your bateys!" The little crowd began shouting, bawling, protesting. François Guillaume threw up his arms, completely exasperated. "Do not insist, Gentlemen, you will not go back to Haiti." "Fine," said a voice. "If that's the way it is, we're going to holler, make a scene." "Please, Gentlemen, please, a little courtesy!" But they did. That's just what they did. They began to shout. They screamed. "*An mwin!* Help!" they screamed. Mad with rage, François Guillaume shoved his clenched fists in his pockets and cursed the Dominicans that had let them leave the batey in such large numbers, let them get as far as here. When they present themselves one by one, they are easily packed off, but here, he was in a jam, felt outmaneuvered by the situation. In Haiti, he would have had them billy clubbed. In open country, he would have had them thrashed. Here, in the middle of the Dominican capital, with the neighbors, the curious, a relatively independent press, political parties in the opposition (can you imagine?), the unions (no, really!), a public opinion, he was relatively tied hand and foot. He cursed the beginnings of democratization in this strange country, and asked himself with irritation how long the military was going to tolerate this...

Meanwhile, the Kongos were entering. He couldn't prevent himself from screeching. "No, not that way, you morons! Go round back! You haven't seen the state you're in!" Yes, they had seen.

He sighed, had the pseudo-identity cards collected, went into his office, started writing, made a few phone calls.

At noon, a big bus pulled up in front of the embassy. "Gentlemen, you may go home."

"Go home, fine! But we are hungry!"

Oh, so now they were hungry! François Guillaume warned them. "Careful, Gentlemen, enough is enough!" They didn't seem to understand. "We are hungry. In fact we are very hungry." They couldn't drag themselves any further. They hadn't eaten since...they hadn't eaten, in other words, for a really long time. "You'll have to make the best of it! I've already spent enough money on the Kongos, I'm not spending any more!" They tightened their belts another notch. They got in the bus, arrived the next morning in Malpasse, still not having eaten. They were dumped at the border, and found themselves in a casern. The Malpasse gendarme, at his wit's end, telephoned Croix-des-Bouquets. At the end of his rope, the captain flew into a rage. "I've spent enough! Him too! Not a penny for these vagabonds. I already sent out five trucks to repatriate all those that got to the border." "Five trucks," murmured the Kongos. "There must be some strange things going on in Dominicanie." All these Kongos, so extremely desirous of working only a few days before, who were pouring back pell-mell to their country, were the harbingers of some catastrophe, some unexplained and inexplicable phenomenon. "Well then, are the Kongos mistreated everywhere in Dominicanie?" asked Jean-René. No one answered him.

They were hungry, hungry until three o'clock. The exasperated gendarme suggested that they sell their last baggage, what was left of pants, shoes, and shirts. Which they did, in the casern, to the delighted wives of the gendarmes. All, or nearly, sold a little something. By now, some were walking around barefoot and barechested. Next, they each paid two or three gourdes. The soothed gendarmes sent for a van to bring them to Croix-des-Bouquets. There they arrived at five o'clock, collapsing, completely wiped out, while an apathetic sergeant made out the report. "Get out of here," he told them, without even bothering to look up. "Pick up your life where you left off. You can thank God to be back alive." Completely staggered, they looked at one another. Next, they went out, crossed the courtyard with hesitant steps, and ran into a captain who stopped them, examined them severely, and ordered them not to leave, not to budge. "What are you doing here? Oh yeah? Is that right? You've decided! Well, we'll see about that. You are going to go back there, I'm telling you so."

They waited until his back was turned, gathered their remaining forces, and fled, running, limping every bit as much as they ran, but they didn't give a damn, they were getting the hell out of there.

In fact, they were very lucky. Very few got out of it as successfully as they.

The whole family watched him do it in silence. Jean-René took a third plateful of bad rice and beans. They were disappointed. When he'd come staggering through the door, then had found the strength to smile at them, they had all thrown themselves on him, convinced he had *anpil lajan*, a lot of money. They were going to improve their everyday conditions. Although, to think of it, he hadn't been gone very long. His ravaged face, features aged by suffering, had stopped them abruptly. He had collapsed, incapable of stammering, thinking, speaking, walking. "*M grangou, m grangou*," was all he was capable of repeating. "I'm hungry." They laid him down and the mother hastily warmed up the big pot.

He was gulping it down voraciously, took a long drink from the plastic pitcher, let a spurt of water run down his beard-blackened chin without reacting. He ate more. No one dared to ask him anything. He put his fork on the cluttered table, slowly took his head in his hands.

He was thinking about Roger, about Ricoeur, about all his comrades, about those he'd lost in Santo Domingo. The others thought they heard a moan. The light of a *gridap* lamp danced softly on the back of his neck. He raised his head, caught a glimpse of the attentive silhouettes in the shadowy halflight. His eyes closed slowly. "I would like to know," he murmured absently, "I would like to know what's going to happen to them, to all my compatriots they took and put in prison. I would like to know what they are going to do to all those thousands of Kongos left in the bateys. I would like. . ."

He got up abruptly, made for the half-open door by instinct, pushed the flap out of the way in an awkward, panicked movement. He leaned against the doorpost. The sweat was beading on his forehead in sickening drops. He doubled over brutally, leaned forward choking, and vomited for a long time.

He had eaten too much.

Article 26: The State Sugar Council agrees to pay the Haitian agricultural worker the sum of 1 peso 35 in Dominican currency for each short ton of cane cut. It is understood that in the event of a wage increase paid to the Dominican worker, in accordance with the Dominican laws, the Haitian agricultural worker will be granted the same advantages, and the Haitian Embassy in Santo Domingo will be so informed.

The night, still full of darkness, a first angry shout, then more shouts, followed by an obscene and continuous thumping on the closed doors. "*Vamos, vamos, Haitianos, vamos!*" The capataz was leaping from cell to cell with a laugh as acrid as sour milk. "Get up, Kongos, get up! Jean-Claude sold you!" They woke up groaning, emerging silently from their night without sleep on the hard, naked cement slab. You could hear long sighs juxtaposed with the voice without mercy, "Get up, Kongos, on your feet!" The zafra had begun. Four o'clock in the morning had not yet struck anywhere, they were coming out of the shacks. The black skin was pale with the unfinished night. They seized the machete without seeing it, got in line, marched mechanically towards the exit of the batey. On waking, they found no water to wash their faces or mouths. And they didn't eat. What would they have eaten? The capataz ran his thick finger over the cutting edge of each tool, grunting a word or two, which they may or may not have understood. Of what importance? They knew they were supposed to show up in the fields with a well-sharpened blade. Next, the boss put them in teams, decided who was working alone, who was working in a group, divided up the work from one point to another after having marked the limit for each group. "You, go over there boy, you there, you there. You can at least do that much today." The field of cane stretched out, immense, like a green sea with no horizon. Estimé Mondestin caught his breath, fearing suddenly to drown in it one day. The expanse to cut could have extended like from the National Palace to the Customs at Port-au-Prince, my friend, patches of cane 200, 250 squares,* really.

When faced with his travail for the first time, Estimé Mondestin saw nothing. It must have been four-thirty in the morning, the darkness hemmed in the long stalks with a heavy protective curtain, he didn't even see the ends of his feet. "There's still too much duskiness." he groaned, alarmed. He didn't cut anything. In this disquieting opaqueness, he could have just as well sliced off a hand. He waited until it was lighter. Around six o'clock, daylight sprang up at one extremity of the plain, and rapidly extended a pencil of light on the dark carpet. The others had already started.

They were three, adrift in the tempest. He was teamed up with his two shackmates, Gérard André from Jean-Rabel and Brutus from Miragoane. Petit Pierre Déroseaux from Pétionville had sort of abandoned them. During the eleven days of inactivity that preceded the actual start of the zafra, in which they were all practically starved to death, he had met a viejo, a vague acquaintance of a distant cousin. The viejo had proposed that they make a team. Déroseaux had accepted. Estimé Mondestin was a little vexed by it. All the viejos display the same attitude vis-à-vis the Kongos. They are always cold, and at the slightest dispute take out their machete. They get along very nicely with the Dominicans. They've got wives, mostly Haitians. They have houses near the barracones. Sometimes they have animals. Often, they have children that roam the batey, completely idle. They live with the Dominican women as soon as with the Haitian women. They don't have good relations with the newcomers. They turn their backs to us. And Déroseaux had gone to work with one of them.

Objectively speaking, Estimé Mondestin didn't know how. He had never worked with a machete in Haiti. This was the first time. Self-conscious, he approached Gérard André, whose arm was rising and falling in a rhythmic, violent cadence.

"*Bon, monchè. Ou a di-m so pou m fè*. Tell me what to do, my friend."

"You don't know?"

"I never learned how."

---

*One square = approximately three acres.

Gérard André rubbed the small of his back, regarded the city-boy with mild astonishment. He had been cutting his whole life.

"Okay, I'm going to teach you how you cut the cane. It's not hard. Watch me" (stroke of the machete). "You have to cut as far down as possible, like this" (stroke of the machete). "The ideal would be to cut under the surface of the ground! *Ou konprann?* Look, I'll do it again" (stroke of the machete). "You have to do it in one clean cut" (stroke of the machete). "You see?"

Gérard André went into action, lowered his body and arms silently, stood up again. "You pull off the leaves, you cut the heart, and you divide the cane into pieces just under three feet long. Now, you try."

Estimé Mondestin turned out to be clumsy. Gérard André corrected him. "There, like that. The tip of the cane has to be rounded so it doesn't hurt the one that picks it up. *Ou konprann?*" Estimé Mondestin understood, but his *mocha*, his full-of-shit, mind-of-its-own machete didn't understand. Patiently, Gérard André started over.

"We're going to need a lot of time," estimated Mondestin, casting his eyes over the immense expanse and depth of the *cannaie*, the cane field.

"That can take a week and a half for a group," estimated Gérard André.

Hearing steps, they turned around. Brutus was approaching, vividly outlined in his bright red shirt whose breast pocket was coming unsewn and which the acrid sweat was already eating into.

"Hey, you two! Me, I'm working, and you, you're talking! That's no good!"

"I'm showing him," explained Gérard André. "He doesn't know."

"Well, let him learn quick," grumbled the robust Kongo. "We're not paid by the day, but by the weight of the cane cut."

"That I know," replied Estimé Mondestin dryly. "What I don't know very well is how to cut."

"You did know what you were going to do here."

"I'm going to learn quickly."

"You're making us lose money. You should have learned before."

Estimé Mondestin shrugged. Brutus wasn't a bad guy, but since their arrival, he was so affected by the situation that had been imposed on them that he didn't say a word all day long, sat withdrawn, jaws clenched, alone in his corner.

"All right, okay, money, we've got six months to make it!"

Brutus was mumbling, something to the effect that it was just his luck to have a beginner for a team member, and other disagreeable things of the same ilk. "Leave him the hell alone," intervened Gérard André curtly. "In three days he'll be working as well as you."

"He better," muttered Brutus, unsmiling. "We came here to make it." He left without adding another word, and after Gérard André had flashed a conspiratorial smile at Estimé Mondestin, all three planted themselves before a veritable forest of tangled cane.

When the sun was vertical — it must have been noon — they stopped for a moment, muscles like mush. They hadn't brought anything to eat. They had nothing to drink. "First of all, we have to buy ourselves a water jug," said Gérard André. "And a lamp for the night," said Brutus, thinking of the darkness. "When are we going to get paid?" asked Estimé Mondestin. "When our cane gets weighed," said Gérard André. "And when will it be weighed?" "No idea. I'm hot."

"It's really rough," said Mondestin.

The planet was nothing more than an immense plantation. Arms already ravaged with cuts, welts, big open scratches burning with omnipresent sweat: throughout an entire country the thousands of Kongos were sweating in rhythm, hanging on to survive the immensity of the plantation. Having left at dawn, they returned at dusk, bellies desperately empty.

They learned the immutable laws of life in the batey. At the approach of evening, one of the members of each group went off to prepare the meal for the others. They took turns. The first arrival brought two loaves of bread on credit. From the day that they had started work, the almost daily allotment of 75 centavos had been stopped. Fortunately, the bodeguero seemed better disposed towards them, they were going to get their first pay. They ate rice, bananas, manioc, especially manioc. Estimé Mondestin saw his friend, Gustavo Perez, regularly, and thanks to him, was able to get his supplies from the bodega without too many problems. Of course, within reasonable limits, however, Scorza had clarified. When the occasion presented itself, he offered the Dominican a pack of cigarettes, a small bottle of rum, in exchange for his helpful services, or to be more precise, Gustavo Perez offered himself a pack of cigarettes, a small bottle of rum, and availed himself of the occasion each time he ran across Estimé Mondestin in the vicinity of the bodega. "As long as I'm around," he said, "you'll have nothing to fear, this old bastard Scorza will give you credit." "Hola Scorza," he brayed, "don't forget to take care of my friend here." Then he added: "Give me a bottle of your cheap rum, my throat's dry from yelling. I'm putting it on your account," he added, in the direction of the Kongo, "we'll settle up." Mondestin was a little bothered, but he was nevertheless happy; thanks to the kindness of Gustavo Perez, he could buy on credit. They would settle all that later. That was how he was able to procure the oil they needed for some light, while so many others were reduced to living in darkness. You didn't find any lamps in Dominicanie. Or even if you do find any, they didn't have enough money, even with credit. Those lamps there, that's for the aristocracy, Scorza had announced, the evening he had asked him the price.

The viejos had thus explained to them the procedure, they weren't all that bad. They took an empty bottle, filled it with the crude oil, fashioned a wick out of an old piece of canvas, and lit it. They had also brought some matches. They lit the *lanp têt zègrè* at the same time as the thousands of Kongos in all the bateys lit theirs.

Petit Pierre Déroseaux rejoined them for meals, good and tired, but who wasn't. He recounted his adventures with the viejo to them. It was a good viejo. He spoke Spanish with the Dominicans and Creole with Déroseaux. They had already filled a cabrouet, the two-wheeled cart drawn by a team of four oxen used to transport the cane. "He said to me, 'Kongo, come here.' I told him, 'one minute, viejo,' ha, ha, I call him viejo since he calls me Kongo. A few minutes later, he said to me, '*carga, carga, pronto!* Hurry up and load!' I did it. He said to me, 'you are a good companion.' He thought a Kongo couldn't work so fast. The viejos, they're used to it, they've done it their whole life. Seeing my good work, he started to sing me an old Haitian song, you know it?" Petit Pierre Déroseaux, seated wearily on the floor, began humming. "*Kalbas kourant ki poté kou li bay maré kod* . . . It's the gourd that carries your neck to put the rope. . ." He was humming away, stopped, lifted his eyes toward the stars. "To quench our thirst, the wife of a viejo brought us a big pail full of water. It's the only drink we can afford, viejos and Kongos alike."

The others were listening and dreaming. "You're pretty lucky. No one gave us anything." "Yes, that's what's good about a viejo. They are bad off but organized." "Better off than us." "Well yes! And more organized! But bad off just the same, I'm telling you — he told me." "Of course, but better organized. Anyway, used to it."

They all quieted down, listening to the murmur of the batey. Déroseaux started up again. "It seems that things were better in the old days, it's the viejo who told me that also. Sometimes, while they were working, a truck from the company arrived, and this truck carried big containers of water and each one received three tablets against the fever. It's the viejo who told me."

"The past is the past," commented Brutus darkly, "we're here in the present." "If only we had some water during the work," Estimé Mondestin was saying, "that would be good. The capataz has a horse and can get around easily to drink some water, I've seen him do it." "The capataz is the capataz," snapped Brutus, hands on the ground on either side of his buttocks. "We are Kongos, we are!" "How much does he make, the capataz?" resumed Mondestin. "I don't know what he gets," grunted an ill-tempered Brutus. "I can't check up on the Dominicans' business." It wasn't easy to talk to him. "...*Kalbas kourant ki poté kou li*," crooned Petit Pierre Déroseaux, eyes far away, "*bay maré kod...*"

They retired, Déroseaux and Brutus each on a bed, Estimé Mondestin on his burlap sack laid out on the ground. Gérard André, also on the ground, on some clothes. It got cold all at once, and they slept like animals, like lambs.

By now they had bought a plastic water jug. They brought water that got hot in the plantation. They drank it anyway. It was disgusting, with the taste of new plastic as well, but it was very good, much better than when they didn't drink.

They were waiting for the collection. They had already cut for three days, and in the morning Brutus had said, "We have to get organized. While two of us are cutting the cane, the third one will arrange the stalks in straight piles. We have to think about collecting it." Gérard André approved, and it was Estimé Mondestin who inaugurated this new system. Stationed upright in his little canary yellow v-necked jersey with three-quarter length sleeves, already ripped at the level of the abdomen, he contemplated the ground littered with cut cane. It was discouraging, there was so much of it, like a storm-racked forest uprooted by a cataclysm. In every direction was tangled cane, mid-calf deep, over hundreds and hundreds and hundreds of square yards. He attacked it methodically. He grabbed the pieces by one end, placed them one on top of another, built a veritable small wall perpendicular to the path. They had cut a lot of cane, really.

There was only one problem. The Dominican cabrouetier, the man in charge of picking up their cane, didn't stop. They saw him passing on the road, steering his oxen, switch in hand, the cart empty in one direction and full in the other a little later. They tried to get his attention, frantically waving their arms, but strangely, he seemed not to see them. That he didn't see them, you could conceivably admit, maybe he was blind, fumed Brutus at the end of his patience, but their shouts? He should have heard! He didn't even notice them.

And he was just going by, the bum!

Estimé Mondestin was worried. Their debt at the bodega must have started to build up, take on proportions, for Scorza the bodeguero had said to him the night before, "Hey, Haitiano, you have to settle up all that! I'm not giving you anything else. *Ya no te doy nada. Nada de nada.*" And Gustavo Perez, whom he had looked for all over the batey to try and arrange things, was absolutely nowhere to be found. Yet in order to be paid it was absolutely necessary that their yield be collected, since they were remunerated according to the weight.

The cabrouet emerged one more time from the principal dirt road and was penetrating into the secondary path which lost itself in the infinity of a horizon convergent with sugar cane fields. All three rushed forward, lifing knees and arms high in the cut cane, still not put in piles.

"*Señor, señor!* You have to pick up our cane!"

The cabrouet came to a halt and oxen behind him immediately lowered their heads to the ground. The man cast an appraising glance over their production lying on the ground, grimaced.

"You've done good work, but I can't this trip."

"We're ready, you can start whenever you want."

"Yes, but I have to go and collect the cane over there, from those Kongos you see."

He pointed to a group of miniscule figures in a zone of cane further off.

"Well then, right after?"

"*Hola hombre*, what do you think, you're the only ones I have to deal with?"

The Dominican babbled in Creole and looked at them as if they were completely out of their minds.

"You are paid to pick up our cane, no?"

"Not your cane...the cane."

"But for our cane, too, you're paid!"

The other took a few steps and his tone changed.

"Paid! You must be kidding! Enough to die of starvation!"

"But you have to collect it."

"That's just what I do. I collect it. All day long."

"Well then, collect ours."

"You aren't the only ones and I don't take orders."

"But why them over there, and not us, since we finished at the same time and we're the first ones on your way?"

The cabrouetier reached out with his hand and patted one of the oxen, a handsome brown beast with GR 620 marked on the neck.

"They're in a big hurry. They need money."

This good joke cracked up Brutus! "We're in a big hurry too! Around here everyone is croaking from hunger, so everyone is in a big hurry!"

"Listen, hombre, they gave me a peso so that I would come right away. I have to do them this favor. They are having big problems."

"One peso," muttered Brutus, eyes blazing... If everybody did the same...! "Well then come and see us immediately after."

The Dominican spat artistically between his feet, dreamily contemplated the little bottle-green spot slowly absorbed by the dust, then smilingly regarded Brutus.

"No, after that I'm going over to the other side, way over there. I promised."

"Promised, promised," exploded Brutus, whom this business was beginning to render beside himself, "and why did you promise?"

"Because they promised me, too."

"Promised what?"

"A little something..."

"What does that mean?" Brutus had asked the question, but was beginning to understand. A violent desire to strangle this guy swept over him.

"That means that I'm very busy. There's plenty of cane to collect everywhere, so naturally there are priorities."

"But how long is that going to take?" asked Estimé Mondestin, very worried. He was thinking of Scorza the bodeguero and of his warning.

The cabrouetier made a coy face, and said in his best Creole: "*Sa kab pran sink jou kon sa*... That could take five days."

Estimé Mondestin was going to reply, with the most extreme courtesy, that it wasn't possible, that he had pressing obligations regarding the bodega, that he was asking with all due respect that he reconsider his position, when a fearsome verbal explosion cut him off. Brutus had just blown up, was looming over the Dominican who calmly took a few steps backward, looking as if butter would not melt in his mouth.

"Go to the Devil, you rotten cabrouetier! You won't get a penny! You are paid to collect, you'll collect! I'm going to talk about it tonight with the capataz and we'll see what's going to happen! And if necessary, I'll talk to the majordomo, to the administrator, to..."

"*Al señor administrador*, you say, Señor the Administrator."

"That's right! To the President of the Republic even!"

"Absolutely, he's waiting for you in his office."

"Really, I'm going to do it."

"Hou la la," clucked the disenchanted cabrouetier, "*qué desgraciado!* If all there were were people like you, we'd never work."

He pulled easily on the reins and the oxen started up. The cabrouet creaked. The cane was left abandoned on the ground.

"We won't be had," pounded Brutus, his face contorted with anger and sweat. "There's the capataz, there's the majordomo, we won't be had! This Dominican, this bum, this good-for-nothing. . ."

Estimé Mondestin and Gérard André moved away slowly toward the green wall, growing out of the hard ground. Their heads were reeling with anger, with misery and hunger, a hunger so stealthily present that they didn't even know it was hunger.

Estimé Mondestin hacked with gusto at the giant plant. The cane remained in his hand. He pruned it, sectioned it, turned around slowly to throw it on the ground.

"Better not cut any more," Brutus shouted to him from where he was standing.

"Don't cut any more!"

"No, it's useless."

"The more we cut, the more we're paid!"

"If it's collected!"

"Yes, but all the same, the more we. . ."

"No, it's not worth it. If they don't collect it right away, the cane left lying on the ground dries out and loses its weight. We work for less than nothing. I'm not cutting any more until this shit has been taken away. *Ou konprann?*"

"I understand," said Estimé Mondestin.

And so my friend, you have probably noticed something in the midst of all this. In the world of the bateys, those who go hungry are called the Kongos. And all the others get fat at their expense.

That night, they were not able to buy anything at the bodega. Brutus came back, jaws clenched, from seeing the majordomo. He sat down, took a while to organize his thoughts, cast an angry glance over the loathsome barracks. Estimé Mondestin and Gérard André respected his silence; besides, there was nothing to ask. "Between the Dominicans and the majordomo, it's one hand washes the other," he finally spat out, his shoulders tense with rage. "Their common enemy is the Kongo." He said a few more words in a low voice which seemed to indicate that the Dominicans, no matter who they were, considered them to be dogs. Then he said no more.

A little later, they headed slowly toward the bodega. Out of boredom, by chance, through weariness, because there was nothing to do, because there was no meal to prepare. Some viejos' kids were coming back from the river, bent over under the weight of big basins of more or less clear water. A little girl in braids proudly displayed her lack of even the beginnings of titties, back arched above torn terry cloth shorts. Seated all along the barracones, the Kongos waited with eyes closed. A billy can of water bubbled over an anemic fire; there were some who were eating anyway. Over there too, a little further.

It was the hour when the Dominicans drank. The Dominicans of the batey. Certain Dominicans of the batey. Bursts of laughter and voices were bouncing out of the bodega. Scorza, *hijueputa, dame un trago mas!* Estimé Mondestin glanced up, full of hope. In vain. Gustavo Perez wasn't there. They recognized the small, nasty-looking capataz, a wagonero and a cadenero, employed in the transportation of the cane when it is sent, compressed in old railroad cars, to the factory, and some guy with a gun in his belt that they didn't know. Brutus stood rooted to the ground, a statue. He had noticed an empty cabrouet pulled over by the side of the dirt road. On the neck of one of the oxen — a brown one, a beauty, a powerful and placid beast — were a few marks he didn't know how to read. GR 620. But he sensed things. Their cabrouetier was there, no doubt about it. They hadn't seen him at first glance, hidden as he was by the wagonero's large build. He was drinking right out of a flask of rum, and he smacked his lips and squinted his small bloodshot eyes.

"That bastard can drink," muttered Gérard André, "he's got money."

"And because of him, we don't even have anything to eat!"

"*Hola, negro,* buy me a drink?" the cabrouetier bellowed, suddenly addressing them, having just recognized them. "I've got one hell of a goddamn thirst!"

"You can drop dead," responded Brutus amiably in a low voice, and only his companions heard.

"These three *desgraciados,*" the cabrouetier explained calmly to his companions, "these three *desgraciados . . .*" And since they had nothing better to do, they started criticizing the Haitians, making remarks.

"Only Haitians cut cane," said one in a loud voice, afraid that the Kongos wouldn't hear. "This type of work is not made for us."

"Not made for them, of course not!" Brutus couldn't contain himself.

"*Blan pa koné travay, mè yo gin machin'.* The whites don't know how to work, but they've got machines." And Haitians. Without their machines and without the Haitians, the cane would rot in the fields and their country would be a desert — feed for the vultures!

For his part, the cabrouetier continued his monologue, staring at Brutus, and his eyes blazed with contempt.

"You, the Haitians, you are dogs and bums."

"You should talk! The Dominicans don't want to work cutting the cane," murmured a skinny Haitian who was standing near them. "They would rather be unemployed. They are lazy and they are thieves."

"Yes, lazy!"

"Hey, Haitians, tell us: so there's nothing where you come from?"

"There is, there is," answered one overzealous voice. "It's a country."

"A rotten country, yes!"

"A country, Haiti!"

"Sure, sure! So why is it that you leave your country to come here and sell your sweat?"

"To eat, that's why!"

Attracted by the start of the argument, a few Kongos had assembled at the foot of the bodega steps, where a handful of Dominicans, drinking and making jokes, were watching them. "Scorza, goddammit, *un trago mas!*" And the rum was strong, raw burning rum.

"We, too, could cut cane," continued the cabrouetier, "but the company would have to pay good money! We don't live like dogs!" He finished his tirade in Creole, immediately translating it into Spanish for his companions, who were agreeing, "Absolutely right, *compañero*, absolutely right!"

"There are no dogs here, but people who are hungry!" shouted the voice of dignity.

"People, people! Your government sells you to Guzman for one million, two hundred twenty-five thousand dollars! Are people sold?"

The cabrouetier turned, laughing, toward his companions. He laughed even harder when he saw that they were laughing too.

"*Ay hombre, qué vaína!* When the President of Haiti signs the contract for the zafra, he has a bottle of rum and a full glass in front of him!"

"Carejo, Guzman wouldn't sell us like that!"

"Guzman gives him a drink, butters him up good, Mister President for Life, and the other one is ready to hock anything!"

"He isn't all that much of a damn fool, mind you! He pockets the money!"

"Ah, hah, hah, that big fat Duvalier is no president, he's a livestock dealer! He's a Haitian-dealer! His country is the most wretched on the continent. Hah, Hah! Big Duvalier!"

The Kongos were not familiar with the Dominicans, but in a few days started to understand. They knew that they had to keep quiet, get used to it. Even if the Dominicans speak badly of you, you get hold of yourself, you pretend not to hear. If you speak out against them, things can turn out badly. Even if you hear them saying something bad, you have to accept it. *Ou konprann?*

The cabrouetier violently stamped his foot on the floor, watched the dust rise, handed Scorza two bills. "So long, you bunch of bastards, I'm getting out of here." He took the two steps like a regular, headed for his cabrouet. "*Hola*, men," he bellowed suddenly, wheeling around toward his buddies, who were continuing to quench their thirst à la Bermudez. "You know my animals?" He planted himself in front of the two beasts that were waiting, heads lowered, eyes lost in another universe. "This one here's name is Jean-Claude," said he, pointing to the first. He burst out laughing. "And that one, Duvalier!"

He laughed, the others laughed. Shit, they laughed.

A Haitian gripped his machete. "I'm going to cut off some Dominican heads." His neighbor held him back, held him back with all his strength. "Stop, that's all they're waiting for, they'll kill you!" The others lowered their heads. "Jean-Claude sold us, we are worthless in the eyes of the Dominicans. For everybody, the Kongos are dogs."

And they remained motionless, humiliated. Haiti will never be great, they were thinking.

They had finally given in two days later, almost starved. The bodega was closed to them, and without Petit Pierre Déroseaux, who had borrowed a little rice from his viejo, they would have already perished from hunger. The discussion with the cabrouetier had put their nerves through a terrible ordeal. Especially Brutus. I need at least fifty centavos! We don't have any money, we don't have anything. That's too bad, I would have liked to help you. Wait until the next load to get paid. Oh, no, there are too many of you, I can't make any exceptions! If you would be satisfied with 25 centavos, we could maybe borrow it. No, it's half a peso or nothing, I'm not a beggar. Well, then, we're going to starve to death! Listen, collect the cane, as soon as we're paid we'll give you the money. You'll forget! We won't forget, we're here with our hands and feet tied! All right; okay, I'll give you credit, but you give me one peso. One peso? But that's double! Yes, sure, but I'm giving you credit, you have to pay for it. You're hard! Come on, come on, hard but fair. Nothing given, nothing gained!

They had accepted.

All the ingenios pay for loaded cane. *Cargar la caña* (loading) is a task as difficult and grueling as cutting it, and is unremunerated. The team closest to their work location came to help them. Some cut in teams of three, others four, and others alone, but to load the cabrouet, it is necessary to establish a system of mutual aid. When the team has enough cane to load, other Kongos come, and vice versa. The Dominican cabrouet driver watches and does nothing. But he is in a big hurry. He doesn't want to lose more than five minutes. As if, in so little time, you could fill the cabrouet. *Vamonos, vamonos* he bellows, and if he had a whip, he would whip them for sure. *Vamonos Kongos!* When a Haitian cuts alone, he has problems loading. If he hasn't previously given a hand to the others, the others will not help him. It's the law of the batey. And the cabrouetier, *vamonos, vamonos!*

He too is paid according to the yield, like the pesador, the one who weighs. He is paid on the cane that's brought in. Thus, on the cut cane. Thus, on the labor of the Kongos. You have to work these loafers hard, if not, you don't make anything. *Vamonos, vamonos, Kongos!*

They were sweating bucketfuls. The cabrouetier says *hola!* The oxen's muscles tighten and the Kongos start cutting again.

Each one hands over the card on which his photo appears to the cabrouetier.

"And how does it work?" asked Gérard André.

"This man is going to bring our cane to the pesador. The pesador weighs it. He'll write down on each one of our cards what we've earned, divided by three, since there are three of us. Tonight at the batey, the cabrouetier will give them back to us."

"And we'll get paid?"

"Of course we'll get paid!"

"How much will we get?"

"How should I know? I don't know. But we'll get paid. It's according to the weight."

"How many tons, do you think, this trip?"

"I don't know, but a lot. We'll know when it's weighed. A lot, for sure."

"I hope they give us a good weight."

Yes, you can say that that day they were hoping.

However, they were not paid any money. That night, the cabrouetier gave them each their card and a slip of paper.

"What's this?"

"*El vale!*"

"The what?"

"The *vale*, the coupon, the voucher, what are you, thick?"

"But the money? Where is the money?"

"They'll give you the money in exchange for these *vales* at the *oficina*."

"Right away?" burst out Brutus, in a hurry. He was so hungry.

"No, they're changed at the end of each week, if not, it's anarchy. They've got other things to do besides that at the *oficina*!"

"But in the meantime, how are we going to eat?"

"Ah, that, I don't know. Go see at the bodega. Sometimes Scorza takes the *vales*." To their great surprise, they hadn't yet thought of looking at the pieces of paper, of asking what they were worth, these *vales*. It was Mondestin who asked the question first.

"How much did we make?"

The exasperated cabrouetier raised his eyebrows, examined the three slips with attention.

"The cabrouet that was weighed gives you 9 pesos 54."*

"Nine pesos fifty-four," repeated Estimé Mondestin softly, without really realizing it.

"Since you are three, you get 3 pesos 18 each."

"Three pesos eighteen," exclaimed Brutus, with a sudden start. "But where is the rest?"

"What rest?"

"The rest of what we're paid!"

"There is no rest, moron! The cabrouetier that you loaded was 9 pesos 54, and that's it."

"It's not possible," breathed Gérard André, and he seemed to suddenly crumble.

They had cut for three days, waited for the cabrouet for two days, had thus spent five days to earn... Nine pesos fifty-four... The cabrouetier's face twisted. It wasn't really a look of commiseration.

"If you hadn't stupidly lost two days with your cane on the ground..."

"But it was you that didn't want to!"

"What do you mean, I didn't want to? You should have been understanding. The next time, make up your minds quickly. In this country, you have to work fast to earn. In fact, while I'm thinking about it, when you've changed these friggin' papers for real money, don't forget you owe me a peso!" He smiled coldly. "If not, the next time you have some cane to load, it's me that will do the forgetting."

He waddled off, and his oxen with him, and his bitch of a cabrouet.

Estimé Mondestin came across other Kongos in front of the bodega. They all went along in silence, lost in their thoughts. He has

---

*Roughly equivalent to $9.54. — Trans.

collected the *vales* of his three companions — Déroseaux's was higher than theirs, 3 pesos 50, he'd earned — and went to pay Scorza. "You take care of all that," Brutus had decided. "I don't understand a thing about accounts."

Mondestin put the *vales* on the counter.

"What's that?" asked the bodeguero innocently.

"The pay slips."

"What do you want me to do with them? That's not money!"

"It is money! It's written how much we earned."

"Well, I don't eat with pieces of paper."

"It's the sum total, señor, it's earned!"

"I want money."

"But we don't have it — it's every week, the money. *Jodi a m pa gin kob!*"

"Well, come back at the end of the week."

"But today is Monday, how are we going to eat?"

"What, eat?"

"*Ou konn situasion-an!* You know the situation!"

"I don't know, try to change them."

"Who's going to buy that from me?" Mondestin shook his head, desperate.

A wrathful sigh spewed forth from Scorza's very guts.

"You Kongos, you're really starting to give me a pain in the ass! You never have anything." He grabbed the three slips, examined them as if he'd never seen one. "All right, let me see your *vales!* There's three for three pesos eighteen, and one for three pesos fifty. That makes...that makes...that makes exactly twelve pesos zero four," he said tranquilly, one peso off, but everybody makes mistakes.

"Twelve pesos zero four," repeated Estimé Mondestin, full of joy and disappointment. It was quite a sum when you've got nothing, it was nothing when you've come to make money.

"I'll take them at ten pesos."

"But it's twelve pesos, you just said!"

"So what...it's not money, it's pieces of paper, I shouldn't even take them."

"But we lose two pesos," rebelled Mondestin.

"And you gain ten! Look, that crap'll take me three weeks to get reimbursed."

"Two pesos for three weeks..."

"Hey, ho, Kongo! I'm not a bank, I'm a grocer! Well, hurry up. I take them or I don't take them, your *vales?*"

"At ten pesos," calculated Estimé Mondestin, disillusioned, "it's not possible." Then, in a low voice: "Take them."

They had to eat, given they had spent numerous days without working, numerous days before their cane was weighed. He waited. He already had his good credit in the bodega, thanks to Gustavo Perez, it's true, and Scorza was in the process of figuring.

"There you go, Kongo, your debts are almost paid."

And how much is left?"

"Nothing. Not only is there nothing left, but you still owe me something."

"How is there nothing? How is there still something?"

"You still owe me eleven pesos fifty!"

Estimé Mondestin frowned deeply. According to his rough estimates he'd spent around six and a half pesos, food for the group and everything else.

"We don't owe that much."

"You're saying I don't know how to count! There was the rice, (but not much, said Mondestin), the oil, (but not much, murmured Mondestin), a can of sardines, (just one can, started Mondestin)...

"Plus the cigarettes and bottles of rum for your friend Gustavo Perez. Five and a half pesos."

"But it's not me that pays all that!"

"Well, who is then? As far as I know, you always agreed, you're not going to refuse now!"

"That's not right, huh, he's got to stop buying like that! I can't pay for him. I'm not paying for him!"

"Fight it out yourselves! All I know is, what's bought has to be paid for. What's more, I'm warning you. I don't like funny business. If you cause trouble like that, I'll close your account, and you'll get no more credit!"

The moral of the story: the assets gained were insufficient. The bodeguero took the receipt, and the debt remained standing, since Mondestin bought more rice, some flour, and, in order to economize, no sardines, no pickled herring, none of that sort of food.

That night, Estimé Mondestin walked silently on the road. He had to be back very quickly. A Dominican gendarme stopped him, ordered him to get back to his barracon, and on the double. "You've got no damn business out of the batey," he'd snarled nastily...

The Kongos are closely surveyed. They are not supposed to go anywhere. As soon as they've finished working, they are to go back to the batey. They can't move, but have to stay there where they are from the beginning of the season until the end. The plantations are surrounded by police, and watchmen make the rounds. In certain bateys there is a gate closed in the evening, a gendarme is stationed there who lets them out in the morning.

When Mondestin was returning, his heart bitter and his belly weary, strange, silent noiseless convulsions shook his shoulders steadily under the starry dome.

Article 8: The Haitian agricultural worker hired by the State Sugar Council will be employed to work exclusively in the Dominican State sugar factory for which he has been engaged.

The State Sugar Council commits itself, with the collaboration of the supervisors and inspectors appointed by the Haitian Embassy in Santo Domingo, to take all necessary measures to avoid having the worker transferred to a private work center having no obligation to the Haitian government.

Mondestin, Brutus and Gérard André stopped working, wiped their foreheads glistening with sweat. Shouts and interjections had just broken out. They were fighting in the plantation. Two Kongos in the team nearby were beating each other violently. "It's no good," growled Brutus, "if the capataz passes by, and he sees this shit, he's going to call for a convention of the guards, and then everybody will get beaten up. It's no good." Well assured of his machete at the end of his arm, he approached the belligerents. Estimé Mondestin followed a few steps behind.

When they fight, it's that things are bad. Hunger gnaws at us, we become enraged, lose control. When one has a little money in his pocket, and he is going to buy something to eat, another one who has nothing sees him, and he becomes even more enraged. We are like animals since we've been here. We can get along sometimes — he thought of Brutus, of Gérard André, Déroseaux, and himself — in the same "household." We can help each other, but individualism prevails. As soon as the Haitians arrive in Dominicanie, they turn into devils, because they understand very well that it is the least diabolical who will bite the dust.

And the Kongos were fighting.

"What's going on?" yelled Brutus, striding over sections of cane flung every which way as far as the eye could see. His machete gleamed in the concentrated rays of sunlight.

It seemed that a son of a *bouzin* was working less than his comrades. Nerves were raw, on the brink. Already, they had all realized that the scales were fixed. No one told them anything, no one explained anything to them, it was the *pesador* who gave the slip to the cabrouetier and the slip was always right, there was nothing to discuss. In order to get one or two pesos from a cabrouet, it would have to be comparable to an enormous dump truck. They could spend a week and a half cutting, and not even make one peso sixty-eight each! Final, net, total! "It is several cabrouets, 1 peso 68," screamed the most excited. "And him, he wants to rest because he's too hot!"

The other did want to rest, as a matter of fact. "We're paid for what we produce. So, if we work at will, when we're tired, we stop at will!" An inarticulate snarl was his reply. "And if we stop all the time, what will we make? Already, when there's a few stacks to load, you have to talk to the cabrouetier, and when the cane is weighed, if it's worth two pesos, you have to pay out 50 centavos! So if we stop, then what do we make?"

"Well then, my friend, you are not obliged to stop." A silence; he spat, then muttered a few cynical words. "We aren't making anything anyway."

"That's no reason, on the contrary." "Oh yes it is, perfectly." "No Sir!" "Oh yes!" And the other continued angrily.

"Sometimes I can cut three tons in one day! Well, my companions better keep up with me, because when I cut a certain amount, the other better not have just done half that!"

"I didn't say half."

"Because when the pay comes, each one has to get an equal share, or else you better leave."

"I didn't say that I do half," contended the dissident, now on the defensive, "but sometimes I need to stop."

"If I get twelve pesos..."

"...I'm no machine."

"If I get twelve pesos, I have to divide it up in equal parts."

"We never got twelve pesos!"

"If it's twelve pesos and twenty centavos, even the twenty centavos have to be divided."

"Sure, sure, but if I want to stop, I stop," repeated the other obstinately. "If I want to stop I . . ."

The malcontent Kongo took a deep breath and spat, more than spoke, at his partner.

"Well then, my friend, after the pay we change teams." He turned toward Brutus and Mondestin who, dumbfounded, were watching the row. "In order to get an equal share of the money, each one should do an equal share of the work, or else leave. Isn't that right?"

"Do what you want," said Brutus with a fatalistic gesture, "but stop your scene. The Dominicans are going to come."

"It's not a scene. It's just that he wants to stop."

"Yeah, well just stop the scene."

"It's not a scene, my friend."

"OK, but stop it anyway."

"All right, we'll settle it at the batey. We won't make a scene."

Estimé Mondestin shook his head and took off toward his section, satisfied with the turn of events. This type of quarrel was taking place more and more often. The exhausted and hungry partners were mutually accusing one another of not working enough.

Sometimes, there are three cutting together. If only one wants to rest, and the others continue to cut, that provokes interminable discussions. If the one who has stopped persists, they kick him out of the group. The other two stay together, and at the end of the two weeks, they give the dismissed Kongo his share. They easily find another, or wait for the opportunity. Estimé Mondestin went back to work, and suddenly felt an insidious melting in his temples on either side of his head. He perceived bizarre stars in a black sky, exploding in his eyes, radiating into infinite space. He staggered, shook his head, awkwardly clung to a stalk heavy with sugar that yielded to the weight. His vision cleared. He rediscovered the green of his interminably green universe, as green as the eye can see. This blackout which left his legs dead, told him that it must be mid day. He resumed cutting.

And so it was weakness personified who murmured to them each day: Gentlemen, it must be twelve o'clock, and one by one, disarmed them.

They held silent counsel a few minutes later, grabbed their plastic gallon jug, went into the field. They pounded some pieces of cane together to soften them, twisted them over a container with a twist of the wrist to obtain the juice. They drank greedily, each one in turn. That saved their lives. Then they slowly went back to work. They had finished their lunch.

They were dissatisfied, starting to grumble. For those who know these things and live on it, it was clear that they were really ready. The Kongos themselves, of course, knew nothing of it. Crazy ideas kept turning over and over in their heads, causing them a strange giddiness, finally obsessing them.

It was the evening, night had already fallen. Petit Pierre Déroseaux was quietly conversing with his cutting partner and another veteran, Antoine the viejo. A truck roared at the other end of the batey, and one imagined, more than saw, the storm of dust in its wake. At a closer look, the truck was not leaving, but arriving. They lost interest. The silence fell as suddenly as it had been disturbed. Estimé Mondestin was dreamily watching a young Haitian woman, her belly slightly distended, who was sitting under the sheet metal roof of a long hangar open to the four winds in the proximity of one of the barracks. In this batey, as in all the bateys, the male population by far exceeded the female population, and that is why Mondestin was staring at her with a certain languor, as if hypnotized. She was laughing noiselessly; he was too far away to hear her conversation with a woman whom misery and privation had already devoured.

They were both born in the batey, as were most of the women there. Others were wives of the viejos, sometimes Dominican, but more often Haitians who had arrived clandestinely in former times, driven by wretched poverty or seeking a man who had preceded them. And then also other Dominican women, wives of the Dominicans in the batey. But these Haitian and Dominican women did not work; they made babies. The girl continued laughing noiselessly, as in a silent movie, and while not really beautiful, she stirred up something sweet and a little hot in the guts and in the soul of Estimé Mondestin. Of course, the Kongos had already noticed certain things, saw girls passing by, but that was of little interest to most, as it was necessary to spend every bit of money to try to eat. That Mondestin knew. Certain Dominican women engage in prostitution, and, beg your pardon, they may not look it, but they are all the same. *Bouzins.* Just that all money has to go for food. And this girl who was laughing over there was not a prostitute, her name was Desruisseaux Simone, he had already noticed her.

He also thought of his wife.

Two Kongos were playing dominoes in front of the open door of their cell. They sat facing one another, clicking down the dotted-white black tiles on a thick sheet of cardboard held on their widespread knees, like the legs of a table.

Through this opening, they heard a moan. A sick and weak Kongo, Necker Marcel was his name, was complaining softly. He hadn't been able to work for two days. Brutus appeared suddenly. No one had seen him arrive. His face was glowing, very excited. He planted himself before the company.

"Well, gentlemen, I have the honor to inform you that I am finally going to accomplish something."

Estimé Mondestin threw him a puzzled look, Déroseaux and the two viejos moved closer, intrigued.

"I'm leaving," Brutus proudly announced.

"Where are you going?"

"With those Dominicans over there, who've come to get us."

"What's this all about?" demanded Antoine the viejo, frowning suddenly; he was afraid he understood.

"There's some men who just proposed something and I'm going with them. I'm leaving. I advise you to do the same."

"Proposed what?" asked Estimé Mondestin, interested in turn.

This is what the guys had said: "Gentlemen, we are here with our *treleu*,* and we have a transfer to propose to you. You are unhappy in this place, they refuse you any consideration. You earn nothing, you live in cages that pigs in Haiti wouldn't even want. Follow us, we have some good work for you, you won't regret it."

"Can everyone get in on it?"

"They choose those who have the most strength, big arms, the gro-nègs."

"And you're going?"

"The Haitians leaving with me agree. They see they are leaving this poverty. They are going to live in a better batey."

"You must not go," Antoine the viejo said softly, sorry to have to disappoint them. "Above all, you must not go."

Brutus threw him an incensed look.

"In Haiti, I'm hungry, I'm sick, I don't even have a place to sleep. Here, with no experience in this country, I don't earn two pesos a day. If they give me the opportunity to go and accomplish something, I better go."

"No, no, no," answered Antoine the viejo, this time with force. "You must not. *Es un négocio*, it's a deal, you understand?"

"What I understand is what they propose."

"Don't go. It's a deal. Crooks. It's a scheme they've made with some owners: I bring you so many Haitians and you pay me."

"Yes, but I'll be paid too. Here I'm not."

"And where do you go to leave?" asked Mondestin, who was dangerously fascinated in the opinion of the second viejo, who intervened immediately.

"There are some *colonos* that belong to the big bosses. It's for

---

Treleu: trailer.

121

sugar cane or coffee. The Haitians who get out of the batey to go and harvest coffee don't get out by themselves. Dominicans come and get them in vehicles. They give 200 pesos to these Dominicans for finding the Haitians. They go out, and when they encounter some, they take them by force, make them prisoners."

"But it's not by force," protested Brutus, shrugging his wide shoulders, "they asked us."

"Same thing. If they don't find any Kongos here, they'll go and get some elsewhere. If they don't find any elsewhere, they'll come and imprison some here. Of course, in the beginning, they ask for volunteers. It's easier for them."

"They buy Haitians in the state ingenios," confirmed Antoine the viejo, gravely. "Eleven pesos a Haitian head. Eleven pesos, my friend! Here, that's all you are worth!"

A sudden silence surrounded them, slowly fading, and merging into the obscurity.

Two raw-boned Dominicans stood near a truck parked with all the lights extinguished. Several silent Kongos were already sitting in back.

The State Sugar Council (the CEA) recruits 15,000 Haitians each year for the zafra. But there exist enterprises other than the CEA, which, having no contract with Duvalier, nevertheless need a labor force. Gulf & Western, an American multinational, and Vicini together represent about fifty percent of the Dominican production. Moreover, the CEA's sugar factories, which transform the cane or refine the sugar, do not own all the terrain on which the cane is planted. They also buy the crop of a certain number of private concerns. Almost all of the high-ranking officers in the Dominican Army are the owners of vast *fincas*, plantations, which are scattered with cane fields. They need manpower, and are obliged to procure illegally about 15,000 extra braceros, which brings the number of Haitians recruited specifically for the zafra to about 30,000 a year. This second contingent of 15,000 is recruited by an organization of veritable slave traders. Of the 15,000 laborers officially imported by the CEA, about 4,000 disappear each year: the pretext put forward by the immigration services to organize forays, the hunt of the Haitians on Dominican territory. The private companies supply themselves at the expense of the CEA. The latter pays around 86 pesos a head to the Haitian government. The private companies, in supplying themselves directly, on the spot, and in paying the reduced price of eleven pesos per individual, benefit from a very interesting financial operation.

The CEA is well aware of this, and in order to avoid the flight of the nègres stuck in the barracones, sometimes locks them in. In certain bateys, especially where there is an atmosphere of rebellion, the gates are locked in the evening and reopened the next morning before sunrise.

The private plantations, and consequently the sugar factories, perpetually lacking manpower, hand over large sums of money to Dominican officials at the border. The raids are carried out by the Dominican border forces, who pick up any and all nègres, in other words, anyone who looks like a Haitian. Like a slave, as it were. There also, $11 a head is paid for each individual recovered. Most of these operations are carried out with the support of the magistrates, the rural police, and other local officials. The administrators of the factories—El Señor Rodriquez, among others, administrator of the sugar factory, *Barahona*, master Haitian hunter—make a brazen and open practice of kidnapping. A sizeable traffic also takes place in the vicinity of the police station in Lorenzo, and at the military head-quarters in Enriquillo. Most of the Haitians are stopped in the mornes of Paraiso and on the cotton plantations in Enriquillo. With the complicity of the military authorities, the human livestock is transported in trucks, by night, away from public view, and dumped in the private plantations, in defiance of their most basic rights. Sold to the coffee, cocoa, rice, and *ganaderias fincas*, they work; their only payment — one meal a day."

"You must not go," said Antoine the viejo once again, gravely. He was worried to see Brutus ready to accept the transfer proposed to him by those people from the mafia. He continued, trying to be as persuasive as possible. "Last year, they took eight Kongos, and transported them to other plantations, very far away, near San Luis. No one ever found out how they live over there. The Dominicans who took them say they are just fine. *Sé manti*. They are lying. These Kongos have no one left to complain to. If they have problems, they've got them for good."

"I've got to leave anyway," said Brutus. "It's too hard here. It's hard to always go with just a jug of water for the whole day, suck cane to hold together."

"It will go even harder where they're taking you, you stubborn fool," exploded Antoine the viejo. "It's trafficking in men, under-stand, trafficking in men!"

"Traffic, traffic," sighed Brutus, more perplexed than he wished to appear. "But these guys promised us . . ."

"Hah! Promises!" The second viejo laughed bitterly. "Promises!" He slapped his thighs theatrically. "Traffic and promises forever for the Haitians!"

He ceased laughing, placed a worn hand on Brutus's shoulder. "My name is Marcellin," he said. "Follow me, I'm going to show you something." Brutus shook his head. "Something?" "Yes, or if you prefer, someone." Brutus hesitated an instant, then, at the man's insistence, followed his steps. "Only," said he, "let's hurry, because those guys are going to leave without me." "Well, let them leave, let them leave!"

The man was now walking in front of them, and Brutus heard him snickering and mumbling, "promises, hah!" all along the way. Antoine the viejo and Mondestin followed.

The shack wallowed and stagnated, vile and familiar, just like the others. The flickering flame of the improvised lamp permitted them to discern a bowed and emaciated shadow, sitting motionless in a broken chair. The old woman looked at them, seeming hardly to see them. Over a table covered with oilcloth hung three pots on the wall, and, in faded colors, an innocent Jesus prayed while watching over some sheep. "He'd do better to watch over some men," thought Brutus in a flash, before noticing a cardboard carton, formerly of Bermudez rum, placed on another table, with a turned-over pail and a big, completely extinguished candle. You could see the bare sheet metal roof in the shadowy half light, and the partition of bare green boards separated the hut into two rooms without reaching the ceiling. The simple absence of boards in this partition, screened at eye level by two old dishrags sewn together, served as a passageway between the two rooms. Through the opening thus fixed up, you could vaguely make out the shape of a real bed. "A Kongo's house and that of a Dominican," mused Estimé Mondestin, "it's the same difference as in Port-au-Prince, between living with the rich at Bois-Verna, and living with the less-than-nobodies, the other Haitians, at La Saline. The Dominicans have nice houses, ours are cages. And the viejos are midway between the two. In the time they've been here, they've bought a little furniture, and their houses somewhat resemble a house. But they are not Dominicans, no way, they are not Dominicans."

Now, standing motionless, the viejo silently contemplated the shrivelled-up shadow of the old woman.

"This is old Suzelle, my mother," he said simply.

"But how old are you?" asked Brutus, in a low voice, as if he were afraid to wake the old lady.

"I'm forty-two."

"And you brought your mother with you?"

Marcellin laughed softly, shook his head indulgently.

"No, she got here before me. I was born in Dominicanie, not very far from this batey."

The light flickered, out of breath; Mondestin thought it would go out. The viejo continued, graver this time.

"All her life she knew promises and traffic. Promises and traffic in Haiti. Promises and traffic in Cuba. Promises, traffic, and death in Dominicanie. If she still had the strength to speak, she would tell you don't go. . ."

"She can't talk any more?"

"I think she still can, but she doesn't want to. She's tired."

"It's always promises and traffic for the Haitians," Marcellin the viejo repeated several times. Then he said nothing. You would have said that he was voyaging in a far away past, one that he'd never known. They heard a dog barking.

She was barely twenty, she was said to be beautiful, and she was; she was also said to be a little wacky, which she was not. But people said it and she laughed. Imagine! She wanted to go to Cuba to get rich washing bottles. It must be said in her defense that she wasn't the only one. And each time she heard the unbelievable news, she said to herself: why not me? She also told herself that she was going. Why stay in Haiti? The Whites had started invading the country five years before, they arrived in 1915, she remembered well the first she'd seen.

This piece of news interested her, and her friend Marisa as well, who brought it up regularly.

"Did you hear, Suzelle? It seems that in Cuba the women earn one peso for washing bottles!"

"You sure of what you're saying?"

Her friend Marisa was sure; as sure as she was sure that she detested these cursed pigs of American Marines who had massacred so many men in the Haitian country, drowning their revolt in a blood bath.

"It's as sure as sure can be. The man that I told you about the other day confirmed it. And he's a man who knows, he's the one in charge."

"He can help us to get by?"

"He suggested it himself."

Cuba! Belle Suzelle started dreaming.

"If all the women earn a peso, how much could we, who are energetic and determined, earn?"

"We could earn a lot."

"But to leave. . ."

"A lot of Haitians do it. We wouldn't be alone."

Belle Suzelle thought about it, it was true that they wouldn't be alone. It was the time of the "Fat Cows," the "Dance of Millions," in Cuba!

The sugar expansion had, since 1915, up until that year, 1920, caused the price of sugar to rise to never-yet-attained heights. The Haitian workers were rushing headlong out of the country in improvised flotillas, pushed by their wretched poverty—already—by the propaganda, and the Caribbean winds that whispered astonishing figures. The cutters earn one dollar per arrobe* of cane! Yes, my friend, a salary of one dollar!

"You won't be afraid, Marisa?"

Marisa burst out laughing, communicating her hilarity to Belle Suzelle. They got along well together.

"Afraid! Did you already forget what we've done?"

Belle Suzelle had not forgotten, and in a flash her expression changed; her eyes burned with powerless anger and rage.

The American Marines threw bombs on defenseless villages, fed their dogs the entrails of still alive women (absolutely true), burned Haitian captives alive, threw babies in the air and caught them on the points of their bayonets, (alas, true again). The American Marines did that to the Haitian people. The bourgeoisie, the landowners, puppets of the Yankees, rented or sold their land to the big companies, to the businessmen, and thousands of small peasants were evicted, robbed, despoiled. So the Haitians struggled. The "marrons," scattered in the mountains, had met up with a leader of an intransigent nationalism, Charlemagne Perrault, the "leader of the Revolutionary Army fighting against the North Americans on the soil of Haiti." And the rebels followed him. Sons of the ragged nègres of former times, they fought with old rifles—one rifle for five men—odd revolvers, sticks, machetes, swords, rocks and pebbles, against a superior army equipped with *Krag Jorgensens*, the most modern guns of the era. And submachine guns, and bombs, and incendiary materials, all that sort of thing. The *Cacos*—which was what the rebels were called—disappeared into the mountains, traversed the mornes, streaked through the plains, elusive like a guerrilla—which they were—waiting in ambush where they were least expected, attacking "Ricains," as they were called in those days. In the incandescent air, drums sent messages as quickly as a telephone.

Belle Suzelle and Marisa, intrepid little girls, belonged to an anonymous "army," the "Madame Saras," an innocent-looking group of women who, in the guise of selling their fruits and vegetables, gathered news and information to transmit to the guerrillas. They travelled up and down the mornes, important news hidden in the secret of their youth, as light as the Haitian wind. A basket of pineapples on their head, a sack of rice in their hand, they, unnoticed and

---

Arrobe: Volumetric measure (Spanish) equal to 10-16 liters—TRANS.

insignificant, regularly brought the information entrusted to them of the North American troops to the rebel headquarters.

One remembers this type of thing.

They remembered 18 February, when the *Cacos* attacked Mirebalais, Ranquitte, Las Coabas, Dessalines. They remembered the day they had seized Maissade, set fire to the casern, destroyed the telephone installations.

They remembered, and they remembered well.

The panic-stricken Yankees sent for reinforcements, companies of fresh men from their base at Guantanamo, Cuba, to back up the occupying troops in trouble. They also remembered, but who didn't remember, the horrifying day when the mutilated corpse of Charlemagne Perrault, the "leader of the Revolutionary Army fighting against the North Americans on the soil of Haiti," betrayed and cut down, had been put on display in the public square in Grande Riviere, his arms nailed to a door in the form of a cross.

They remembered.

But today, 1920, vanquished, humiliated, without hope, the flocks of peasants dispossessed by the occupier and his accomplices, were surging to Cuba. The agricultural companies of that country sent agents to Haiti, charged with engaging thousands of workers. Legally established taxes were collected by the Haitian government. The consuls made a big profit on the control they exercised over the hard labor of their nationals and on the cost of their visas. One would have thought it was already the Duvalier era. That was between 1915 and 1920. The traffic continued on a lesser scale until the decade of the fifties.

Siméon was Haitian, and had himself called "boss." He was a trafficker.

The choppy waves, breaking in the obscure night, loomed out of nothingness, only to die in the same instant on the beach. The night was almost cool. Belle Suzelle and Marisa were standing very close to one another, shivering a little, vaguely impressed; and the moon, emerging from behind a cloud, revealed them standing motionless in the middle of a group of men who were silently assembling. They were arriving in little parcels of six, of twelve, of twenty, guided by the lesser traffickers. Siméon looked them over with a connoisseur's eye, muttered a few indistinct words, and made them immediately pay up. They didn't pay the whole amount—two hundred dollars, they would have been quite incapable—only a deposit. Some, like the tall, well-built nègre stretched out near the boat, the one with a big scar on his forehead, were leaving a shack as guarantee of payment. Others, a tiny piece of land. Or something. All settled the outstanding balance of the trip in installments, it was understood, in salary withheld, sometimes for two years.

The old tub smelled of fuel and coal tar. Siméon the boss had Suzelle and Marisa sit next to him, trapped right against him by the masses of men piled in, maybe a hundred. When he looked at the two girls, he smiled, and despite his efforts to make it look simply friendly, his smile was a filthy smile.

The small, anemic lights of Saint-Marc disappeared in the night, there was a great silence, soon you could hear nothing more than the mysterious lapping of the sea on the gunwales. Occasionally, a man coughed. They were so jammed in that no one could budge, and sometimes the water rose very high around them. They were a little afraid, and the two girls a little more afraid. It took them twenty-four hours to cross the Windy Canal, only about forty-seven miles wide. All night long, Siméon the boss let his greasy, dirty hands wander over Suzelle's tense body; it was disgusting. Especially for her. Eyeing Marisa, he'd made vaguely obscene gestures. With daylight, they had found a semblance of tranquility, but were presently darting somewhat panic-stricken looks about them.

And all these men who were looking at them.

All at once it was very hot, their hearts skipped a beat, and Cuba appeared.

Another coast, another beach, more confabulation, a port that they might not have seen, a rattling, clanking truck, piled in like cattle, the bumps and jolts, the miles of route.

"*Cosados! Cosados! Hola los cosados!* Hurry up, *cosado!*" They didn't understand this Spanish language, but had immediately grasped that they were nothing more than a herd of *cosados*, anyway. In another time, in another country, they would say "Kongos."

On the third night of the escapade they arrived at the plantation, a sea of cane in the Camaguey region. Belle Suzelle had only one thing in mind: to start working. No one seemed to be concerned about her, whereas the men had immediately been taken in hand, sent to the scene of their travail without losing a minute. "Later, later," the boss Siméon put her off when she tried to approach him. "Come and see me later, over there, at my house." She sighed, disconcerted. She didn't like this place, hated the fixed gaze of certain ragged Haitians who were already living in the camp. Who did they think they were? Even more, who did they think she was? And Marisa, her girlfriend, from whom they had already separated her, and whom she hadn't even seen leave! Where did they take her? Maybe she had already started to work.

Belle Suzelle waited as long as she could, then headed toward the shack where Siméon should be found. Night had fallen. She made out a faint light, and in front of the camp, the solitary silhouette of

Siméon. Seeing her, he grunted loudly.

"Ah, there you are!" he said. "I was waiting for you." Then he grunted again.

Belle Suzelle felt an unidentifiable malaise invade her.

"We've arrived now?"

"That's right, we've arrived."

"Well, when and where do I start washing the bottles?"

The trafficker slowly looked her up and down. An unwholesome smile appeared on his face.

"In Cuba," he started slowly, and his eyes stopped unequivocally on Suzelle's body, "what we call a bottle is a man's penis."

He burst out laughing. Aghast, she thought she couldn't breathe. He casually moved closer and she was enveloped in a hot odor of rum.

"Since you are in such a hurry to wash some," said he, "you can start by washing mine!"

Then he grabbed her savagely by the shoulders, forced her brutally to her knees. With the other hand, he was feverishly unbuttoning.

The guy was at least forty-five, a cane cutter for eternity. He was a Haitian immigrant with a little more seniority, called Saint-Aubin. He made her understand that at the present, he was master of her destiny. "You cost me three hundred dollars, my dear, it's in your interest to toe the line." "What does that mean?" she managed to whisper, her heart horribly constricted. "That means that I bought you." She couldn't believe it, and at the same time she knew it was true. He had signed a contract with Siméon, the purchase would be paid for in installments, with each paycheck. In the penitential world of the plantations, it was difficult to obtain a companion any other way. She didn't have the choice to accept or refuse. She shared the miserable existence of this Saint-Aubin. He parted her thighs any time he felt like it, even when the work had exhausted him, and pounded out his all-powerful thrusts with a leitmotif that enraged her: "Three hundred dollars, uh! Three hundred dollars . . . uh!"

This guy used her at will, enjoyed himself at a brisk pace, and invariably terminated his performance with a poisonous stock phrase. "Shit! Three hundred dollars! It was too much to pay!" That was all he ever said afterwards.

One stormy night, the electricity in the air, perhaps, gave him some ideas. He decided to amortize this purchase beyond his means. He started quite simply by lending her to a barracks mate. Just to be a nice guy, without an afterthought. She refused out of instinct, then, as always with women, stopped refusing. The second round of slaps had really hurt, fear took hold of her. "He's my friend, he's always so alone, you can do that for him and for me." She did it, got no pleasure from it. The guy, yes. "She was good?" asked Saint-Aubin of his beaming companion. "Well, be nice, give me a peso to help me make the monthly payment, this month is going to be rough." Then, since the other balked: "I'll lend her to you again."

It started to rain very hard and Belle Suzelle stayed out a long time, a very long time in the rain, trying to wash herself. Since her face was soaked, no one could see she'd been crying.

As for Siméon, he usually lived in the plantation. He often went back to Haiti, sometimes every two weeks, to look for new groups..It was according to the demand. As for the rest; it wasn't for nothing that he was called the boss. He took care of everything — work, supplies, clothing, really everything. Every two weeks, when the cutters got their pay, Siméon buried himself in his little notebook, noted the amount of the paycheck, indicated to each one the situation of his debt, encouraged them to work more. He was a very amiable and very methodical man, who knew how to make himself attractive to women, with punches in the ribs, if necessary. Saint-Aubin could refuse him nothing, especially not Belle Suzelle, and he didn't deny him Belle Suzelle.

It was in May of this same year that Siméon arrived one evening, sweaty, perspiring, very excited. He rounded up a group of about fifty Haitians, posthaste, apparently chosen from among the recent arrivals, but also among the most senior. Belle Suzelle and Saint-Aubin were among the lot.

"Quick, quick," Siméon told them, "get your things, follow me!"

As if he had gone mad. At first, they looked at him without moving.

"For the love of heaven" — that was a new one — "hurry up! They are going to kill you!"

"Who's going to kill us?" asked ten appalled voices.

"The Cuban rural police!"

"But why? Why?"

"You've been denounced! They are going to kill you!"

Denounced! But why denounced? You didn't denounce people just like that. You denounce them for something, and they hadn't done anything, were just there to work.

"I don't know, I tell you, but you have been denounced, they have decided to kill you. By miracle I was warned, there's not a minute to lose."

"But the rural police, even if they are bastards, don't just kill people like that!"

"You don't know anything about this country! They kill when they feel like killing, I'm telling you, and you, they're..."

"It's not possible. You'll see with those people. We are in Cuba." "But there could be a reason! Don't forget that we are Haitians. Besides the harvest is almost over, even if we die, they don't need us any more." "So what do we do?" "Siméon says we better go." "Go where?" "I'm going." "Wait, we better think about it, you can't ...Besides, we haven't been paid!" More than any other, this objection made them stop a minute. Siméon threw up his arms, broke into obscenities, showered them with a string of oaths. He had come to save their lives, and all they could think of was their piece of shit of a miserable rotten salary! Were they nuts or what? Did they realize the risks he was taking to save them?

"We can't leave without getting paid."

"We're supposed to get paid tomorrow."

"Ah, yes, tomorrow."

"Look, you idiot assholes, I'm telling you they want to kill you tonight! You can't understand that?"

Well, of course, they were certainly not unaware of the cruelty of the Rural Guards, the well-armed mounted police who put to death the *cosados* caught trying to flee, that they knew. But why them, who precisely had never dreamed of fleeing up until now? Huh, why? That is what it would have been necessary to know. Now, if Siméon said so, there must be something to it, where would his interest lie? Yes, exactly, where would his interest lie? He had none. Better listen to him.

They fled from the colony. They marched in silence through the dark, hot, gloomy countryside. The trafficker was in the lead. They were afraid, fearing at every moment to be surprised by the rural guards launched in their pursuit. Siméon had told them. Don't panic, but they are surely in our pursuit. And they walked, turning around at the least suspicious noise. In that unknown country, all noises were suspect at that hour. Their nerves took a beating. Siméon marched them a good part of the night, fortunately he was there, as far as a crossroads where "they" were waiting for them, as if everything had been carefully organized. They hastily boarded a truck, and the truck vanished, all lights extinguished, and they with it.

In the morning, they discovered a new camp. They sighed, completely exhausted and very relieved. They had had a narrow escape.

Siméon discreetly went where he was supposed to go, collected a substantial commission, received a cordial handshake. Next, still unshaven, he paid a brief visit to his dear *cosados*. "Thank you," said one of them to him, "in the name of all of us, thank you." "Not at all," protested he, "it was only natural. Only," he added immediately, "I took enormous risks to save your lives, and I had some expenses. You have to give me something in compensation." "Compensation!" A cry burst forth, "but you know very well that. . ." "Ah, yes, that's right," said he, understanding, "you haven't been paid. That won't be a problem. We'll mark that in the little notebook." Which was done. And they wondered if they had been right to thank him.

He had already left, returning in the empty truck to the original plantation where he received, of course, another commission. He had ridded the camp of some people they no longer needed, and allowed them to avoid paying the last two weeks' salary. There, too, they shook his hand.

They had to start all over again, which only meant, in reality, to suffer and to sweat. Times were hard, and life without pity. Saint-Aubin had to lend Belle Suzelle more and more often to more and more numerous friends. One day he announced that his situation was improved. He was very happy about it, he'd never really felt attracted by sugar cane. He stopped working. He started to save in view of his return to Haiti. He must have lent Belle Suzelle rather often, for they say the day he left, two years later, he had amassed a nice little pile. He wasn't ungrateful. He abandoned her, of course, left her two dresses and one pair of shoes when he took off.

She didn't mourn his departure. She didn't have time to. Some other guy was already ogling her, one of Saint-Aubin's buddies whom he'd advised to take care of his wife. Fortunately, she met Ti-Jacques. He wasn't very sweet, he wasn't very handsome, he didn't have a cent, but he was a man, a real one, a former "Caco" rebel who had had to flee the North American repression. He told her the story of his participation in the attack on Port-au-Prince, on 7 October 1919, at four o'clock in the morning, and how they had occupied a part of the city. How, on the eighth, armed with clubs and machetes, they'd had to fall back under a deluge of automatic weapons, armored cars, arms of all types and all calibers. Of other battles and other flights, pell-mell, over hill and dale.

It was he who had told her, he who never talked about it; besides, afterwards he didn't talk about it again. But after having recounted it, he had said to her: "I will never sell you to anyone, you can stay with me. I'll kill the first one that touches you."

And no one else, except him, whom she respected, and who respected her, ever touched her.

In a way, they were happy in their adversity.

They knew the Great Depression in the thirties. From 1931 on, the Cuban government began repatriating several thousand Haitians each year. At that time there were three to four hundred thousand, concentrated in the Camaguey provinces for the cutting of cane, and in the Oriente region for the harvest of coffee.

Nineteen hundred thirty-four. The American troops leave Port-au-Prince. An unknown, insignificant fellow receives his medical degree. His name is François Duvalier. They were going home.

They headed instinctively towards the northeast, to Fort Liberté, Ti-Jacques's home town. They rediscovered with pleasure the fantastic Marion River, and discovered the immense American sisal plantation presently devouring the nourishing earth from which thousands of peasants had summarily been ejected. There was no work for them. At this time, there were only two large concerns in Haiti: this one and the Hasco sugar central, whose domain extended over several thousand hectares in the plains of Cul-de-Sac and Leogane, near Port-au-Prince. The total amount of the concessions made by the government to the foreign companies would amount to 28,000 hectares, but was far from being exploited in its entirety. For the little guy, there was no means of subsistence.

They had vegetated for two years. Ouanaminthe and the Dominican border were not far. In 1936, they made the leap with Marcel, their first child. The traffickers brought them in an old truck, as if they were transporting livestock. Ti-Jacques quickly found work — he has both his arms — in a *finca* close to the border in the Dajabon region. And 1937 arrived.

The dictator Trujillo was then governing the Dominican Republic. Son of a small merchant from San Cristobal, successively a telegraph operator, a delinquent, a *pesador*, then *guarda-campestre* (rural police) in a batey in the eastern part of the country, he had presented himself in December of 1918 to the American authorities — who also occupied the Dominican Republic — to join the National Guard, a repressive organization which they created and which served simultaneously the function of army and police. He was well liked by those great humanists, the Americans. In 1922, he was named captain; commander from the beginning of 1924, then lieutenant-colonel of staff headquarters of the National Police at Santo Domingo that same year, when the Yankee occupation troops withdrew. Colonel and chief of police in 1925, he seized power definitively in 1930, to conserve it in one form or another until 1961.

He was a demagog, one of those Latin American *caudillos* fascinated by European fascism. He dreamed of becoming the Mussolini of the Caribbean.

The sugar trade was almost entirely in the hands of the American companies. As long as the price of sugar was high, the Haitians were welcome. Which is one way of putting it. The Dominican oligarchy had never looked very favorably upon the immigration of the black braceros. Article 90 of the 8 July 1911 law on agricultural franchises even specified that the agricultural enterprises could only use immigrants of the white race, "except if the zafra was endangered by a lack of workers." In this case, and in this case only, the Executive Power could authorize by decree, as a provisional measure, the immigration of Blacks. But Trujillo himself had not been able to succeed in making his Dominican compatriots—subjects would be a more exact term—work in the infrahuman conditions rampant in the bateys and on the plantations. Thus, in a way, the Haitians, in spite of all the hostile talk, were, as a last resort, hypocritically welcome. Just as today, they were needed. They had just made do with a vague treaty to codify and legalize this immigration, signed in 1929 between the Dominican president, Vasquez, and the Haitian president, Borno. New negotiations took place in 1933 between Trujillo and Sténio Vincent, and again in 1934 and 1936. That was all. Nothing of any consequence.

But in September, 1937, crisis was at the door, in fact was already in. Trujillo had made promises to his People that he couldn't keep, that is, if he ever had any intention of doing so. Fiscal resources were running dangerously low. The axe was not long in falling.

"It's the immigrants' fault," rumbled the rumor, carefully nourished, as always in such cases, by the authorities and the media. "It's the Haitians! They must be driven out."

His excellence the Generalissimo Dr. Raphael Trujillo Molina, honorable President of the Republic, Benefactor of the Fatherland and Reconstructor of Financial Independence, summed up the situation in a few words which evoked the admiration of all the brown-nosers in his entourage: *these are foreign negroes in our country; contemptible livestock thieves, practitioners of voodoo. Their presence on our territory can only deteriorate the living conditions of our citizens.*

There was really nothing to add, and no one added anything, except the press, which launched a virulent anti-Haitian public opinion campaign.

No one ever really confirmed that the fatal order was given in the course of a drinking bout one night, in which Trujillo wanted to please one of his mistresses who was irritated by the presence of the black workers in the countryside. But no one ever really refuted it. Anyway, what is certain, and the rest is of little importance, is that the order was given, and given good.

Ti-Jacques and Belle Suzelle were unsuspecting. Ti-Jacques did, at a certain precise moment, begin to suspect something, but it was too late. The horrifying blow of a machete had just split his head open lengthwise and for eternity.

He was walking in the countryside, drowned in sun and fierce heat, holding little Marcel by the hand, when three individuals accosted him, three guys looking grim and determined. Eyebrows raised, they had stopped him. The smallest was holding in his hand what appeared to be at first sight the leaf of some green plant, and he held it out in the direction of Ti-Jacques.

"*Hola hombre, como se llama esa cosa?* Tell me, what is this thing called?"

Ti-Jacques had looked at it, astonished. Funny question.

"Why, it's *pe'sil* (parsley), of course!"

Exactly what they were hoping. The three were not peasants, but Trujillo's soldiers in disguise.

A Haitian, even when he can speak Spanish well, which was the case with Ti-Jacques, experiences serious difficulties in pronouncing it. He has an especially hard time with the "r" and the "j". As for articulating the word parsley, *perejil*, obstructed with "r" and "j", which rolls on the tongue, and scrapes the back of the throat, that one is practically impossible. *Perejil* becomes pe'ejil, or pe'e'il, or yet pe'e'i, but never, ever, *perejil*.

"It's pe'sil, of course!"

"You are a Haitian, you! A brigand, a bandit, a horse thief!"

"I am Haitian, Señor, but I never..."

He didn't have the leisure to explain that he had never stolen the slightest animal. That wasn't really the issue. In the border region, any black individual incapable of pronouncing the word *perejil* was henceforth a condemned man. Uncomprehending, little Marcel saw his father collapse, losing buckets of a red liquid that seemed to never stop. His eyes opened wide, and his cry of terror was drowned in the flood of his own blood. He wasn't quite two years old, but that day, a Haitian was a Haitian. "Operation perejil" was in full swing.

When she learned the news, from the mouths of completely panicked men and women, Belle Suzelle, pregnant to the teeth with her second child, went literally mad. She ran screaming in every direction, weeping tears of blood. Why, why, why? No one had time to answer her. It was each one for himself, and terror was leading the band. It was first things first, and that was try to stay alive.

The planned massacre started in Dajabon, after Trujillo's personal visit. It was the night of 2 October. Crazed with terror and incomprehension, sobbing Haitians hurled themselves on the banks of the Rio Massacre — oh, the name, that name — attempting to get over the border. They didn't succeed. In thirty-six hours, the number killed exceeded 20,000. One week later, 40,000 Haitians scattered throughout sixty-five localities had been coldbloodedly assassinated.

How Belle Suzelle survived, she was never capable of recounting. She had at first rushed for the border, saw shadows, heard cries of agony, sweated with fear, wept with terror in the depths of a night blacker than the darkest gloom. Then she'd run without even realizing she was running, her big belly bouncing between sweat-soaked hands, then walked and walked, hallucinated in labyrinths of unfamiliar countryside. Whipped by tall grasses that she didn't see, treacherous branches tore into her that she didn't feel. In the early morning she had fallen, then awaited death with her expressionless face lying in the dry dust.

Some Dominicans had taken her in, and hidden her. Prostrate before the body of the semi-unconscious Haitian woman, dazed with fear and suffering she could never have imagined, they wept for a long time with shame and despair. Horrified, they in their humble shack were not responsible for the abominations perpetrated by the dictator and his henchmen, but it hurt to be Dominican.

Relations became tense between Port-au-Prince and Santo Domingo. That was the least they could do. Then it relaxed. It must be said that Trujillo, with the aid of the United States, had set up a force of 30,000 men, armed to the teeth, with tanks, a dozen ships, and twenty or so airplanes. One of the strongest armies in Latin America. Facing them, Haiti disposed of 2,000 gendarmes armed with 1,000 nonfunctioning rifles. Which, in fact, was of no importance whatsoever. Those then governing Haiti didn't ever think to formulate a protest on principle. On the contrary, they claimed an indemnity. A sin paid for is a sin half pardoned. The United States, Mexico and Cuba mediated. It was decided that 750,000 dollars in damages would be allocated to the victims by the Dominican state, which, in reality, however, only paid 500,000. And not to the victims, it goes without saying. The representative from Santo Domingo who went to Port-au-Prince to make the last payment closed the incident in distributing 25,000 dollars, in ten and twenty dollar bills, to the Haitian politicians and party leaders. Well-bred people of society won't haggle over so little.

The holocaust momentarily interrupted the Haitian migration to the neighboring republic. As far as the Dominican oligarchy was concerned, the "leader" was glorified for accomplishing the "dominicanization of the border." A quarantine line of villages and churches, primarily destined for the Spanish, Japanese, and Hungarian immigrants, was erected to protect the country from a new Haitian invasion.

Meanwhile, Belle Suzelle's baby was born and the price of sugar was starting to rise again.

Once again, Trujillo needed manpower. The Spaniards,

Japanese, and Hungarians weren't going to work in the bateys! Discreetly, immigration was encouraged to recommence on a scale of three to four thousand vigorous males. Nothing official yet, just the early stages of the mafia.

It was during this era that a well-known Haitian, a certain Garcia Marquez, bought himself a truck and started making the rounds of the impoverished rural areas of his country. "Come to the Dominican Republic, you don't have to pay for your trip, I'll bring you. You'll find work right away." He was making about two dollars a head.

On the European continent, the ultimate of ultimates was unleashed.

Belle Suzelle and her son Marcellin sojourned in one batey, then settled permanently, a few years later, in the barracks of Batey 7A.

Later, after François "Papa Doc" Duvalier and Rafael Leonidas Trujillo Molina, dictators, had met in Jimani in 1958 and had made a mutual agreement to neutralize any possible attacks of their respective political oppositions by means of the frontier, it was Clément Barbot, the all-powerful head of the Tonton Macoutes — Duvalier's future private secretary — who was to furnish the Haitian manpower for the Dominican neighbors' sugar plantations. This operation would, in passing, leave him a comfortable profit. The bitter Haitians began to talk about "slave trade."

The viejo stopped talking. One would have said that he was voyaging far away, in a past that he hadn't entirely known. He sighed, seemed to emerge. "All her life, she knew nothing but promises and traffic," he said. He took a few steps, moving closer to his companions, and lowered his voice. "Soon she will die in this batey without ever having seen her country again."

Brutus was pensive. Estimé Mondestin was staring at the old woman with a mixture of awe and silent admiration. An entire Haitian life in this rickety chair. They went out.

"Even so," said Brutus, emerging from his silence, "this isn't Cuba! It isn't 1937 any more in Dominicanie!"

"They don't massacre us any more *en masse*," admitted the viejo with a smile, happy again, "but as for the rest, nothing has really changed."

Then he let escape a brief laugh, elbowing his old companion Antoine the viejo. "Tell him the story of Bernardino."

Antoine seemed to hesitate, his eyes lost in a fog. "I don't really know the Bernardino story. There were a lot of different versions. But I was mixed up in another affair, not long ago, it was still under Balaguer. It happened at Isabel, on a *finca* that was privately owned. Two compatriots were having a dispute. A Dominican with a gun had gone to talk to the two Haitians and ordered them to calm down. Which they did. After the incident, one of them, on his way back to the barracks, machete in hand, encountered the man with the gun next to a cabrouet of cane. The other one saw him coming, and fired on him without warning. The Haitian was shot through the chest and left arm. That night, we buried the lad, among Haitians, and afterwards, I did something that wasn't my job, because I thought the Haitian Consulate was there to defend us. We formed a delegation. When this delegation went before the ambassador, he replied: 'this Haitian was not here legally, he came here fraudulently, *au ba fil*, it's not my problem, he has nothing to do with the Embassy.' The other guy was never prosecuted. He was arrested, but less than two weeks later he was let go."

"You see," said the viejo, smiling slowly at Brutus, "that's still the way it is." Then he gazed at Antoine and whistled dreamily. "I know the Bernardino story. I met someone who saw it with his own eyes. And it didn't happen in 1937, but in 1974, gentlemen."

They were slowly going back towards the center of the batey. They passed a figure not yet completely ruined by the unfortunate conditions of existence. The girl was walking with a nonchalant step. Estimé Mondestin recognized the regular features of Desruisseaux Simone, caressed by a moonbeam, foreign to all that depressing universe. For an instant, his mind wandered, languid, adrift.

The small hills in the distance contrasted with the dazzling light of the immaculate sky. The Bernardino *finca* stretched into an infinity of sun and cane dust. Rhythmic and monotonous, the Haitians were cutting. In the intermittent silence between the shock of crashing blades on long stalks, now and then a sigh burst forth. Hearts were no longer in it. On 18 June 1974, theoretically, the zafra was over. They were still working, eyes burning with sweat. Didn't even really know where they were. A truck had arrived in the batey at night. They were piled in without anyone asking their opinion and brought to this remote place. A curt and merciless foreman distributed to each of them a machete and fifty centavos. They read in his face how much he scorned them. Fifty centavos!

Occasionally, between gasps, the verdict fell. "It's no good, huh! It's no good! We're not going to keep on working like this, it's no good."

Only to stoop once more, backs bent and arms raised, in the absurd, eternally repeated movement.

Around midday, the sun got the better of their great courage and their feeble strength. They decided together to take a break. Exhausted. Immediately the foreman sprang out.

"What's going on here?"

"We're hungry."

The man spat out an oath. They were hungry. The Haitians were hungry.

"And what else?"

"Nothing else. We're hungry."

"Get back to work, we'll see about that later."

"We're hungry, we're stopping right now."

"Get back to work, I tell you, the harvest is already late."

"We don't want to work for fifty centavos any more."

Little by little, the Haitians had gathered together, facing up, standing up, and quickly came to life, too long suppressed, a black wall of anger against a green wall of cane. The foreman started by haranguing them, "troublemaking...," continued by commanding them, "chrissake," became enraged, "will you understand," spat in their faces, "you'll wish you did." Nothing doing. They'd said no and it was no. They were too hungry. And besides, they had decided to leave. They rested a moment, then started back home. Frothing with rage, he jumped on his horse and took off in a gallop, after having heaped them with insults one more time.

He crossed the plain. His mount galloped as fast as the dust. They heard nothing more.

The noise of an engine brought them out of the exhausted torpor hanging over the little group prostrate on the ground. They lifted their heads. Félix Bernardino, former Trujillo henchman, was advancing towards them, stamping his boots, lips curled in a snarling grimace. He glanced at his watch, bright flash on his bronzed arm. Two o'clock. Sole owner of his finca, he had no contract whatsoever with anyone to obtain Haitian braceros, and didn't need any (contract, that is, not Haitians). He'd gotten in the habit of buying, through more or less specialized networks, Kongos under contract with the CEA. He made them work for a mouthful of bread, that was still too much to pay. And here these lousy Kongos were rebelling. These nègres thought they could abandon the finca. He glanced quickly at the revolver in his belt, secured the butt of his automatic rifle in the crook of his arm. His foreman and his men were following two steps behind.

The violent blow of a rifle butt struck down the first Kongo. Cry of surprise and pain, disapproving murmur.

"And now, back to work, cursed dogs!"

That was how he talked to them. They got up hastily. Bernardino brutally shoved another one of them.

"They tell me you want to leave..."

"Yes, we're going to leave," replied a gnarled stocky nègre.

The reply cracked, curt and dry.

"No one will leave here."

The nègre with the powerful muscles stood up straight, keenly annoyed.

"We're not your slaves, our contract is finished, let them take us back to our country."

Bernardino and his men advanced, menacingly.

"You will leave when my plantations are clean and not before! And now, enough said, back to work!"

He cocked his rifle, very calmly fixed his gaze on his herd of slaves. Colonel Simon Tadéo Guerrero had sold them to him for ten pesos a head, and whether they wished to or not, they were going to work, and hard.

"We want to leave," shouted a furious Kongo.

"Let them take us back to Haiti," clamored a few others.

Bernardino's men continued to advance. They, too, were armed. A sudden hesitation seemed to run through the group of Kongos. Frightened, a few backed away. "I think maybe we should stay." "Out of the question," rebelled the most determined, "our contract is finished." They forgot about the rifles pointed at them, and curiously, began to bicker among themselves. Bernardino was showing signs of getting closer and closer to the end of his rope. He blew up, beside himself: "Are you going to cut this cane of mine or what!" Then he understood that the most determined would not give in.

"We're going," said the short, stocky nègre, and he moved away suddenly with an assured step. "Yes, we're going," said another, and still another, a whole bunch, "yes, we're going."

And they were leaving in numbers, *nègres marrons* in revolt.

Bernardino barked. With blows of rifle butts, his men stopped the procession, seized eight Kongos, and lined them up. Bernardino, white with rage, but very calm, planted himself in front of them, rapidly raised his gun and coldly fired. Eight bodies fell, eight men, one after another.

A howl of fear answered the volley. The other Kongos, crazed with terror, defenseless, scattered in every direction. Once again, the rifles cracked, and you could no longer tell which made the most noise, the rifles or the screams, the screams or the rifles. Wails of agony slithered over the plain. A heap of black bodies littered the brown earth, pathetically curled up.

The exact number of victims was never known. They brought many dead to the hospital — what hospital? The one in Seybo, maybe — to make it look as though they were still alive. They buried the bodies on the spot, in the strictest secrecy.

Officially, five deaths were announced. The people of the finca themselves claimed there were thirty. They were very likely the closest to the truth.

From two o'clock, Tuesday, 18 June to Thursday, the 27th, the Dominican authorities and the Haitian Embassy whispered not a word to whomsoever of this massacre.

Later, rumor had it that they had arrested Bernardino. It was false. He never went to jail. In order to protect him from any possible reprisals, his finca was henceforth under military guard.[*] As for President Balaguer, he may have paid 73,000 pesos — to whom? — to cover the affair. Duvalier and his lackeys, as usual, lived up to their reputations. The Haitian ambassador at Santo Domingo made the following declaration: "An incident is being blown out of proportion, in order to exploit it politically against the two regimes. After all, it is not an exceptionally grave matter. There were only five dead."

He didn't dare add: it was only Haitians.

Brutus did not leave. The mysterious truck, with its cargo of Kongos, moved away in the night without him. For a good while they could see two persistent red lights blinking on a dark horizon disappearing in an unknown direction...

One more time, they went to bed hungry.

Estimé Mondestin had a hard time getting to sleep. He heard his companions' irregular breathing interrupted by dreams that elicited brief exclamations. Lying on the hard ground, he groaned silently, trying to shift out of the cold pain that had been preying on his back since the cursed time he'd been sleeping on the ground. He didn't succeed, any more than he succeeded in falling asleep. He sighed again, mentally going over his universe. He thought with anguish of the money he had to reimburse upon his return. Eighty dollars. He still didn't have the first cent.

---

[*] He would conduct his affairs in a perfectly normal fashion up until May 1980, when he sold his plantation to multinational Gulf & Western, for a considerable bundle of dollars.

Article 11: The Haitian government authorizes the State Sugar Council to deduct one (1) dollar every two weeks from the wages of each Haitian worker; the sums deducted in such a way will be converted to American dollars and will be given to the Haitian Ambassador in the Dominican Republic at the end of the harvest, to be distributed to the Haitian workers as withheld wages upon their return to Haiti.

Article 22: The State Sugar Council agrees to instruct the State sugar factories to grant the Haitian agricultural workers free time from 12:00 PM to 1:30 PM for a meal. Also, Sunday will be a holiday. The State Sugar Council will also put at the disposal of the Haitian agricultural workers recreation centers organized by the Department of Social Affairs of this organism.

The capataz was banging on the doors. It was four o'clock in the morning. *"Vamos! Vamos! A cortar la cana!"* When they took too long to wake up, he would push the door right open. "Get up, Kongos, Jean-Claude sold you!" And they got up groaning, didn't know any more how long they had been there, left in the cool dawn, just like Zombies. The capataz didn't cut cane. He was just there to get them up, and to inspect the fields, to make them go back when they forgot some stalk of cane. They left to cut with an empty

143

stomach, started work immediately. They couldn't do it any other way. They stopped at noon to take a little rest if no authority was lurking round about. They twisted the cane to drink its juice, far from the eyes of the Dominicans. They could go for three, four days, drinking only the juice of the cane. Afterwards the monotonous sound of thousands of machete strokes beat out the time and the hours once again. Shoulders breaking, they suffocated in the stifling heat that gave them no respite until the night. The Dominicans kept watch, sitting up very straight on their horses. There were always two or three bosses, with an inquisitorial eye and a curt, belligerent word, patrolling the edge of the cane. The Kongos weren't allowed to talk, to tell each other stories, or to take a walk. They went to bed hungry, got up hungry, and worked hungry. If they stopped their toil for an instant, they insulted them. If they were found sitting down, exhausted, their ravaged faces did not constitute an excuse. They hit them. The bosses said, "We're not going to let that money spent on you go to waste! You don't want to work, you bunch of loafers, but we already paid!" That is what the bosses told them when they were dragging themselves on, completely exhausted. The Dominicans who surveyed them from the edges of the plantation understood and spoke Creole. Some very well, others not so well, but they all knew some. Every year they worked with Haitians, they picked up in passing the words they employed, reusing them haphazardly when the need arose.

The Kongos couldn't leave the plantation before six o'clock. Sometimes after a day of work, their legs betrayed them. They dragged themselves along, eyes empty, completely worn out. The capataz was on their ass continuously. One pathetic piece of cane was lying on the road. A cutter was passing at a certain distance. The order cracked: gratuitous, immediate, and savage. "Go pick it up!" For one piece of cane, when there are thousands and thousands of tons of it. "Go pick it up!" And you had to go and do it.

The moment it was time to go back, the cabrouetier would suddenly arrive, whereas they hadn't seen him all day long. They stayed loading until an advanced hour of the night. They could work to any hour of the day or night. To one o'clock in the morning! To four o'clock! Stopping was the same thing. The Dominicans decided.

If a Kongo doesn't work, he doesn't eat. If he works, he doesn't eat much more. There was not the slightest possibility of protesting. Even on Sunday they had to work. They needed to rest, but they were hungry. The two did not go together. "The cane will be picked up next week," the capataz would say. Then, with a glacial smile: "Or else on Sunday, if you work!" They worked.

One Monday, when they were starting to cut, the train broke

down. They stopped weighing the lots of cane. In the course of the week they had to resort to credit. Afterward, when they were paid two or three pesos, they handed it over to the storekeeper who had advanced them some money. They always owed something. The process continued, week after week.

But why recount all that?

When a Haitian is caught in the trap of the plantation, only the total and definitive loss of his strength could bring him to stop.

He is literally crushed. As the cane is crushed in the factory.

The pesador mechanically pushed back his long-visored red cap, scratched his hairline with a dirty fingernail. He remained still for an instant, his pencil in the air. A limber green lizard scampered over the conglomerate board wall, near the open entrance in the interior of the little shed. The noisy clumping of boots on a metallic surface brought him back to reality. He leaned his forearms on the brown plank that served as his desk, unstuck his rear from the uncomfortable stool, and leaned forward. Light flooded in through a narrow opening over the counterweights, which, when he had finished moving them over the two graduated metal bars, generally gave the result of the weighing. He recognized Lorenzo. The cabrouetier maneuvered his oxen, letting fly a few interjections, and the cabrouet came to a halt face to face with the pesador, in the precise spot where he knew the pan of the scale was situated.

"Ho, Lorenzo!"

"Hola, pesador!"

"*Como estas?*"

"*M pa pi mal mersi,*" tossed Lorenzo in Creole, in imitation of the Kongos' speech. "Not too bad, thank you." Then he burst into a boisterous laugh. "Ah, the turkeys!"

The pesador smiled silently, sat down again. He snapped the catch that was holding the two parallel bars horizontal. They fell roughly to the left with a dry bang. He slowly moved the counterweights in the opposite direction to make the balance. The two rules, one for the tons and the other for the hundreds of kilos, moved, little by little, back to their original, perfectly horizontal position. The pesador read out the result of the operation. "Four and a half tons." He put the catch back on and rapidly slid back the counterweights. Lorenzo's heavy bulk was framed in the entranceway which had never boasted a door.

"Jesus Christ, I'm dry!"

"How's it going, Lorenzo?" asked the pesador again.

"It's going drier and drier."

"What else is new?"

"Besides that, I'm dry."

"Right. And besides that?"

"So-so. You gotta make these friggin' Kongos produce. That's what makes me so thirsty, *puta*, trying to make these friggin' Kongos produce."

"Are they tough?"

"No. That's just it. This year they're soft."

"Ay, hombre," laughed the pesador. "The Kongos, it's like butter. The hotter it gets, the softer they are."

Lorenzo snickered. He indicated the scale with his chin.

"How much did they do me, those loafers?"

"Four and a half tons."

"Shit! Those motherfuckers only did four and a half tons..."

The carretero, or cabrouetier, makes something on each ton brought in to be weighed. When he's made four trips in a day, bringing in three or four tons a trip, he's earned just enough to eat. Could he survive without his little "on the sides?" Without the Kongos, from whom you can squeeze out around three pesos a day, he'd starve, and that's that! Shit! It's a good thing there were Kongos!

"Four and a half tons," he muttered, lost in his thoughts, "could you survive?"

He dug in his shirt pocket and came up with four cards that he threw, more than put, on the pesador's desk. The latter grabbed them, examining in passing the photos stapled on the corners. Three real nègres, good and black, with strong features, thick lips, and kinky hair. Like all the Kongos. He grabbed the book of coupon stubs on his right, glancing again at the names, which he recopied, one by one, each at the top of an individual sheet. He was applying himself. He looked up, made a rapid calculation. Four and a half tons divided by three. He took the *vales*, one by one, and carefully entered the results in the corresponding column. Estimé Mondestin, one point one tons, one peso, forty-eight. Gérard André, ditto. Brutus, the same. He took a look at the whole lot, clicked his tongue, and handed the sheets, as well as the cards, back to the cabrouetier.

"Here you go, cowboy, for your indians."

The carretero grabbed the papers, slowly added up the tonnage marked on the slips, and nodded his head, winking in the direction of the pesador.

"Three point three tons...It's good pay. Don't make a mistake now, you sonofabitch, mark me my four and a half tons."

The pesador shrugged. There wasn't much chance he'd make a mistake, he did it all day long.

"Don't worry, chump, you're no Kongo!"

"*Carejo!* I'm thirsty," said the cabrouetier again. "I'm going to have a drink to your health."

"Thanks," said the pesador. "That's nice of you."

Lorenzo left. The pesador almost immediately heard the slow step of the team of oxen which was moving away in the direction of the crane and the railroad cars. He grimaced with pleasure, and grabbed from the opposite corner of his table another book of *vales*, special vintage, and went about filling out the sheet after having rapidly scribbled a subtraction on a slip of crumbled paper. Ramirez Garcia, one ton point two, one peso sixty-two. Then he brought out the company register. Three tons three for the Kongos, plus one ton two for Ramirez, that gave him his four and a half tons. Of course, the Kongos lost out a little, but he and Ramirez could share a peso sixty-two. Especially since it wasn't all that serious for the Kongos. They didn't know how to count.

Another cabrouet slowly moved on to the weighing pan.

It was that the sun beat down so hard. When there were a few piles of cane to pick up, you always had to talk to the cabrouetier. When he made the trip for two pesos worth of cane, he required one peso in damages. Or sometimes for three pesos, sixty-five centavos. It was as he pleased, or according to the day's needs, the weather, the debts contracted (he too), the rum consumption of the day before, a sick child for whom it was necessary to buy medicine. When the Kongos refused, the cane was not carried away. They debated, haggled, argued endlessly, like in an African market, and the Dominican got really angry. "You're wasting my time," he hollered. "That guy, the more he carries, the more he makes. He's always in a hurry." In the end the Kongos gave in. It was they who loaded, the sun beating down on their backs, and, on top of it, they had to pay. Sometimes they asked themselves how all this was possible. The carretero left for the weighing and they had no idea what happened over there. Sometimes they spent eight days cutting and only made three pesos. The *vale* was always right, no way to discuss it. One time, Brutus, just to get it clear in his own mind, accompanied the cabrouetier to the scales. "To see," he said. The carretero had made a long face, forbade him to follow, declared that he had better things to do than to have a Kongo under his feet all day long, and that he, Brutus, instead of wasting his time, would be better off working. "You are perfectly right, cabrouetier," said Brutus, conciliatory, "but I'm coming with you anyway." "It's just to visit," he'd added. They cut and they cut, and they were making practically nothing. He suspected that the scales were fixed. The cabrouetier shrugged and called him a damn fool. Brutus said, "Yes, but I'm coming with you." So he did, he walked for a few miles behind the heavy metal cart raised on two wheels equipped with tires, and saw perfectly well that the cabrouetier was fuming, but no one could have prevented him from walking behind this cabrouet, the reason was understood. Arriving at the *chucho*, the scale, he installed himself in front of the instrument, in the site office, determined not to budge until his cabrouet was correctly weighed. It seemed to him that he waited a long time, and that other cabrouets were passing in front. But it was the pesador who decided, and he didn't seem to be in a hurry to let him pass. As for the cabrouetier — after a short discussion with the pesador, he had completely lost all interest in the operation, abandoned his oxen and vehicle, and went to have a drink at the *colmado* near the crane and the railroad. He, who was always in such a hurry! Not to mention that, in a moment of calm, the pesador had gone to join him over there, and they, Brutus was privately convinced, had flashed looks charged with irony in the direction of the disillusioned Kongo. Brutus waited and waited. When the weighing was finally finished, in the course of which he had surveyed every step of the operation, he rushed for the *vales*. A victorious smile illuminated his face. Tonnage and total appeared to him to be superior to the average of what they ordinarily received. He spat absentmindedly, passed the cabrouetier and the pesador, covered the same route in the opposite direction, crossed immense fields of cut cane, perceived his companions from afar. Estimé Mondestin and Gérard André ran to meet him when they saw him appear at the bend in the path that led to their prison of cane. "Well, gentlemen," he said to them, "I do believe that I was right." Making a rapid estimation, it seemed to them that they'd gained about a ton over what would have been credited them if Brutus hadn't been present. It was great. From now on, that would be the necessary procedure. They went back to their work stations with lighter hearts. Suddenly Brutus stopped, put his hand on the back of his neck, and stared at the heap of cut cane cluttering the uneven ground. "But tell me, is that all you cut today?" Gérard André halted, eyes opened round. "But we have not stopped, my friend!" He contemplated the tangle of sugared stalks. "There were only two of us working. You were gone all day long!"

They looked at each other in silence. By and large, things presented themselves as such: Brutus's presence at the weighing premises had permitted them to gain about a ton. His absence from the plantation made them lose about one and a half. They lowered their arms and started back slowly. Once again it was they who'd been screwed.

Every weekend, on Saturday morning, they were supposed to

exchange their *vales*, or what was left of them, at the office in the batey. Or what was left of them, because as soon as they received the paper, during the week, they had to bring it to Scorza, the bodeguero, to pay for their purchases. Or their debts. They didn't know what money was. For example, with a slip worth two pesos, if they bought a peso's worth of merchandise and were given twenty-five centavos change, they had to take it. Or, if they held out the slip, the storekeeper would say, "you have to buy for the whole amount, I don't give change." They went before the majordomo to protest, but he regarded them with a bored air, wiped the hint of sweat that pearled on his brow with a nice silk handkerchief, and replied: "What do you want me to do about it, I'm not responsible. I'm not in charge of the bodega." From time to time they managed, anyway, by depriving themselves, to hold on to a few left over pesos. At the "oficina," part of their salary was confiscated for taxes. They were paid a dollar thirty-five a ton, but 10 centavos was taken out for the cabrouetier; 30 for the *seguro social*, dues for the obligatory insurance, whereas they never received anything when they were sick; 15 centavos to pay back the advance which had been accorded them in the beginning (the 75 centavos a day), when they had stayed without working for the simple reason that they weren't given any work; and one dollar every two weeks for President Duvalier. That particular sum, said the Dominicans, was held by the Haitian government and would be given back to them upon their return. Fine. In a sense, that gave them a savings. They had only one vague fear, that once returned, they would forget to give it back to them. You never know with the Macoutes and Duvalier! It's easy to forget.

Thus they were officially deprived of around twenty percent of their income. With the rest, they...

With the rest! With what rest?

They worked, that's what they were there for. They couldn't do anything. They resigned themselves. Lived their wretched poverty.

Petit Pierre Déroseaux from Pétionville was literally popping with joy. He downed another hit of rum, smacked his lips, his eyes rolling around in his head shiny with perspiration. With all his heart, he thanked one more time *Bon Dié bon*, the Good Lord, and all the saints in his acquaintance, his own as well as those in the paradise of "my father," as well as the mysterious *loas* of voodoo. Déroseaux was Protestant, voodoo mixed in, of course, and even a little Catholic on occasion. Just as well not to forget anyone after such a stroke of fortune. He handed the bottle to Mondestin, then to Gérard André, and they felt the fire seize their gullets. Rum! It had been a long time since they had tasted any of that! Their heads swam slightly.

Petit Pierre Déroseaux had won in the *bolita*. They couldn't get over it and neither could he. Up until now, their minds were made up concerning this game in which they'd never seen a Kongo collect. And here, Petit Pierre Déroseaux had just won.

In all poverty-stricken countries, the hand of God is the hope of men. The lottery, the numbers, the *bolita*, the Dominican equivalent of the Haitian *borlette*. The game is played with a hundred numbers, from 0 to 99. No tickets are sold. It suffices to sign up, to say "I'm in." The Dominican in charge of the game in the batey writes the number chosen in his notebook and pockets the amount played, minimum, 25 centavos. The three winning numbers are announced on Radio Venezuela, where this lottery has its store front. The jackpot pays 14 pesos for 25 centavos played. The second prize, four pesos. The third, one peso. The winner, or winners, if there are any, are paid in full, even in the bateys. The whole Dominican society plays this game. Hundreds of thousands of dollars circulate every day. Many Dominicans only work to be able to play; if not, what's the use of working. Such a meager salary.

"How much did you win?" asked Estimé Mondestin one more time, fascinated by this incredible luck.

"Fourteen pesos, the jackpot."

"That's a lot," said Gérard André, "and at the same time, it's not a lot."

"My friend," said Brutus, "we can never win a lot, we don't have enough money to do it, *ou konprann?*"

When they had a few coins put aside, it was so little that it was pathetic to keep them. They were better off playing them, trying their luck. They rushed to put down their 25 centavos, and in general, lost them. Between nothing and less than nothing, there wasn't a big difference.

"If you could put down more than 25 centavos," said Déroseaux, "you'd win a fortune."

"How much would you win?" asked Mondestin, who was thinking, with anguish, of the eighty dollars owed to his usurer.

"A fortune."

"Yes, but how much?"

Petit Pierre Déroseaux thought a minute, making a difficult mental calculation, and stepping into a fairy tale universe.

"Well, my friend, if you could play ten pesos, and you won the jackpot, you would collect 560 pesos."

Five hundred and sixty pesos! In the silence that reigned you could have heard their hearts pounding. Five hundred and sixty pesos! But who could stake ten pesos on such a big chance? When they managed to throw 25 centavos into the pool, it was already a big event.

"Fourteen pesos is already a small fortune," said Mondestin enviously, coming back to earth. "What are you going to do with it?"

"Have a drink," said Déroseaux, joyously, suiting the action to the word. They all burst out laughing. "Then, eat. And then. . . Ah, then. . ."

"Then what?"

His hips undulated gently, placidly obscene, and they understood very well what he was going to do next. They were more envious than ever of his good fortune.

Sometimes, in the batey, the Haitians feel like getting laid. When they need to spend some time, they go and find the girls who walk a certain way, for among the ladies of the batey, one can distinguish two main categories: the *mujeres* (mu'eles, as the Kongos say), and the *señoritas* (senolitas). The *mujer* is a woman who has a husband. The *señorita* would more or less resemble an easy woman. Whose life was far from easy. Without counting certain *mujeres* who. . . In order to find these girls, you have to have money. Estimé Mondestin sighed. He didn't even have any to eat with.

"You are going to go and see a Haitian girl?"

Petit Pierre Déroseaux hesitated for an instant, a delighted smile spreading over his feverish face, then shook his head no. To celebrate such a big day, he wanted better than that. The Haitian women in the batey will go to bed for the evening for a bit to eat. For twenty centavos, a guy can go to bed with a Haitian woman, and for twenty centavos, it's for the whole night. The Haitian woman has no value, and she starves to death, like the Kongos. He was savoring the moment.

"No. I'm going to see La Rosita."

"Her? That Dominican girl?" asked Estimé Mondestin, impressed.

He would never have dared. He regarded his companion with envy and admiration. La Rosita. This girl was always laughing loudly in the batey, hanging around the men, but especially the Dominicans, brushing too closely against them, swinging her hips, giving off an arousing odor of love and coupling.

"She won't want to," stated Gérard André firmly, whose opinion no one had asked.

"She's a Dominican who practices prostitution, I don't see why she would refuse."

"She's white, she goes to bed with Dominicans! She won't want a dirty Kongo like you! Look at yourself!"

Petit Pierre Déroseaux burst out laughing. "But my friend, I'm going to go to the river, and put on my clean shirt. I'll be very handsome, she won't get over seeing such a good-looking Kongo!"

"She's white, she sleeps with the Dominicans."

"You don't understand at all. *L'a vand nèg la ti kouleu a ke li ginyin!* It's her color that she sells to a man. That's her greatest treasure. Especially for us, the Kongos! I don't want to blow this experience."

Gérard André shrugged. That beautiful, attractively vulgar, Dominican woman with the very heavy and very white breasts and buttocks wouldn't want a nègre, black like Déroseaux. That Kongo there was kidding himself.

"She won't accept."

"You're just saying that because you're jealous," tossed Déroseaux, with a stiff little laugh.

"Me, jealous?" It was Gérard André's turn to chortle. "I'm being realistic, that's all. *Ak déryé ron monchè ou vlé pété karé!* With a round rear-end, you want to fart square!"

"Talk all you want!" Petit Pierre Déroseaux remained steadfast in his idea.

"I won fourteen pesos, I'm going to see this Rosita. *Koko li pa gin zorey mé l tandé brui lajan.* The vagina doesn't have ears, but it can hear the sound of money!"

"After all, do as you like." Gérard André conceded that it was certainly worth a try.

Estimé Mondestin watched Déroseaux move away; tried hard to get rid of the large lump of bitterness stuck in his throat. He really would have liked to have a little sum. "*Fam yo rinmin lajan,*" he murmured, distraught, in a barely audible voice. "Women like money." He felt a wave of anger overcome him. Those women there are nothing but a flash in the pan! *Yo arona; yo bouzin!* All whores!

He hadn't found a girl yet. He'd never won at the *bolita*. He didn't know about the others, but for him, no. He didn't have any money for that sort of thing. He was very much chagrined about that.

That night, he had a very hard time getting to sleep. He was imagining Port-au-Prince, the waterfront, the crowd, the sounds of the booming music on Dessalines Street. He saw his wife and his children. Next, the image of La Rosita's full body imposed itself in his mind against his will. Then his wife again. Without his knowing exactly how, an unfamiliar, but at the same time strangely familiar, face suddenly floated before his eyes, wide open in the darkness. It took him a moment to recognize Desruisseaux Simone, that Haitian girl he'd noticed. His wife's image came back, but was immediately chased by that of La Rosita's belly. Something hurt somewhere, and he felt like...felt like what? His right arm rose, moved restlessly, in

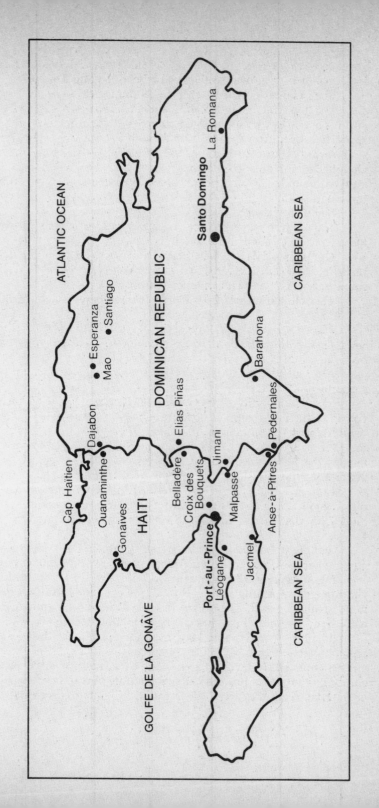

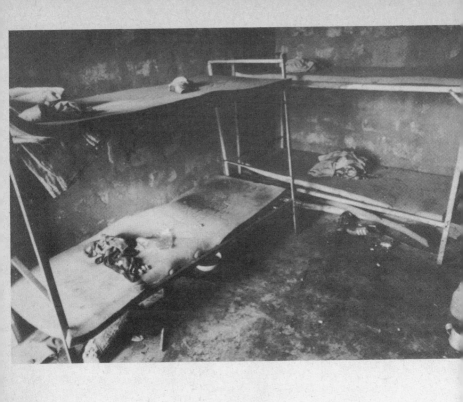

Bodega, or batey store. Place of obligatory passage where the Kongos are forced to get into debt.

To prevent all escape attempts, armed militiamen, police, rural guards surround the plantations.

Owing to the repression launched in Haiti in 1980, and for reasons of security, this photograph has been deleted.

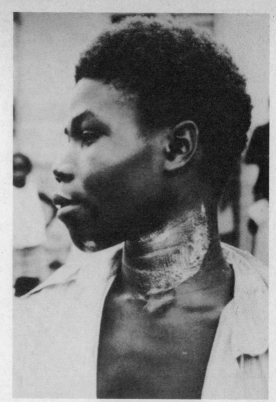

aint Lima. Ill, the hospital
sed him admission. Strangers
sted him, beat him up, tied
up, and put a rope around his
with which they dragged him
e street. Miraculously escaped,
nded, weakened, shocked,
matized, he asked to be
triated to Haiti. The Haitian
ector's reply: "Out of the
tion, get back to your batey!"

This Haitian "supplétif" (auxiliary "police") is paid 4 pesos a day to stop all the
Haitians passing on the road (to San Isidro). They were going to a funeral.
They will find themselves back in the plantations.

They are between eleven and thirteen years old. They cut cane every morning. They are paid two and a half pesos ($2.50)...every two weeks!

Gulf & Western: the bateys

Gulf & Western: the headquarters in New York.

the black of the night, seeking a presence, perhaps, but only fanning the warm, muggy air, full of unwholesome odors.

The hand fell back on his thigh, moved slowly back towards his belly. Estimé Mondestin, Haitian Kongo, groaned in despair, tried not to make any noise.

That night, like other nights, he married his solitude.

It was not a very senior viejo: if so, he would have known. The capataces had trampled everything on him, had savagely kicked everything all to hell. He was choking with indignation, and asked the same question of everyone he met. Whom could this garden have bothered? No one, was the response. Literally no one. The little piece of useless land lay idle in a remote corner of the batey, was not planted with cane, served no purpose whatsoever, and he was starving. You couldn't even say that he had appropriated it; he had simply turned and sowed it. He'd dug the holes one evening after a hard day, very carefully placing the potatoes, yams, and manioc in the earth, according to the immutable laws, as he would have done in Haiti, taking into account the moon, the date, and the rainfall. He had even chosen the best day of the year, in all cases and for all things, the Holy Saturday, the *samedi dlo bénit*, as they say in Creole. Everyone knows it, certain dates for sowing or planting are particularly favorable. For instance, the first of January, St. Jean's day, and the famous Holy Saturday. Thus, all the chances of success were on his side. In addition, he had done what was necessary to increase them. On a moonless night, in the greatest secrecy, he had placed a *mygale*,* *krab arénié*, in an empty bottle that he then filled with water and buried in a corner of what was to be his garden. It would henceforth be protected. Anything harvested prior to the uncorking of this bottle, of which he alone knew the location, would be irremediably poisoned. For there was no reason why the Divinities would not function in Dominicanie as well as in Haiti. He wasn't going to go to the trouble to plant and look after a garden for others to reap the benefit.

And that is how it happened.

Basically, it was nothing new. In the days of slavery, that is, the other, the first, the one which was not disguised, the one of the colonies and the French, there existed, besides the work in the plantation, a small, subsistence agriculture on what was called *places à vivres*. These were small patches of land that the master left at the disposal of the slaves, on which they could cultivate what they

---

*Mygale: tropical spider. — TRANS.

153

wished for their own consumption. Their daily two hours of leisure (?) time, plus Sundays and religious feast days, were devoted to caring for their little plots. Later, after Independence, the law of 20 April 1807 recognized the equitable allocation of these *places à vivres* among the families of those who were made to cultivate the plantations. And so you see, my friend, you could almost say those were the good old days.

The capataces had pulled up everything. When the young viejo was informed of the act, he rushed to the scene, but was only able to view the extent of the damages. The crime had already been perpetrated.

"But capataz, what are you doing?"

"We are getting rid of your crap! Where do you think you are?"

"It's a garden!"

"On company land!"

"But it's land not used for anything!"

"It's the company's land. What the company does with it is none of your business."

"But if it serves no purpose, and if I'm starving to death. . ." He took out his latest *vale*, out of his shirt pocket, held it out to the Dominicans. "I spent seven days cutting the cane, and since it wasn't collected, I bought on credit in the bodega until the pay came in. And finally, the cane I cut only paid 3 pesos 50. I'm not going to spend my life starving to death!"

"Cut more and you'll earn more."

"But it's not possible to cut more — you know that."

"You are not supposed to be planting, but cutting."

"It's just to eat."

"You are not here to make roots. As soon as a Haitian arrives somewhere, he starts scratching the ground! You think you're at home? Here it's the company."

The capataces appeared to be uncompromising. The majordomo, one day, had explained to them the whys and wherefores of the situation.

"You can't let them grow anything. A patch of land, as small as it may be, quickly becomes their garden, which they exploit, and whose product belongs to them, do you follow me?" Sighing, he'd mopped his brow; for although he did not cut the cane, he endured the implacable heat with difficulty. "If they have to choose one day between working an extra hour in the plantation for a few centavos and taking care of their garden which permits them to eat, you can guess right away which will be their preference! They will leave our sugar cane and look after their vegetables. An hour here, two hours there, and we'll soon find ourselves like a bunch of damn fools, if I may say so, with our plantations abandoned."

At the time of the General Emancipation of the slaves, it was so much the same situation that Toussaint Louverture himself, who believed the strength of the new nation depended upon their raising agricultural production to a maximum by whatever means, had to force the recently freed peasants to stay on the plantations they wanted to desert. He instituted an agricultural plan which, if not formally bondage, recalled certain facets of it: including discipline, severity, and corporal repression.

"Gentlemen," said the majordomo, "you know me, I am not cynical, but there is one thing that you must never lose sight of." He had left them in suspense for a moment. "They only continue to work, in the conditions of which you are aware, because they are starving to death. We can regret it, but the whole system, the entire economy and wealth of our country, depends upon this. Give them the slightest means to produce anything at all, they will eat at will, and we can anticipate the worst calamities. I know that in certain bateys, a few viejos, after several years, are authorized to have a garden. To my knowledge, these bateys are rare, and in any case, it is out of the question here. Quite often, mind you, these viejos who have been accorded a handkerchief plot of land have it worked by someone poorer than they." Then he changed his register. "In 1977, gentlemen, the State Sugar Council showed a deficit of 26 million pesos, and last year, a deficit of 24 million pesos." They all shuddered, extremely impressed. "Taking into account the ups and downs of the market, and in the present conditions, only draconian measures imposed on our cane cutters can ensure a profitable production, a recovery of the CEA, and can safeguard your jobs. Mine also, I might add, by the way."

The majordomo had observed a brief silence, then had managed to somewhat soften his remarks. As he had already said, he was not a cynic.

"Enforce these orders and don't let it bother you. After all, these Haitians are paid a salary. Besides, if they were given more, they would spend it on drink. Where would be the progress? As for the viejos, they have nothing to demand; they are all illegal, we would be within our rights to have them arrested. So let them not complain. They are not slaves. Their ancestors didn't have as much."

They listened to him. They enforced their orders and didn't let it bother them.

The fields were very long. Estimé Mondestin, who knew—he was a driver, eternally unemployed, but even though not driving, he still had distances in his head — Estimé Mondestin said it was as far as from the customs in Port-au-Prince to Pétionville, where Déroseaux was from. Then he began to dream. He imagined Pétionville, the luxurious villas belonging to the big, important nègres, the hotels for white tourists which dotted the somewhat dry greenery on the hillside, three miles from the capital. The fields were long, really. Dozens of Kongos had to be thrown in to chew up these immense surfaces, and they cut the cane so rapidly that they could finish one field in a week and a half. But it was really hopeless. The more they cut and the more they cut, the more the cane stretched on and the more the cane stretched on. When they had carved up one field, they were sent to another. In the beginning of the zafra, the expanses of cane literally surrounded the batey. But the time was passing, and now they had to walk for a long time to start work. It was a few miles they had to cover. That is, some left at three-thirty in the morning to arrive at the site at five o'clock. The Kongos complained about the length of the route. Sometimes, they were packed into trucks like sardines. In other bateys they were transported by rail, in "MacDonald" cars. Kongos, capataces and their horses, cabrouetiers and their oxen and their cabrouets, the merchant women and their merchandise, all were thrown in pell-mell. The merchants, wives of viejos, or else Dominican women, traveled up and down the fields selling a little bit of everything: bread, dried codfish, drinks. When the week had been good, the Kongos chipped in together at noon to buy 60 centavos worth of cake. But most of the time, they didn't have five *cheles* in their pockets to get anything to eat. They didn't eat anything before six o'clock.

They walked in the plantations, covered miles and miles and miles.

One morning, which should have been just like the others, Estimé Mondestin, Brutus, and Gérard André came to a sudden halt, machetes in abeyance. Three viejos were working in the good spot which had been assigned to them, the Kongos, by the capataz the day before.

"Oh, hey, viejos! That's our cane you're cutting," shouted Estimé Mondestin from the edge of the route.

The three viejos accorded them no more than a half glance, and continued their work as if nothing had happened. The three Kongos advanced briskly into the field.

"Gentlemen! You are in the wrong spot!"

"*Ki sa li mandé?*" asked one of the viejos, insolently, addressing one of his companions. "What is he asking?"

"*M pa konprann sa li di,*" replied one of the others. "I don't understand what he's saying."

Then they calmly began talking among themselves, in Spanish, before the three speechless Kongos.

"You are in our spot," said Brutus once again, raising his voice.

"So what? It's no big deal! The plantation is big, go somewhere else."

"No. It's the capataz who gives the spots, and this is the one he showed us. Yesterday you were over there."

"There's been a change," said the first viejo. "This morning he put us here."

"This morning is now."

"Yes, but we got here first."

"We were here, that means we were here. The time you arrive has nothing to do with it."

"There's been a change, we're telling you," snapped the second viejo.

"If there had been a change, the capataz would have informed us."

"He didn't have time, he told us to let you know."

"*Se manti*. It's a lie," accused Gérard André.

"The capataz does what he feels like. He doesn't owe any explanations to the Kongos. He changed the places and that's it."

"*An alé! An alé!*" cried Estimé Mondestin. "Get out of here! We work here!"

The viejo let out an exasperated sigh.

"*No an alé!* Here we do what we want, we're not Kongos!"

"You know what the Kongos say to you?"

"We work where we want, we've got priority."

"*An alé*, viejo!"

"Filthy Haitian," spat the viejo with disdain.

"Filthy Haitian, hah, hah! But you, too, are Haitian, my friend!"

"I will never go back to Haiti. I'm staying here, I have nothing to fear, no problems in life."

"You're nothing but an exiled Haitian!"

The second viejo, a skinny nègre missing one finger and with a wide scar on his arm, advanced toward the Kongos.

"You, the Kongos, you've all been bought! It's Duvalier that sold you!"

"But you too, you are also Haitians, sons of Duvalier!"

"We haven't been sold, we got here secretly, *an ba fil*, by our own courage!"

"Sonofabitch of a viejo," growled Brutus, nervously gripping his machete. He called his two companions to witness. "The worst in this batey are not the Dominicans but the viejos!" He thought he would suffocate with rage. "These viejo bastards get along fine with the Dominicans. They don't like us because we come to Dominicanie each year."

"Kongos bought and sold," insisted the viejo, his face exuding contempt.

"They say we've been sold," Gérard André laughed brutally, with a sharp, high-pitched laugh, "but they are nothing but bastards! They don't even know who they are any more! They aren't Haitians any more and they'll never be Dominicans!"

"*Hijueputa vendido,*" spat one of the viejos, surprised.

"The sons of Haitians born in this country — they don't give them any documents, they don't get a birth certificate, they don't get a *cedula* to justify their origins or their nationality. They're nothing at all."

"They are batey-shit!"

This time, the viejos took it very badly. "*An alé, an alé,*" they began to shout.

"Rotten bastards!"

"Dirty Kongos!"

At that point, Brutus had had enough; he declared that they would not give up the place and advanced, machete held high. These viejos thought they could get away with anything, under the pretext that they'd been in Dominicanie longer, spoke Spanish, had wives and children, and because some of them lived a little better, were masons or carpenters, and even sometimes married a Dominican woman! Let them go to hell! Besides, they could pretend whatever they wanted, in the last analysis they were here, just like them, and they were cutting cane. Brutus announced coldly that he would not leave. For once they'd inherited a field of good cane, and they weren't going to let it go. They weren't paid by the day, but by the weight. It wasn't the first time that this situation had come about. They'd come across a spot where the cane was good and heavy, good and plump, and others had come to take their places. There was nothing academic about the question. There were times when you could make 12 pesos when the cane was good, but only three and a half when it was bad. They weren't going to budge. Already, they were circling one another, machetes in hand.

Not one among them saw the capataz arrive, but they all heard him when he got within earshot. The viejos seemed very reassured by this propitious intervention.

"What the hell is this shit?"

He'd taken off his white plastic safari hat, dismounted ponderously from his horse, and was advancing with a rather uninviting air. He was greeted by a string of vituperation which seemed to say that everyone wanted to work in this spot, and that this spot was not big enough to accommodate all those who wished to work there. And vice versa. Or something like that. These morons were really starting to give him a pain in the ass. He started bawling his head off, got worked up into a good lather, threatened to stick them all in prison to teach them to piss him off with their damn Haitian foolishness. In between two strings of abuse, he perceived the discreet signal addressed him by one of the viejos. He calmed down like an old, worn-out storm.

"*Bueno*. Kongos, get the hell over there!"

"But we were here yesterday!"

"Yesterday was yesterday, today is today, and until proof to the contrary, it's still me who gives the orders!"

"But it was you that decided..."

"Are you going to stop pissing me off, or am I going to have to call the police, you friggin' full-of-shit Kongos?"

They indulged in one last, vain protest, just for the record, but were forced to give up; moved away silently, crushed by the injustice.

One of the viejos, with some difficulty, pulled a soiled peso out of his pocket, handed it to the capataz, who grabbed it without a word. Their problems among nègres weren't any of his business. Let them figure out how to get out of their own damn mess. He didn't have any favorites. Now, of course, it was only natural that the good shares of cane be granted to those who participated. There has to be some ethic in this life.

The Kongos began to cut without saying a word. The stalks in this new spot were tough and light, dry and shrivelled up. It took them three days to fill up a cabrouet.

The sky was undulating in gloomy whorls, swept along by a nasty wind. It had rained. The batey, disgraceful human cesspool, foul blister of despair, was decomposing, lost in the dripping immensity of the cane. The miserable huts were huddled against one another along alleys transformed into sewers. You could hear fits of coughing. It would be cold that night. Kongos with vacant eyes were trying to light fires for the evening meal on the bare, mirey ground turned into a swamp by the rain. Others were walking barefoot in the mud. They were coming out of the plantation, their faces ravaged, their clothes soaked, going along silently, expressions stamped with a painful dignity. Those with a pay slip in hand went to the bodega. Those without, went to bed with nothing, or else gathered their last bit of strength to go and pound a few pieces of cane. They drank the cane juice down to the last drop. Others were passing silently like zombies. Near an open door, a woman rubbed the skinny body of her child with a mechanical gesture.

An insistent odor was lurking around two cells curtained by a few rags. A broth of excrement was gently overflowing the camp latrine. An exhausted viejo swore with lassitude, went to shit far into the cane, holding his belly. Another, overcome with dysentery, brutally emptied himself in his *barracon'*. No doctor, no clinic, no clergyman, no union. No money, no food. Their only relations were with the cane, the horses, the oxen, the bosses, living completely isolated — with no radio, no newspapers, no nothing. They felt very dirty, they who had been so clean in Haiti. Poverty and filth don't necessarily go hand in hand. They could go a week without bathing. The river was far, they didn't have the time, they didn't have the strength. At night, they scraped the mud and their skin off with the machete blade. Sometimes they didn't have any water. The Dominicans had some, were always supplied with several drums, permanently full. They wouldn't give them a glassful, even when the Kongos were gnawed by a terrible thirst. They didn't give a shit, they considered them dogs.

In the evening, after their sorry homecoming, they talked about their conditions of existence and went to sleep. It was the Dominicans who spent the night having a good time. You often heard them in the depths of the obscurity, laughing, drinking, and singing. But not the Kongos. The Kongos hardly exchanged two words. They didn't have leisure time. They got up too early, were much too exhausted. They didn't sing. They didn't play music as they did at home. They didn't feel like playing the drums, they, who would play at the drop of a hat. They didn't know what it was to dance any more. In order to party, they would have needed a happy heart! Sometimes they were so hungry they couldn't even speak. When you have gone two or three days without eating, drinking only water or cane juice, you can no longer even speak. You can stew, but you can't speak. To party, you have to have your belly full. Then you can have a good time. But with a hungry body, you haven't got the heart for that sort of thing.

They dragged themselves around, destroyed by fatigue, crippled by humiliation, without joy, without laughter, without identity, completely alienated.

They lived in cages. Sometimes it was so hot that they had to go outside, to sleep inside would have been impossible. But they were freezing to death after the rains, and lived plagued by the mosquitoes.

That week an old Haitian died as he had lived, in silence. The hospital had refused him, he'd been given no medicine, no one lavished any care upon him. He croaked like a dog in a corner of the batey.

It was a very out-of-the-way spot.

Sometimes they call for help, but no one hears them.

Article 6: The State Sugar Council agrees to report to the Haitian Embassy in Santo Domingo and to the Dominican Institute of Social Insurance of the Dominican Republic, any accident befalling the Haitian agricultural worker in his work center or in the course of his duties.

In the event of an accident at work leading to the death of the agricultural worker, it is expressly committed to bear the expense of any damages and compensations resulting from it in accordance with the legal provisions. Any death of a Haitian agricultural worker must be reported the same day, by a detailed report to the Haitian Embassy in Santo Domingo and also to the concerned Dominican civil and military authorities.

Article 25: In the event that a Haitian agricultural worker is the victim of an accident, the State Sugar Council is committed to provide him with free transportation from the site of the accident to a Health Center where he must be treated.

"A *msyé, sé gro blan!*" The winded viejo stopped running. "The white man's here!" he shouted once again, "and it's a big wig!" The little group broke off their conversation. In fact, it was even a whole bundle of whites! On the road in front of Scorza's bodega, three carloads of bosses, including some very important ones, had just come charging in, full tilt.

"They are here about it," affirmed Gérard André immediately, a gleam of satisfaction in the back of his eyes.

"For that?" scoffed Antoine the viejo, more than skeptical. "That would surprise me!"

"But of course, that's why they're here. What else would they be doing here?"

Each one echoed the question. Ordinarily, it's true, the highly placed Gentlemen of the Company never pay them a visit. Now as far as thinking that they came for that . . .

"I'm telling you that's why. The capataces and the majordomo are going to get yelled at," continued the voice of common sense, which then became indignant. "Really, a thing like that just isn't done!"

That was true. On that point, they all agreed. A thing like that just wasn't done.

"We'll have to go talk to them," said Brutus. "We'll all go."

"As for me, I'm of a mind not to get mixed up in it," said another Kongo. "If that's what they came for, they'll take care of everything."

"Of course that's what they came for."

"Well, I, gentlemen, would be quite astonished. It would certainly be the first time."

Someone voiced a rather disagreeable remark. Antoine the viejo was a pain in the ass. Under the pretext that he had the advantage — a sorry advantage, by the way — of seniority, he claimed to always know, better than the Kongos, what was going to happen. He was all right for a viejo, but he was a pain in the ass. They slowly advanced in the direction of the extremity of the batey, examining from afar all these big whites with a mixture of fear and curiosity.

"I say we better go there," repeated Brutus, who pursued his ideas.

"Let's wait. We'll see what happens all right."

At a closer look, and at the sight of their somber expressions and concerned air which clearly indicated that something serious had occurred, Antoine the viejo somewhat qualified his position. After all, maybe that's why they had come. The rumor had seeped out, gotten past the limits of the batey, reached as far as them, and there they were, to find out what the story was . . . But he would be mighty surprised, anyway. It wasn't their style. No, to tell the truth, he didn't believe it.

"Because really," said an irritated Brutus, "it has to be very clear, you don't just throw people out like that!"

"We've seen worse," said Antoine the viejo.

"We might have seen worse, but that's really going too far."

"Oh, yes, too far!"

They didn't look it, but they were in a stew because of the fact that Célestin Pierre-Henri, the man with two fingers cut off, and Méral Joseph, the worn-out Kongo, had been expelled from the barracks by an intransigent capataz. As Gérard André had said, to resume the situation, the limits had overstepped the bounds! Enough was enough.

"Couldn't we complain at the Embassy?" Estimé Mondestin had initially suggested. They'd smiled about that, especially the viejos. An old-timer with an unbelievably worn-out face had told him no with a shake of the head: "You can't. My friend, no one can get to where the Embassy is. There, where it's called the Embassy, is the '27 *febrero* street'; you have to go to the capital, and the bus is two pesos sixty-five. The bosses don't allow us to go there. All along the way, watchmen are on the lookout for Kongos. When they meet up with you, you've got problems. We're not allowed to go all the way there. The Dominican bosses know that they have mistreated the Kongos, they don't want us to go talking about it. Besides, even if you go there, the Ambassador is bad. You arrive, and right away, it's back to the cane again."

"Fine," said Estimé Mondestin, frowning, "but what exactly should happen if you are sick?"

"If a person gets sick, say, malaria, fever, etc., the Company doesn't compensate," Antoine the viejo explained calmly.

"Doesn't compensate!"

"No, doesn't compensate."

"However, in the contract..."

"Don't talk about the contract, you've never read it," chortled Gérard André, who was listening with only half an ear. "None of us have ever seen it. They have us make an X on a paper that we are all incapable of reading, hah! hah! Without that, we certainly would not be here!"

"Yes, but anyway, the contract... They told us, when someone is sick, and can't work, he's put on *Seguro Social*."*

"Please! The only thing put on the *Seguro Social* is the tax that's withheld from us!"

"This is what I've seen," cut in Antoine the viejo. "A Haitian suffering from malaria spent a week in the hospital. The diagnosis revealed his physical incapacity. He was fired, pure and simple."

"Fired!" Mondestin couldn't hold back an exclamation. "But that's like..."

"Exactly like."

Seguro Social: health and welfare insurance.

Mondestin pondered for an instant. Fired. It was exactly like. . .
At bottom, maybe they hadn't come here for that. "And when you
have an accident?"

"If the accident happened at work, you have the right to a
compensation."

"How much is the compensation?"

"I don't know the amount of money they give to the victim.
They compensate."

Célestin Pierre-Henri, for example, had received 25 pesos,
everyone knew that. Méral Joseph received nothing, everyone knew
that, also.

Méral Joseph had already been taken with fever for several
weeks. At the batey's *consultario*, the foul, empty room where a
practicante, not a doctor, but a *practicante* in a dirt-stained white
smock passes from time to time, he hadn't received any medication
for the good and simple reason that there wasn't any. As for the
Dominican Institute of Social Insurance, they paid him absolutely
nothing, in spite of his recognized disability. Besides, each time it was
the same thing. They paid taxes for social security, health insurance,
and never reaped the slightest benefit. There was no doctor in the
batey. There was one at the ingenio, the Dominican factory, but it
was too far to go on foot in a very weak condition, and too expensive
to go by taxi in a state of complete destitution. All that was not for the
Kongos. When, in a bad way, they asked for help they were told very
nicely: "Work!" and when the claimed their due: "You'll get that
money in Port-au-Prince, after the zafra!" In a sense, it was better
than nothing. But they didn't do much for anyone who got sick. He
was just simply left sitting, sweating with weakness, dying in a corner of his cell. His closest companions helped him as much as they
could. If one ate, the other ate, too. But otherwise, his problems
went unnoticed. Each one had plenty to do looking after his own
survival.

According to a report submitted to the United Nations, a large
proportion of the 250,000 immigrant workers in the Dominican
Republic die from chronic malnutrition and disease, while the infant
mortality rate of the children of viejos attains frightening
proportions.

It would take a really extreme case, urgent, spectacular, with a
lot of blood, for an automobile to make the trip to the hospital. Not
counting therein the open wounds, or those badly healed, the
purulent gashes, the oozing boils, the terrible swollen scars, all too
numerous in the batey to be listed. It would have been necessary to
organize a veritable airlift! They weren't about to do that. Those
were the occupational hazards.

Célestin Pierre-Henri, for example… Célestin Pierre-Henri got up one morning at four o'clock, as usual. Around seven o'clock, while trying to cut the cane in such a way that it would fall directly on the pile, two fingers placidly parted company. He never knew exactly what happened. His two companions had held him while he screamed. They'd called the capataz, who'd taken his time to arrive and began by yelling at him, but had called for an auto, anyway, that had taken him away. They bandaged him at the ingenio, then transported him to the hospital, for the wound was really deep. Upon arrival, he was refused admittance. "You are not insured!" Meanwhile, they regularly deducted from his pay! He'd had to really insist, in spite of the pain, and raise hell, in Creole, which obviously no one understood, and show, with his good hand, his batey card, and explain, up and down and all around, that he was sent by his government, that he was not an illegal immigrant, in order for them, finally, around six o'clock, with tight-lipped looks, to consent to take care of him. Next, they refused to give him a bed. Every time someone indicated a spot to him, others arrived menacingly. "*Haitiano, Haitiano* out! No nègres here! These dirty immigrants are invading our hospitals! Go sleep in your country!" As if it were next door. He'd dozed in a chair, even though he paid for their hospitals with his sweat. The next day, he left, thanking them. Since then, every week he went down to the ingenio to get taken care of. He had been lucky to be paid 25 pesos by the *seguro* for his two fingers. He spent it on transportation, to have his bandages changed, and to eat, naturally. Out of the question to pick up a machete for quite some time. He was worried, wondering what was going to happen when he'd spent everything. A sick Kongo isn't paid. The Embassy refused to repatriate him. Out of the two jeeps in their possession, they had explained to him, one was broken down, and the other was at the service of the Ambassador. It's asking for the impossible — only in the most extreme cases… Besides, if they had to repatriate all those who cut off pieces of hands, they would need ten Embassies and an entire fleet of buses!

As for the Dominicans, they weren't much better. One day when they were lavishing some care upon him, the doctor was inadvertently rough, hurting his badly healed scar horribly. Célestin Pierre-Henri was not able to hold back a cry of pain. The doctor looked at him and said to him just like this: "You got nicked by a machete, it's nothing! It's really nothing in comparison to the ill treatment you inflicted on us when you invaded us! Stop whimpering!" In other words, even in the hospitals, where one might expect a little humanity, they were not welcome.

Célestin Pierre-Henri had had time to see some of his compatriots, victims of all sorts of maladies, of weakness, and of fever. He wasn't able to count them, but had been able to exchange a few words.

No one pays attention to Haitians in the hospital. There are Haitians who hurt themselves, and can go for four days before the nurses dress their wounds — not even necessarily because they are malicious, they are just afraid to approach them.

He'd had time to see severed hands, broken feet, all the injuries from the bateys.

The machete constitutes the principal cause of work-related accidents of the cane worker, making up 44.3 percent of the total. Hands and arms receive 41.7 percent of the lesions. According to the *Oficina Nacional de Estadísticas*, 11,670 work-related accidents were recorded in the sugar industry during the period between 1970-1974, of which three-quarters occurred in the plantations. At the present time, of 880 work injuries in the Dominican Republic in a single month, 804 are from sugar production.

The sugar is not white, but red with the blood of the nègres.

Now, to be more precise, and to leave off the abstractions, here is exactly what happened.

Four Kongos had arrived one morning, emerging from the almost icy mist, four Kongos no one knew. They said they were from the Catarey ingenio, that they'd fled because life there was impossible, and they were looking for work. The authorities were not men to refuse them that. It remained to lodge them. "We'll get rid of the dead wood," pronounced the small nasty-looking capataz. Célestin Pierre-Henri and Méral Joseph were the first ones picked out. They were sick, they were not working, and were taking up space.

Méral Joseph was dozing on the bare ground, shivering uncontrollably with fever when the man shook him violently by the shoulder.

"So! Snoozing again!"

The Kongo looked up, glassy-eyed, with an expression full of incomprehension and great fatigue. He was obviously in bad shape.

"You can't cut cane?"

Méral had gathered his feeble forces to shake his head no.

"You can't cut cane? Well, then, old man, a batey is not a vacation camp. Get up and give up your place!"

The Kongo seemed not to understand, it was necessary to push him a little.

"You're no worker! Those who live in these lodgings have to produce, understand? *Pro-duce!* Come on, move!"

"Capataz, it's impossible! I don't have any strength. I don't know anyone here in the Dominican Republic."

"Don't wanna hear it."

"I've got no family, no friends. Where will I go?"

"You can go wherever you want, I don't care."

"But where?"

"How should I know? There are workers to lodge. Hurry up."

The two nonproductive, sick Kongos were presently on display, in their misery, in the central square of the batey. Méral Joseph was lying in the dust, weeping. He felt himself growing weaker.

Estimé Mondestin was glad that the authorities of the ingenio had come to solve the situation. In the hour they had been there, they'd walked around a lot, arms behind their backs, interrogating the capataces, also speaking with a cabrouetier. Now they were headed in the direction of a long building which wasn't one of the Kongos'.

"I'm going to talk to them," said Brutus, abruptly, "give them our feelings about it. We can't let this happen."

It was thus that he boldly approached the group of big Whites, pulled on the sleeve of a capataz who didn't even look at him, exchanged a few words with the majordomo who, irritated, turned him away; tried unsuccessfully to attract the attention of a señor, *muy bien vestido*, very well-dressed, and *muy culto*, very cultivated. He got himself very politely thrown out. They would be greatly pleased if this full-of-shit Kongo son-of-a-bitch would be so kind as to, *por favor*, go and take a walk elsewhere, stop pissing them off for two minutes, they let him know with the utmost courtesy.

An ox was found dead that morning, which no one had expected, and they still hadn't discovered why. They had other things to do at the moment, besides worrying about the fate of the Haitians.

It was at the end of a day, a short time later. A cloud of gray smoke was rising in the immaculate sky. It seemed to hesitate, then moved away in dense wreaths before completely spreading out over the horizon.

Arde la caña! The entire *cañaveral* held its breath at once. Dozens and dozens of Kongos stopped cutting, shading their eyes with their hands, and turned toward the patch of darkening blue, steadily growing like a cancer of soot. They understood, with some anxiety, that it was not a matter of a small fire. The fire was spreading too fast, you could tell by the more and more obscured sky.

They finished up their day as if there was nothing amiss, they had nothing else to do; but every time they looked up they couldn't help sizing up the advancing line of the upheaval and feeling a dark menace hanging over them. It was progressing steadily, far away, there, beyond the horizon, but it was progressing.

When night fell, they slowly returned to the batey, turning around at regular intervals. An entire side of the obscurity was now burning silently, swallowed by a long incandescent streak. The black sky glowed red.

Arriving at the camp, they realized the gravity of the situation. A multitude of faces, familiar faces, unfamiliar faces, were passing to and fro, covering the batey in every direction, panic-stricken insects in a trodden-upon anthill. "It's panic," pronounced Antoine the viejo, placidly, when his companions stopped wearily in front of the barracks. "It's one big panic. A fire has broken out, a huge fire." "Yes, we saw." "No," said he, "you haven't seen anything, it's much worse than you think. It's not stopping. There's several contingents of police there, cars are arriving from everywhere, plenty of whites from the capital, and the administrator himself even came out. Again! It's the season! All you see around here is them."

Antoine the viejo had already lived through numerous disasters since he'd been there. When fire spreads in the cane fields, all the Dominicans, including the *gran nègs*, have to lend a hand to stop the plague, for the cane represents the greatest part of the economy in Dominicanie. But this time around, it's really a panic! There are at least ten thousand police in the fields! Antoine the viejo was laying it on thick. It must be said in his defense that he'd never seen anything like it yet. But he, ordinarily so level-headed, was exaggerating. There weren't ten thousand police.

However, there was reason to think so. In the midst of an impressive cloud of dust, a replica in miniature of the cloud of smoke, there were innumerable automobiles arriving, stopping, pulling away, doors slamming, and chauffeurs honking; it was practically impossible to get through.

A jeep screeched to a halt, sending gravel flying in front of the majordomo's cute little house. Two armed men brutally dragged out two Haitians whose faces were covered with blood. They'd been beaten with rifle butts. You could hear remarks rising from the center of a small group of Dominicans who were assembled there to comment upon the event, as always whenever anything was happening. Then there were cries.

"Here are the culprits! *Matanlos! Matanlos!* Kill them! Bastards!"

"They were working there, they started the fire!"

The two Kongos were looking around them, eyes blinking, completely terrified.

Fires break out daily in the plantations of the Dominican Republic; Haitians are always the first accused.

A big hefty capataz stopped ranting and raving an instant, took off his wide-brimmed hat, and furiously scratched his head.

"They set fire to the plantations, these shitheads! They don't dare to do it in Haiti with Duvalier, so they come here and do it."

"They're Devils, demons," screamed one frenzied Dominican. "Devils! Kill them!"

"It's not us," one of the two accused tried to say, raising a timorous hand to his broken nose. "We were working there where the capataz put us."

"And the box of matches, huh? The box of matches?"

A hostile roar shook the little crowd. They had found a box of matches on one of the Kongos, the batey already knew all about it. This guy had a box of matches in his pocket the moment when. No need to look any further. They were financed by the troublemakers to set fire to the sugar cane. By what troublemakers? By the troublemakers!

The Kongo shook his head, distraught. A policeman ordered him to get in and immediately lie down in the back of a van that had just pulled up. Then he violently loaded the other Kongo.

Regrouped a little further away, the Haitians silently contemplated the scene, their faces set in a mask. They did not protest. There were sub-machine guns everywhere. No boss went anywhere without at least a rifle and a revolver.

There are always things like that.

Chita tandé! From mouth to ear, the rumor was spreading, silently. The Kongos were whispering, mechanically raising and lowering their arms without even realizing it, and continuing to whisper. From group to group, under the pallid glow of the starry sky, they were commenting on the events of that afternoon. Ear to mouth, *chita tandé, chita tandé!* The Dominicans set fire to the plantation because they knew the Haitians would be blamed. Yes, my friend, set the fire because they knew very well. The one who did it was sure the bosses would see the two Kongos and that they would be accused. Yes, they were sure of it. They don't like the Haitians. Ah, no, they don't like us. They don't like us, don't like us, don't like us. That Dominican that set the fire, nothing will happen to him, the Kongos are charged. As for me, my friend, I'm tired of being Haitian. And now, they are in prison? In prison. They took them away. At the Dominican prison, *el cárcel*, they mistreat the Haitians. Ah, yes, they are mistreated. They get no aid, no help. They've got no friends. They can die under the weight of the repression, we've seen that.

Chita tandé, mouth to ear, *chita tandé*...

"*Vamonos, vamonos, perros haitianos, vamonos!*" They'd wakened the Kongos and viejos at midnight to go and cut the burnt cane. They knew that had to happen, but couldn't help groaning anyway when the capataces came violently banging on their doors. "When the cane burns," Antoine the viejo had warned them, "we no longer have the choice to rest."

When a plantation goes up in smoke, the stalks of carbonized cane are not irremediably lost. You can still extract the juice, on the condition that it is cut immediately and transported to the factory within twenty-four hours. After, it is too late. It can't withstand a delay of several days before being crushed.

The race against the clock had begun. At midnight, in a confusion of shouts, they had been thrown out of their bedless sleeping places; at half past midnight, bodies still aching from the effort all day long, they were piled into old trucks that lumbered painfully through the night to the edge of the scorched black earth. By the feeble light of an uncertain moon, they groped their way around, awkwardly seizing the stalks of cane, still hot, dry, and full of soot. They spoke in lowered voices, full of fatigue, grief, and resentment.

In the darkness, a recently arrived Kongo, punctuating his story with machete strokes that pierced the night, told about the big fire at the Monteco batey where he'd lived before coming here to try his luck. "It was even worse than today," he began. "It was the end of the world." It was the end of the world, relayed immediately, *chita tandé*. And a shudder went through the plantation. "9 February 1979 still stands out in my memory. A huge fire broke out in forty-two fields of cane. Forty-two, gentlemen! It was fearsome, you would have thought the sky itself was ablaze. Well, there too, they grabbed some Haitians. Pierre-Richard was young, twenty-two years old, a *gro nèg* there, good and black, from Jérémie. He was my buddy. They said he was responsible and he wasn't. I know, he was my buddy. It was he and another Kongo; they were arrested, they were beaten, they were taken away, and no one ever saw them again. The Dominicans were so mad they were beating all the Haitians. It was their wealth that was going up in smoke. What we did, we were afraid, we didn't do anything. We became nègres marrons. We hid. When the bosses found us, they mistreated us. In that fire, nothing happened to me because I ran really fast. I left the batey, not to return until the next day. But one of the Haitians was named Pierre Richard. His fate is unknown. They beat him up and they took him away. I saw it happen, gentlemen, in my very presence, even."

In his very presence. The spreading whispers of *chita tandé* echoed from the depths of the plain, humming with activity. In his very presence.

"They made us get up at midnight and you had to cut. If you don't want to," groaned Estimé Mondestin, in an exhausted but active half-stupor, "if we don't want to, the stick gets us up, the stick throws us out."

They were imprisoned by the long night, a fortress painted in gloom.

A machete escaped from a hand whose strength had abandoned it and cruelly gashed a leg, its muscles lean and taut. It wasn't the only one. Another, deceived by the moon's opaque reflection, screamed in pain as he severed his entire thumb.

Ups and downs. They weren't going to stop for so little.

When the dawn, unconscious of the unfolding drama, blew softly over the last remnants of obscurity, when the morning twilight gave way to the first rays of a well-rested sun, an army of zombies, spiritless and expressionless, stirred in slow-moving gestures in the returned light. Under the already dauntless blue sky, those who were tuned in to the happenings in the lives of men believed they perceived a long sigh of disappointment. The incinerated hell in which they were struggling extended as far as the eye could see.

They distributed to each of them a piece of bread. "On the house," the majordomo had announced. Then they were ordered to continue. There was still a good day's worth. And they had started working at midnight.

It is generally believed that the Haitians are black. Well, it's false. You can say they are completely washed out in comparison to the color they are when they've spent the whole entire night sweating in the burnt cane.

Each one of his movements was slower than the preceding. He tried, at times, to speed it up, when the capataz stopped and bawled him out, but you could tell his heart was no longer in it. Every movement of his worn-out body, as black as a kettle on a wood fire, wrested from him a dull moan. He made a last desperate effort to fell a long stalk strangely diffused with darkness, his arm fell in slow motion, and he collapsed, human cane on the pile of burnt cane.

It was six o'clock in the evening. In a cottony fog, the Kongos shouted out to one another in panic. "Brutus! Mondestin! André! Come quick! There's a guy who had some symptoms and he's fainted." The man was resting now, his arm strangely dislocated, prolonged by the ignoble reflection of a machete that no longer moved. They all came running, without realizing that they were no longer capable of running and were dragging themselves along. They stretched him out as best they could, and someone gathered his last remnants of energy to go in search of the capataz.

He arrived around seven o'clock, his horse lumbering along. Pains in the ass, these Kongos. What else could they think up to piss him off? What else? He, too, was exhausted. His sleepy red eyes blinked above an already well advanced beard. His horse's hooves clip-clopped in slow motion. No one could stand up any longer. He dismounted, and as tired as he was, still found the strength to yell. "Well, loafer, wake up!"

The Haitian didn't move. There wasn't much of a chance he'd wake up. He hadn't fainted at all. He'd died. He was lying there motionless like an old worn-out machine.

A piercing, chanting cry— the *rèl*—announced the mournful news to the plantation, which came to a standstill. The soul of a Kongo had parted.

The capataz broke out into quadruple oaths. Shit, shit, shit and shit, and piss, sonofabitch! Doesn't he think we have enough shit to deal with, this moron?

He had finished his funeral oration. He pushed back his hat slightly. Next, he grabbed his horse's bridle, put his foot in the stirrup, mounted painfully in the saddle.

"All right. We'll pick up the body tomorrow morning."

The dozen or so Kongos, completely disfigured with grime, raising their ravaged faces toward him, all jumped at once.

"But we're not going to leave him there!"

"Don't piss off the caballero, will you! If he's really dead, he won't be going anywhere."

"We can't do that."

"We'll pick him up tomorrow, before sunrise, he won't have time to stink."

"We have to bring him to the batey," insisted a viejo who had approached, "so that we can have the wake."

"The wake! In the state you're in? And who's going to work tomorrow?"

"But you have to sit up with the dead, you have to help them pass their last night on earth."

"Out of the question. That will lower the yield!"

He was a Haitian, he was their Brother, they had to carry him, and in spite of their incredible fatigue, they would pass his last night with him. The capataz laughed in their faces. And he didn't have the dead man taken away. "Why not embalm him while you're at it?" He was no undertaker. His horse's hoofbeats grew fainter in the night.

Rage in their hearts, they covered their companion with leaves, remained for a moment of silence around the leafy mound, and left for the batey, dragging their feet. They felt sad, and tired, and dirtier than ever. If only it would start to rain, that would have helped them clean up.

Arriving at the barracks, they all collapsed, and more passed out than fell asleep.

At five o'clock the next morning, a van went to pick up the body. It was a beautiful day. The Kongos were waiting in front of the bodega, saw the cloud of dust coming closer, getting larger, as the roar of the motor swelled. An old Dodge, all its roundness dented in, stopped before them. The capataz, pushing the Kongos out of the way, went up to the back of the truck, and, satisfied, turned around. "Well, here he is, your pal! You see, no one stole him!" Then, an ironic look in his eyes, "We aren't nègres, we don't eat corpses!"

They shrugged, vaguely disgusted. As weary, worn out, hardened and blasé as they were, they couldn't repress a fit of indignation when they saw the coffin in which he was "laid to rest." Their companion's remains had been unceremoniously chucked into a crate made of rough boards, untouched by a plane. A chorus of protests rose, assailing the capataz, who, head held back, hands on his hips, was frankly irritated.

"You're not going to bury him in that!"

"What, not in that? He's fine! He doesn't look like he's complaining!"

"It's not even planed," launched an appalled voice.

"That's not a coffin!"

"What can I tell you..."

And they told him. "That's not a coffin, it's a wooden crate, a rotten old rum crate!" They must not have had a trash can handy, or they would have put him in that! A wooden crate that didn't cost two dollars. Not more, my friend. If that, two dollars...

"Perhaps you'd like a state funeral in the cathedral in Santo Domingo? I'm very sorry, but the archbishop is on sick leave." A delighted pause, for the effect: "He got the clap!"

He could joke, but the Haitians didn't see it that way. Brutus became violently angry and a cordon of Kongos, machete in hand, encircled the vehicle to prevent it from starting up.

"You have to have some respect. Poor as he was, if he died in Haiti, he wouldn't be buried like this."

Back home, even the most impoverished family doesn't hesitate to sacrifice its last resources to give one of its members a decent funeral.

The indignant rumbling started to swell all around. To swell. It's like that these things happen because they sold us. That's how they treat us. They treat us like slaves. That's how it is, that's how it is.

The capataz threw up his arms, lowered them immediately; he

was in no position to wash his hands of it at all. "Go talk to the major-domo," he said. "Me, I'm in charge of the plantation, not the fer-tilizer!" And he started to laugh, "not the fertilizer, hah, hah!" He parted with dignity. "He'll lose sleep over it, I'm sure," he couldn't prevent himself from adding.

It took them more than an hour of discussion with the major-domo before coming up with a good understanding and a real coffin. "In our country, he wouldn't be buried that way," they insisted, very politely, while he, impatient, wiped the nape of his neck with a nice dotted handkerchief. The lovely Manuela Garcia y Garcia was awaiting him in the next room.

"You must understand, gentlemen, that the DEA doesn't have the means to offer a luxurious coffin to..." Then he stopped. He almost said: to all those who die in the bateys. "It's a question of budget..."

Finally, the State Sugar Council not being in a position to bear superfluous expenses, it was unanimously agreed by the majordomo that if these rich Kongos wished to offer their compatriot a luxurious burial, which furthermore, he perfectly understood, and which, he added, was to their honor, they were authorized to take up a collec-tion. Which they did, in their infinitely wretched poverty.

Everything should have then gone well, their demand having been satisfied, the real, modestly polished coffin with four handles having been brought in from the nearest pueblo: if they hadn't ex-pressed the imprudent desire to accompany their compatriot to his last resting place. The majordomo, up until now extremely patient, became incensed this time.

"Gentlemen, we've lost enough time. You will now do us the favor of going to cut the cane!"

All the more so since other Kongos had just put forward a gro-tesque exigence. It was necessary to wash the corpse with an infusion of aromatic herbs, plug his ears and nostrils with cotton, close his mouth by means of a chin strap knotted around his head, and tie his big toes together, as it is done in Haiti.

"Enough eccentricities! Here we are Catholic and civilized and don't practice your voodoo witchcraft!"

"But can't we say a prayer?" asked Gérard André, backed up by the approval of the Kongos who believed in Heaven. "Can't we?"

If a Haitian wishes to pray, he is free to do so. He can pray in his heart while working, the two are not incompatible.

They understood that this question of Church and respect was not for them, either. They were not part of the Dominican society, there was no church in the batey, no chapel, no voodoo temple, no señor the parish priest, no protestant pastor. God himself had undoubtedly deserted this cursed place.

A Kongo had only the time to turn out the dead's pockets, according to custom, and to take off his incredibly down-at-the-heel shoes, so that the sound of his steps would not disturb the peace of the living. The lid was closed with a dry bang.

Four Kongos picked up the genuine, nicely polished coffin with four handles, hoisted it up on the platform of a cabrouet drawn by four oxen. Gérard André, his muscles tense with effort — how could a guy so skinny, get so heavy, all of a sudden — awkwardly stumbled in a rut, almost lost hold of his compatriot's last resting place, caught himself in time, as best he could, but couldn't, however, avoid scraping it violently on the metal post of the cart. He abused himself heartily, while his companions told him to be careful. A long, unsightly scratch now spoiled the right side of the coffin which they had all paid for, and which, in final homage to the unknown Kongo, they had wanted to be as handsome as possible, from the bottom of their hardship.

"Fine. Now go to work, it's already seven o'clock; we'll take care of the rest."

"We have to go, too."

"*Vamonos, vamonos! Al trabajo!* To work!"

"He's our brother. We want to see where he's buried."

The Dominican capataces, whom this business was beginning to seriously annoy, lost their patience. The cabrouet started up with a jolt, and a funeral procession of about twenty Kongos formed spontaneously behind the heavy cart. They walked, lost in bitter reflection. The comrade had been devoured by the plantation, he would never again see Haiti, the wild and high land of his youth. Gérard André was making his way in a confused fog. How many unknown Kongos, forgotten viejos, never see their home again, he wondered in anguish. How many? He felt Estimé Mondestin's habitual presence on his right. He glanced quickly. Estimé was praying silently, his lips moving imperceptibly, eyes half-closed.

> *Mwin kwè nan Bondyé*
> *Papa-a ki gin tout pouvoua*
> *Li kréye sièl la ak tè-a*
> *I believe in God*
> *the Father Almighty*
> *Creator of Heaven and Earth . . .*

Others, in their secret hearts, were afraid for the deceased and for his far-away relatives. The tie between him and his *loa* — the voodoo spirit created by the Great Master to come to the aid of men — had not been broken as required by the traditional *désounin* ceremony. The *loas*, it was certain, would avenge themselves in bringing disaster upon his family. And this long advance... That's not how you conduct a burial. A *pere savane* must bless the dead, sing the cantiques, recite the prayers. You're not supposed to just go straight ahead. This Dominican was going straight ahead. It would be necessary for this cabrouet to make some brusque detours, some about faces, to prevent this Kongo from finding his way to the batey again. What if he, despairing in the solitude of his unknown tomb, came back to earth to haunt the living? It was a great misfortune to die in Dominicanie.

Some of them were very frightened. A voice was heard, then two, intoning in a wail the name of the departed, followed by a long modulation.

Célestin O... Célestin Ooooooo... Célestin Ooooo...

When they arrived at the exit to the batey, police armed to the teeth prevented them from passing. They protested, only to receive blows of rifle butts in return. Five more determined Haitians, who knew the deceased well, had lived with him in the same room in the barracks, insisted, hung on. "We want to accompany him."

They were hit, mistreated, arrested and thrown in jail.

The others fled, tears in their eyes, overcome with misery, running to take refuge in the plantations.

The lone cabrouet disappeared on the trail without end.

When it returned that evening to the sleeping batey, they silently removed a long, empty rectangular box, which they discreetly stored in a warehouse. A Kongo who was passing by on his way back from a bout of dysentery, whom no one noticed, saw that it was a new coffin. A long unsightly scratch spoiled the right side.

It would be unfair to claim that the sugar authorities took no measures following these diverse occurrences.

Firstly, as a result of the fire, the capataces went through the entire barracks and confiscated all the Kongo's candles.

Secondly, concerning the death, they perfected a diet based on molasses and protein supplements which minimizes, during dry periods and in disadvantaged areas, the weight loss and mortality of oxen.

Article 14: It is agreed that the Haitian Embassy in the Dominican Republic has the privilege to appoint 75 (seventy-five) inspectors and 15 (fifteen) supervisors in order to protect the Haitian agricultural workers.

Article 18: The supervisors and inspectors will be free to visit, without restriction, the cane fields where the Haitian agricultural workers work, the weighing premises of the cane, and the places where payment is effected, and will be entitled to intervene to defend the interests of the Haitian agricultural workers, whatever the rank of the employee may be, in any circumstance in which such an intervention is required.

Article 20: The standard salary of each supervisor will be $350 (three hundred fifty dollars) a month, and the standard salary of each inspector will be $200 (two hundred dollars) a month during the harvest. The sum total of these salaries will be sent directly to the Haitian Embassy according to the instructions of the Haitian government by the State Sugar Council, in order to be delivered to their beneficiary.

Since the fire, the atmosphere had become as imperceptibly

unhealthy as the tropical climate that deadened the batey. In the evening the Haitians bought their handful of flour, handful of beans, handful of corn at the bodega, looking at the Dominicans with mistrustful eyes. The Dominicans passed alongside the Kongos, walking tall in their cowboy hats, stomping their boots or their run-down clodhoppers, and quite inadvertently jostled them, letting curses fly. "Dirty Haitian!" "Dominican bastard!" Plus all sorts of things in the secret of their hearts.

Brutus had had a violent row with Gustavo Perez one night, when the latter's consumption had a little too much exceeded their very meager budget and when Estimé Mondestin had come back to the barracks crying with rage and despair. Scorza had immediately cut off all possibilities of credit since these dirty *perros de negros sucios*, these ungrateful dirty dogs of dirty nègres had made trouble and insulted his friend. The three Kongos decided to no longer buy at the batey except once every three days, in order not to have to ask anything of these hot-tempered Dominican bums, assassins of Haitians. During the other two days they lived on cane, were accompanied by cane. It was lucky—lucky...anyone could go into the fields and help himself to satiety without laying out a cent. There was so much of it! The majordomo had said to them one day, in what they had at first taken to be a gesture of generosity, "Help yourselves! It's part of the fringe benefits!" Then he laughed.

They went around penniless. Their shoes were falling to pieces—when they still had any at all. Their hands trembled, rougher, more scraped, more bruised, more unbelievably ravaged than those of a Christ of the plantations carrying his cross in the blazing sun, wearing a crown of sugar. They walked limping on their poor broken-down feet, bodies barely clothed in rags and tatters. These were men. Other men subjected them to this treatment.

Gérard André was suffering from a big, purulent abcess; he could no longer bend his knee, but bent it anyway, groaning. What else could he do? Estimé Mondestin secretly dreamed of buying himself a bar of soap. In their barracks alone, five men were sick, festering, eaten up with stomach pain and fever.

The stormy sky didn't help matters any, hanging like a purple crepe over a casket.

Concerning the question of finding out who, in fact, stole the life's savings of a Kongo who, crazed with anger, covered the batey screaming one night, all renditions are possible. What is undeniable is that during their long daily absence, no one kept watch over the habitations. Shoes, pants, shirts disappeared regularly. Even in the cells with padlocks on the door, they swiped everything, including the padlocks. What is also true is that certain *ladrones*, small-time

Dominican bandits, were stealing and pilfering while the Kongos were cutting. But it is just as true that the Haitians were no angels. It would be unjust to systematically accuse the Dominicans. Be that as it may, the Kongo had won a small sum in the *bolita*, and now found himself with nothing.

That is what made the temperature rise in the batey. All the more so because the overdose of misery, the unbelievable accumulation of racism, humiliation, and injustice that the Kongos had been enduring for several months had already rubbed their nerves more than raw. Irritated, they talked among themselves, got worked up, and the tone rose all by itself.

"The Dominicans don't cut cane, but they eat well!"

"They're thieves! All thieves!"

"Yes, thieves! The Dominicans' houses are very nice! Even those guys that don't work have nice houses!"

That is what Estimé Mondestin thought, too. Once in a while you come across one miserable little Dominican in the cane; but in general, the cane is not their affair. The Dominicans who cut, black Dominicans, by the way, are in a bad way. Those are the ones at the very bottom of the ladder. But this Dominican in rough shape is worth a rich Haitian! Our living conditions are very bad. No matter what kind of a small cabrouet a Dominican fills, they pay him good money!

"Who is it that works around here?" demanded a big, very angry Kongo suddenly. "Who is it that does the dirty work? It's us! And these Dominicans who don't want to work, drink, pickle themselves in alcohol! It's always a party for them!"

"I wonder where they find the money," asked a young Haitian, in a shrill voice.

"Why don't you ask that Kongo they robbed?"

Several Kongos backed away, suddenly silent. Viejos' wives grabbed their children, whose underfed bellies protruded.

"I'm going to tell you something... The Dominican... he gets up Saturday morning, does one row of cane, and earns ten pesos," declared the big Kongo with rage. Then scornfully: "Ten pesos to go and get drunk, to drink wine and rum! After that, Monday, Tuesday, Wednesday, he does nothing!"

He was boiling, hadn't noticed the subtle change that had just come over the assembly, took a few steps to and fro, and jumped.

"Hey you, you follow us," one of the two guys that he hadn't heard arriving said coldly.

He looked at them, laughed in their faces, these two Dominicans, Gustavo Perez and Ramirez Garcia, the bodeguero and pesador's great buddies.

"I'm not following you, because what I'm saying is the truth! Around here everyone lives off the Kongos: the majordomo, the pesador, the capataz, the cabrouetier, the. . ." He broke off, stared at them with a baleful eye. "And you, Gustavo Perez, and you there, the pesador's good buddy, how do you live? We've never seen you working!"

"Don't worry," spat Perez, "we're going to explain that to you in detail! Let's go—follow us!"

"No way. I'm staying here. You're nothing, you're no boss, I'm not following you! You're nothing but a rotten *ladron*! Besides, all the Dominicans are rotten! And all the Dominican women are whores," he added for good measure.

"All you had to do was stay in your own rotten country, we didn't come looking for you."

"Oh, yes you did, as a matter of fact, come looking for us," the Kongos growled, sticking together.

Then, of course, things began to happen all at once. Insult added to injury, the abuse incited even more abuse. The big Kongo didn't want to follow, and the other Kongos sided with him. He wouldn't follow them and he was right, and they'd had it up to their necks with all the humiliation, and who were those two to think they were better than the Haitians?

The fight, completely impromptu, broke out. Estimé Mondestin felt himself take fright, but didn't back away. The Dominicans don't like the Haitians, he thought in a flash; at the slightest quarrel, it's the machete in full swing, causing a lot of people to get hurt. The Haitians sometimes get their heads or their limbs cut. But at first, he didn't back away. Confusion reigned, cries rebounded between the wooden walls and cement slabs, other Dominicans arrived, the rumor spread very fast: the Kongos are revolting and one of them is defiant, knife in hand. No, I won't follow you.

The Dominicans were mobilizing. The nebula of blows was moving in anarchy, arriving near the bodega. Scorza hastily shut down the wooden swinging door, and his wife made the sign of the cross. Other Dominicans were arriving, notified by the tumultous commotion that distance hadn't muffled. Bosses, this time. They had guns. One of them, seeing the knife, but unthreatened, leveled his gun without aiming. "*No disparen! No disparen!* Don't shoot!" screamed a Dominican *gruero*. "Don't shoot, these are men!"

The first shots rang out. Two Kongos fell, another had his leg broken. But it was the big Kongo with deep-set eyes, very angry, knife in hand, that they wanted. They fired at him seven times; he was lucky, he ducked, he fell, not one hit him. He was a guy from Port-au-Prince. No one ever understood how he wasn't killed. He had to have a mark, divine protection. He was holding his knife in his hand, and nothing hit him. And yet it was he they wanted, they wanted him, that was obvious. In a shack slightly set back, a very frightened pregnant woman was screaming, holding her belly. She shouldn't have stayed there, planted in a patch of sun, as if she wanted to defy destiny. The fifth bullet missed the Kongo, and this woman was hit, this woman *ki té gin gro vant'*, this poor pregnant Dominican, and she dropped dead, without realizing what happened to her.

After that, *kako kanpé!* General mobilization. The Dominicans were wheeling in every direction, mad with rage and uncontrolled insanity because of this woman who'd just been killed. This trouble didn't help matters any for the Kongos. The majordomo had left the lovely Manuela Garcia y Garcia to call the police, who soon arrived. The capataces joined the forces of order, nervously and longingly fingering the triggers of their guns. All this repression turned loose, and again it was the Kongos who tasted the bitter fruit. There weren't two dead, as they say in Haiti; in other words, this figure was far surpassed.

They rounded up everyone who resembled a Haitian, and who hadn't had time to take flight. The big Kongo with deep-set eyes, very angry, his knife in hand, they put him in prison, they put plenty of people in prison, including Gérard André. They were never seen again at batey 7A.

Whatever you do, don't think that this was an isolated incident. In another batey, Antoine Blanchard, from the Delmas quarter, died in just about the same conditions.

He had arrived, dressed to the nines, attaché case in hand, very anxious not to crumple his impeccably pressed trousers. "Gentlemen," declared he, to the first two Kongos he'd encountered, looking mildly disgusted by their appearance, "I am the Inspector from the Embassy (giving a certain emphasis to the capital letters), I am here to monitor the situation. Have you anything to say?" Oh, yes, they had. A bit foolishly, the first Kongo launched into a long tirade. They never got anywhere, they worked for days and days, they couldn't even eat, hunger was killing them, no one gave them anything, they put them in prison, the cane sat then without being picked up, the. . .

"Tttt ttt ttt," interrupted the "gran nèg," a little irritated, and at the same time, but maybe it was just an impression, looking at him as if he were looking at a dog. "Tttt ttt tt! You have to work, my friend! Tell your companions that if they have any complaints to express, I am at their disposal." Then he glanced at his watch. "Don't be long, I'm going to have to go back soon."

The Kongo took off running to spread the good news. "There's a Haitian inspector! There's a Haitian inspector!"

An old Kongo who was painfully going through his third zafra, and who asked himself in heaven's name why, couldn't help laughing in his face.

"My friend, you must have been dreaming. You can croak, the supervisor doesn't come. When you get sick and you can't cut any more, you're starving to death, a Dominican passing by'll help you, pay your transportation, take you to the hospital, but you'll never see either an inspector or a supervisor."

"But I saw one, there is one."

"He didn't have the Ambassador with him?" said someone who didn't believe it either.

"Oh, no," protested a viejo whose old, badly-cared-for leg injury made him limp. "The Ambassador never comes to the bateys. The day when you'll see the Ambassador is the day of return, at the Cité 22, that day and that day only."

"There is an inspector," insisted the other one, who knew what he was talking about. "I'm telling you there is one!"

The old Kongo looked at him strangely. He was wrong. There was, in fact, an inspector.

The Haitian Embassy receives an overall sum of $32 thousand a month to pay seventy-five inspectors and fifteen supervisors. The number of these civil servants whose function is, theoretically, to see that the rights of the Kongos are respected, is very much smaller than the figures indicate. It's all profit. First, for the Embassy and the Haitian government who pocket the difference between the salaries declared and the salaries paid. Secondly, for the State Sugar Council which closes its eyes, and thus pays to be left alone. No waves and as few outsiders as possible in the plantations. Besides, even if the initial number were respected...

They gathered around the man. He eyed them up and down, scornfully, as if indifferent, then annoyingly interrupted the rising chorus of lamentation, firmly ordering them to speak in turn, and preferably, in brief. "If you please, gentlemen!" They had a hard time controlling themselves, their hearts were so overflowing with all those things they had to say which filled them with such a great, deep-rooted rancor.

The inspector looked up and sought out a spokesman. One Kongo made up his mind.

"We're sick, we can't work, we are paid nothing by the *seguro*!"

"My friend, you are here to work, not to live on the *seguro*!"

"They also take a percentage, one peso every two weeks, and they say it's for the President," launched one old-timer in an unsteady voice.

"For the President . . ."

"Yes, for the President!"

"And that shocks you?"

"Well, it's just that . . ."

"You don't love your President?"

"Fine, okay, if it's for the President, we have nothing to say," granted the other one, who felt the wind turning.

"In any case, it's not for the President," said the inspector, an unpleasant look in his eye. "It's a sum that is put aside for you, which you'll be paid upon your return."

A satisfied hubbub rose forthwith, even though . . . "We'd rather have it now, to eat," remarked an anonymous voice. "It would be more sure," an insolent one even added very low.

They stopped talking. A well-built, bare-chested Kongo politely called out to the official.

"Mr. Government Inspector, sir, the Kongos' conditions must be changed. If I told you that I had five cents to eat, I'd be lying."

"If you please, let us not enter into the domain of individual cases. I am here for the great problem of general interest."

"But Mr. Government Inspector, we can go a week eating nothing! Nothing! We drink the cane juice."

"I have the impression that you are exaggerating. You look healthy to me."

"*Nèg noua toujou gin plis fyel pasé lot yo*," declared the Kongo, as if he were stating an obvious fact.

His companions agreed. The Blacks are always more resistant than the others!

"That's fine! You are an honor to the Haitian people. Keep it up!" Then with a knowing smile: "We are proud of you. *Blan travay ak plis prékosyon, yo vine ak machine, tout' bagay!* The Whites work with more precautions, use machines, all those things! You are tough, real men, real Haitians!"

The Kongo stood up tall and proud, discreetly flexing his shoulders, and Brutus couldn't restrain himself from giving him a shove to make him stop his comedy. That damn fool was letting himself get screwed. "This inspector isn't on our side," he breathed angrily. "We explain our working conditions and he doesn't give a damn! Stop clowning around!"

"I'm not clowning around. Mind your own business."

"Moron, you're even stupider than I thought."

"Your opinion doesn't interest me, bum!"

They ceased this affable exchange delivered in lowered tones. A Kongo with meticulous speech, ceremonious in his rags despite his situation, tackled the heart of the problem. "Mr. Inspector," said he, as if he were beginning some important discourse, "Mr. Inspector, here is the truth about our bad conditions. Concerning bad conditions, the Haitians are obliged to drink the dirty sugar. The workers who have nothing, absolutely nothing, are obliged to wring out the cane to extract the juice, which they mix with flour in a plastic container. Sometimes we fall ill. This type of dish causes diarrhea. When sick or hurt, we are very neglected. Mr. Inspector, these are also things that can kill the Haitians: hunger, sickness, injuries, machete blows. Sometimes the Haitians can also die in prison. In prison, they can die from hunger, a firearm, or else their head cut off. Mr. Inspector, I . . ."

The inspector stopped him with an imperious gesture, laughing in his face, asked him if he was talking about a soap opera. The Kongo didn't know what a soap opera was. Despairing, he shut up. However, another picked up the torch, telling himself to heed the lesson and only tackle one very precise, very concrete theme. "Mr. Inspector . . . Permit me to sum up my true situation, and I'm not the only one in this situation. I don't have a bed."

A rumbling broke out spontaneously. He doesn't have a bed. Me neither. And you? I guess not! Ground so hard. No bed either. Oh, no. People sleep on the ground. Really. Oh, yes, really.

The inspector, annoyed, raised an arm. He motioned to the plaintiff to continue.

"Since my arrival in Dominicanie, I have been sleeping on the ground on a sack. I came to get out of wretched poverty. I left my home to come and sleep on a sack."

"But really, I presume that it suffices to ask in due form, gentlemen!"

A chorus of denials cut off the city man's élan; he obviously didn't know much about things, that was for sure!

"They told us we could work and earn enough to feed our families. We can't even do it for ourselves! That's how it is. And we don't even have a bed to rest in."

"All you have to do is look," broke out the angry voice of Brutus, who could no longer contain himself. "When you look, you see these places. In Haiti, that's where you'd put the pigs. Here, that's where they park the Haitians!"

"You surprise me," declared the inspector pensively. "You really surprise me. I've had the occasion, in my functions, to visit numerous bateys. I've never heard anything like this business of beds."

A few almost derisive interjections rang out in the starless night, from Kongos who had been through other seasons in other bateys. "First time he ever heard anything like. . ."

"Very well. I'm going to clarify all this. We can't let such a thing develop."

Unanimous approval rose from the assembled group of Kongos.

As far as they could tell, the Dominicans, ordinarily so distant, gave him a welcome without a hint of chill. They conversed briefly, but the Kongos weren't able to hear what they were saying. The inspector came back towards the shacks and the majordomo was accompanying him. An astonished gasp sprang forth from several mouths. The majordomo in person was going to look after them. The two men were chatting animatedly.

"Show us this bed business," ordered the inspector with authority.

All the Kongos were rushing toward their cells at once, opening the doors, not one that wasn't lacking one, two, three beds. The majordomo entered the first cubbyhole holding his nose, came out again, very surprised, and very angry.

"But there were mattresses here!"

A stupefied silence greeted the assertion. The majordomo was entering one room, then another, into a fourth, a sixth, kept on going in and coming out, the Haitian inspector more or less on his heels.

"There were beds and mattresses!" A moment of reflection. "These people sold the mattresses!"

The accusation fell on them like the sudden rain of a summer storm. They had seen the clouds coming, but didn't expect such a drenching.

"They've sold everything! Just look at this filth! They were given clean buildings in the beginning of the zafra, just look at that!"

"It's scandalous," agreed the inspector, examining the premises, thin-lipped. "But the culprits are going to pay! We must get to the bottom of this, find out who indulges in this traffic. Rest assured, my dear majordomo, I will take care of it."

The Kongos had to make themselves scarce to avoid having several among them sleep in prison that very night. Positively furious, the inspector made it no secret that they were the shame of the country of Haiti, which he was assigned to represent here.

Brutus quickly spun around on his heels in order not to explode, dragging Estimé Mondestin by the arm.

"Come on," he said, "we have nothing to do. The inspectors aren't for us. Those guys have more sensitivity, more contact, more friendship, are tighter with the Dominicans than with us. They consider us like Kongos, get it? Besides, it's not hard to understand. They're paid by the Dominicans. It's in their interest to walk all over us for the benefit of those who pay them."

They didn't attend the inspector's departure. He carefully dusted off his trousers and turned to the Kongos one last time.

"My role is to inspect your working conditions. I will remain in permanent contact with you."

The Kongos saw him disappear without a hope, without regret, with perhaps a little more hatred deep in their hearts. They wouldn't see him again. Those guys do very irregular work, can go for months, an entire season, without visiting a plantation.

By now, what was left of these individuals should have ceased to exist. However, in an unbelievable rebound of human dignity, they defended themselves fiercely — be it in silence — tooth and nail, body and soul, against the inhuman degradation. They remained Men.

That was displeasing.

They had to be broken to their very marrow, the only means of survival for a system based on the most shameless exploitation.

Brutus was hard-headed.

When the cabrouetier had yet again increased his demands while they had practically nothing left, they told him to go to hell. Mondestin, of a more or less conciliatory nature, had vainly tried to cajole him. "You can't do a thing like that to us!" He didn't want to hear it. He always operated according to the rapidity of the cutters, leaving the cane of some, favoring that of others. Since the disappearance of Gérard André, they, who were only two, didn't interest him. Or else, they had to really encourage him.

Brutus, with a malevolent gleam in his eye, had told him that he'd better profit by the situation as much as he could because one day he was going to split his mug open with a machete.

The other didn't say a thing.

They had cut two long days' worth of cane; it stayed on the ground in the oppressive sun for eleven days. They didn't know what to do; they were going mad, becoming like famished wild animals whose claws had been removed. Their cane was shrivelling up under the cabrouetier's indifferent eye.

When their cane was finally weighed, at the end of eleven days, they each earned one peso sixty-five.

The next day, Brutus, who had been completely silent for many days, suddenly opened his mouth and emptied his heart with a flood of bile that no obstacle could have contained.

"This cane that made us one peso sixty-five, it was a lot. It was some major cane. It was two piles of cane that filled the cabrouet, it was a lot.

"Well, you see, my friend, since I arrived in this country, I haven't had any good times, not one instant of joy. I look at the miseries I live, *misé m ap pasé*. When I was in Haiti, it was better, I had my family. Here, I've got no one.

"I'd compare this life to hell."

"I see that I left all my plans, all my work in Haiti to come to Dominicanie; and here I find nothing. My family thought I was going to come back well off. I don't even have five cents.

"Instead of taking a step forward, I've moved backwards."

Brutus had lowered his head, ruminating unfathomable thoughts. He slowly turned his face heavenward, staring fixedly past the stars. For the first time, Mondestin noticed the beauty of Brutus's massive features, sculpted in pure ebony.

"Mondestin," he finally heard, "I'm leaving tomorrow."

This Dominicanie was filing past slowly, with no major change since the morning. Cut cane, cane to cut, multitudes of dark figures lost in the cane fields, tiny motionless cabrouets in the distance and regularly, in the dilapidated silhouette of a batey. Brutus was walking along at a brisk pace, his straw hat well placed on his streaming forehead, sure of himself. His red shirt, the breast pocket completely torn, had lost its color, stood out anyway—too much, perhaps—against the immense, limitless verdant ghetto.

With three pesos in his pocket—the little savings put aside had melted away during the eleven days their cane was boycotted by the cabrouetier—he was heading toward the border.

He didn't really know where he was going. A *gruero* from the batey that he'd questioned in secret—one of the few Dominicans who communicated with the Haitians—had told him: go down to the capital, then take a bus that goes to Elias Piñas, by way of San Juan. Elias Piñas is on the border, you'll have arrived. I think it's the bus "La Experiencia," he'd added. Brutus dared not admit he only had three pesos, had thanked him.

He was feeling a bit lost at the moment.

A crossroads in the sun, one bigger, well-asphalted road, no longer snaking its way, a good and straight route of a civilized country, and on the other side, undulating, verdant fields, which were not of cane. Brutus had a hard time figuring it out. Gentle slopes, groves, a few well-outlined palm trees, a herd of handsome animals scattered in the distance, and no more cane. He'd just reached another planet. He thought to himself it must be nice to live here, took a deep breath, felt the perfumed air fill his lungs, found it almost cool. He indulged in another long look in order to better persuade himself. Without looking back, and he had no desire whatsoever to do so, there was no sugar cane in any of the places his gaze fell. He had a sudden desire to laugh and sing, to seize a drum and to beat it with his hands in a long, syncopated roll of exhilaration.

But he was a little lost.

This perpendicular and seemingly better route, should he take it to the right, or to the left?

He waited until the Dominican he'd seen appear in the distance, who was little by little approaching, finally arrived within hearing range. Brutus laboriously mustered up his limited knowledge of Spanish to address the old *campesino.* "*Eské ce carretera est la route là pour s'aller sur la frontiera?*" he asked.

The man stopped as if dumbfounded, and broke into a long whistle.

"You are going to the border? *Hasta la frontiera?*"

"*Si. Me voy a la f'onte'a!*"

The man looked at him from head to heels, manifestly alarmed.

"How? On foot?"

"Si Seño'."

The campesino spread his arms as if he wanted to take flight.

"But that's impossible, young man! *Eso es muy imposible!* Very impossible! The border is 240 miles from here! You can't!"

"But is it this way, or that way?" insisted Brutus, turning his head successively in the two directions.

"You can't do that!"

"This way or that way? *Por aqui o por aqua?*"

"It's that way, *muchachito*, but you'll never make it."

The sympathetic campesino was shaking his head as hard as he could. "Don't do it!" He screwed up his old wrinkled face. "If we weren't so poor, I'd take you home, you could rest a little." He laughed. "*Carajo!* There's not even enough room for a newborn baby! Hombre, don't do that!"

"Thank you, seño'," smiled Brutus, "but I've decided that I'm going and I'm going."

"Well, adios hombre, and may God protect you!" murmured the old-timer, despairing. Then he thrust a dry, calloused hand into the pocket of his shabby pants, came up with a few coins that he contemplated, imperceptibly nodding his head. He held them out to Brutus. "Here. Here's twenty-five centavos, it's not much, but take it. You'll need it more than me."

That was a lie. In reality, he needed it a lot.

They parted, each in his own direction, glancing backward several times, one Dominican, the other Haitian, poor among the poor of the world full of poor, saluted each other one last time with a wave of the hand.

Fifteen minutes later, Brutus encountered the soldiers.

The jeep had at first whizzed by him, helmets and guns in the whistling wind, then he heard it slow down, then stop, and he didn't need to look back to understand that it was turning around. He was alone on the big road. In his head he repeated three times and at top speed a little word that had been with him all day long: Freedom, Freedom, Freedom! Then he stopped, for the khaki vehicle had just caught up and pulled in front of him. Two pairs of impeccably polished "rangers" were crunching the gravel on the side of the road, and a massive shadow spread out full length on the grass, yellowed by the sun, now very low on the horizon. Brutus looked up, glimpsed the gun belt and pistol in passing, fixed on the expressionless face.

"*Tiene usted su cédula?* Identification?"

Brutus dug into the back pocket of the remains of his pair of pants. The frayed cord that served as a belt chafed his lower back. The two soldiers were watching him attentively, calmly, sure of themselves. He handed them his batey card. "*Haitiano?*" barked one of them, grabbing his card.

"*Si Seño'.*"

"*Eso no es una cédula.* This is no piece of identity."

Once again it was necessary to juggle with the words, a pathetic mixture of Spanish, Creole, and anxiety.

"*Sé cédula pa'a el batey!* It's the identity card from the batey!"

"Yeah, but you aren't in the batey any more."

"*Me voy.* I'm leaving."

One of the soldiers burst out laughing, abruptly regained a menacing impassivity.

"You're leaving! But you're not allowed to go!"

"Ah, si seño', but *los condiciones* are *muy* bad *en el* batey. *Muy malas condiciones!*"

"But, tell me Haitiano, don't you know you signed a contract?"

"No, *el contrat* for me is *terminado.* I'm going to Haiti."

"But in God's name, sonofabitch," suddenly burst out the one who seemed to be the most senior and highest-ranked, a sergeant, maybe, and who up until then hadn't said anything, "you don't break a contract like that! The Dominican government bought you. You're here to cut the cane, not to stroll on the roads!"

Brutus shook his head, uncomprehending, shaken by this sudden furious outburst.

"*Sé pa un contrat bueno.* I saw *mucho* misery and *mwin vlé* go back *nan pays mwin.*"

"Not a good contract! But we paid your President, el señor Duvalier! And he pocketed the money! You have to work to pay it back!"

"Or else pay back the money that we spent for you," suggested the second soldier in outraged tones of ridicule.

"You have any money?" asked the other one maliciously. "You can reimburse us?"

"*M tengo trois pesos*," stammered Brutus.

The two soldiers looked disappointed.

"You can't pay it back with that."

Then with anger! "You cost us one and a half million dollars, Haitiano, you understand what that means? Guzman bought you from Duvalier! That's what that means! We didn't import you so you could go sightseeing on our roads! One and a half million dollars you cost us, you and your pals! All right, let's go, *vamonos*. Do us a favor and follow us, and quickly, please."

Guzman and Duvalier, repeated Brutus slowly, his brow strained in a violent effort to think. Guzman, Duvalier. . . then, getting hold of himself:

"You don't have *el derecho* to arrest *mwin!*"

"Don't have the right! You're walking around perfectly illegal, Haitiano! What are you doing here in the Dominican Republic? Show us your passport!"

"*El esta* at the Embassy and. . ."

"You don't have it?"

"No. *El esta* there."

"But you don't have it?"

"But no, because they. . ."

"That's just what we're saying. You could be a trafficker, a bandit, a smuggler, you are swimming in illegality! Let's go, *vamonos!*"

"I want to go back to my country," he cried very loudly. "I want to go back. . ."

Brutus could have wept with rage. Perhaps he was crying. But the hot wind swept his face as the jeep plunged into the beginning of the twilight, and dried up the visible signs of his despair.

While the countryside streamed past unnoticed, he attempted to calm himself, succeeded, and undertook a calm deliberation of his situation. So if he well understood, and he was just about certain of having well understood, he had crossed the border and reached this promised land under the jurisdiction of a contract drawn up by others than himself, precisely those who, on both sides of the border, were filling their pockets. If he continued to well understand, this famous contract that they talked about so much to remind him of his duties, contained a certain number of clauses that were also supposed to protect him. It allowed for social advantages, medical assistance, accident insurance, a weekly day of repose, habitable units of habitation, precisely, social protection, and theoretically a decent wage. At this point in his reflection Brutus paused, gazing at the creased necks below the helmets of the two men who were taking him, top speed, to the. . . to the what? *M pa konin.* He dismissed the anxiety, made his mind a blank, and took up his analysis where he'd left off. One fundamental thing occurred to him immediately. To his knowledge, and to the knowledge of all the Kongos he knew, not one—he repeated, struck by the evidence, NOT ONE—not one of the terms of the signed agreement is respected by the CEA. NOT ONE. And those two guys, who'd just intercepted him, claimed that he had broken the. . . Something flashed through his head. But it wasn't he who had broken the contract! It was the CEA! And if he refused the inhuman treatment which was imposed on him, he was perfectly within his rights! He could leave, do whatever seemed to be a good idea to him, go back to his country, or go and work elsewhere! He could even demand damages and compensation with a good lawyer or a good International Court! Within his rights! Perfectly within his rights! They didn't have the right to hold him against his will!

Yes, but his passport? He had no passport! There, those two were surely right. That was a hole in his argument. He leaned forward, thinking intensely, threw all his good sense into his mental struggle. He had no passport. . .

Of course not! Of course not, because they had confiscated it from him! Well, if. . .

Brutus was illiterate, but in this jeep which was carrying him, posthaste, towards an unknown destination, he put his finger, in his own way—that is, not exactly highbrow, but did it need to be?—put his finger on one of the vilest machinations of the exploitation to which he and his were subjugated.

The article that suspended their freedom of movement through the confiscation of their identity papers condemned them to forced labor. They were OFFICIALLY and openly kept in servitude by. . .

Two names suddenly sprang into his mind. GUZMAN. DUVALIER. Guzman and Duvalier! Brutus sat up, overcome by an insane rage and a sudden fear, which was not at all irrational.

"But it's slav. . ."

A sudden jamming of the brakes hurled him forward.

The pale green walls on the outside were replaced by partitions of the same color on the inside. It was dim and stuffy. Many generations of flies had orbited the light bulbs, diminishing their feeble luminosity. Brutus was unceremoniously pushed toward a long wooden bench, on which were already huddled three nègres,

Kongos undoubtedly. He sat down.

"You were arrested too?"

His closest neighbor acquiesced with a movement of his whole body.

"We wanted to change. Where we were, the cane was too light, they didn't pay us the right price."

"Same in my batey."

"So we wanted to go to another batey, to get better pay. We didn't want to escape, just go to another batey."

"Me," said Brutus, "I wanted to go back to Haiti."

"It's no good in Dominicanie. The Haitian has no value to the Dominicans."

"Some of them bad-mouth the President of Haiti," said the last Kongo in the row, leaning forward to see Brutus.

"Yes, I know. They say the Haitians are dogs."

Two soldiers were confabulating, leaning on a wall. Nearby, on a color poster, a certain President Guzman was proclaiming that they were going to finally build up the country, one for all and all for one. A little more to the right, another great poster. No doubt the instruction sheet. "Soldier, your enemy is Communism!"

A third soldier appeared, held a brief pow-wow with the other two. They looked at the Haitians. The newcomer designated Brutus's neighbor with his finger.

"That's the soldier that stopped me," murmured the latter.

The man mechanically hoisted his gunbelt, approached, invited the Kongo to rise.

"Haitiano! *Parece que tienes un poco de dinero!*"

"*Si seño*'. I have a little money."

"Fine," said the soldier. He leaned over, pointed to the little door hidden in the back of the room, began again in a confidential tone. "You know what's awaiting you?" The Kongo shook his head no. The soldier grimaced. "*Malas cosas*. Listen, if you have ten dollars, I'll try to speak up for you to the sergeant."

A sort of despair invaded the Kongo's face, and he rattled off a short phrase. "That's all you've got?" Brutus heard distinctly. The Kongo groped in one of his pockets, came up with a few crumpled bills that he slowly counted. He shook his head no.

"It's eight pesos, seño'."

The soldier chewed his lower lip, disappointed.

"All right. Give it to me. It'll be harder, but he might accept."

He pocketed the bills, turned on his heel, a thin smile on his lips. Brutus rose abruptly.

"*Seño', seño'*..."

The soldier turned around, frowning, and looked Brutus over.

"*Seño'*, I have a little money, could you speak for *mwin* self also?"

"How much have you got?" asked the other, surprised and interested.

"It's three and a half pesos that I. . ."

"Three and a half pesos!" The man couldn't suppress a start, and broke out in a nasty laugh.

"Three and a half pesos! You don't say, Haitian, you breaking my balls? You take me for a beggar from your rotten country?" He stood up straight. "Here, the law is the law, illegality is illegality. Sit down, and make it snappy!"

With a baleful look in his eye, he headed toward the small door, grumbling. "This isn't Haiti."

Haitians are often imprisoned by members of the army who are dispatched to the batey zones. Then everyone gets a piece of the action. They are only freed—in the exclusive direction of a plantation—if they pay between five, seven, or ten pesos, depending on what they have available. If they have nothing with which to buy their freedom, they are dispatched to prison.

The cell was big, contained about forty prisoners. "*Gran bagay*," observed Brutus. "It's big." The walls appeared dreadful to him, covered with graffiti and suspicious traces. The inside of this prison was just like a dirty toilet. It was a hodgepodge of Dominican and Haitian prisoners living together in the same room. The Dominican prisoners beat up the Haitians, mistreated them. Brutus realized, taking inventory of his numerous compatriots, that a rather large number of Haitians try to get out of the bateys. It didn't surprise him.

These Haitians looked as though they were prostrated, saying nothing about the conditions of their arrest. Many had undoubtedly been picked up in the same conditions as he. One of them kept repeating softly, as if something had snapped in his head, like a litany, that the Dominicans didn't want to let him walk, the Dominicans didn't want to let him walk, the Dominicans. . .

Brutus sat down in a corner, the only available spot he could find. A pestilential odor enveloped him, the same one that was hanging over the entire little community, but more directly invasive, permeating his body and clothing. He was three steps away from the collective latrine, overflowing with shit. He couldn't prevent himself from gagging. If he had eaten, this foul exhalation in his face would have made him vomit in disgust. Fortunately for him, it appeared that no one dreamed of bringing them anything to eat.

Without knowing why, he thought about Guzman's and Duvalier's beautiful palaces.

An old, resigned-looking Kongo smiled at him.

When it was time to go to sleep, Brutus threw himself on the cement.

The old Kongo with the resigned air befriended him. This old Kongo liked to talk, and was happy to have found someone to listen to him. He pointed out to Brutus an old, completely decrepit Haitian, incarcerated since December, the beginning of the zafra.

"When you land in prison, no greeting, no dialog, nothing. No trial. The Dominicans beat us. The capataces arrest us when there's trouble in the bateys. Some Kongos run away and head for the coffee harvest. Others try to reach the capital. You, you wanted to go back to Haiti. Each his own. When you get to the police, if you don't know how to speak Dominican, it's hopeless.

"Well, my friend, as far as I'm personally concerned, they threw me in prison while I was running away to go to another batey. We're almost all here for the same reason, because we were moving from one batey to another.

"The Dominicans here don't like us, they treat us like dogs, like thieves. They are here for different reasons, for personal affairs. No, we're locked up for no legitimate reason. If, for example, you are living a miserable life in one batey, you want to look for another, I don't see why they put me in prison for this reason.

"We don't eat. As you've noticed, we can't see outside. We sleep on the bare ground."

Brutus was listening to him attentively, asked him if he hadn't seen a Kongo named Gérard André pass through recently.

The old Kongo had not, to his knowledge.

"Could he have been here? Could he have been sick, and died here?"

"No, my friend, not in prison. As soon as the authorities see that someone's going to pass away, they send him to the hospital to die. The prison bosses don't let the prisoners die; but when they get to the hospital, after two or three days they are dead."

"Well, where could this companion be?"

"Well, my friend, as far as I know, there is a prison like the National Penitentiary. It's called Mexico, near Macoris. When Haitians are arrested, they first go to an outpost in Consuelo, then to Macoris. You don't see them again. There are other prisons. There's San Luis, but I don't know it, someone told me about it. Many Haitians disappear, you don't know what becomes of them. The soldiers also sell them to the 'colonos.' "

On his third day of captivity, when he was desperately wondering if he weren't going to stay there until he died—no one had paid any attention to him, no one had interrogated him, he was undoubtedly not even registered by the prison authorities—a big, well-nourished soldier, gun in hand, entered the cell. He looked the prisoners over, solely the Haitians. You would have said a dealer at a horse fair, a colonial "Gentleman" in the days when one bought "pieces from the Indies," coming from Africa, at the slave market.

He designated fifteen Haitians. The sturdiest. Brutus was among them.

Shortly after, he was very amiably received by a guy with lots of brass who was marvelously adept at making himself understood. He was tall, dry, impeccably shaved, even distinguished. A very civilized man.

"Listen to me, young Kongo! I'm going to offer you a deal…"

He stopped a moment for the effect. Brutus waited, holding his breath.

"You have a choice. Either you stay in prison, and in my opinion, taking into account the gravity of your charges, you aren't close to getting out, I'm telling you quite frankly. So. Fine. Second solution: we send you back to Haiti…"

Brutus started, stood up straight, a smile illuminating his eyes. He dared not believe it.

"…To Haiti. But I'm warning you, we cannot do otherwise than send you with a whopper of a report for the authorities in your country. In my opinion, not to offend you, you are headstrong, a dangerous rebel, maybe even an opponent of the established order. A communist, to tell the truth. How do you people say it, a, a, oh yes, *a Kamokin*…"

Brutus had gone pale. He wanted to go back to Haiti, but certainly not with a report calling him a *Kamokin*! Singled out as an opponent of Duvalier's regime! Had this guy decided to have him killed?

"…Or else, to show you that we can be generous, and pardon the errors of youth, there is a third possibility. You are free!" The officer rapped the edge of his desk three times with the pencil he held delicately between his fingers. He was watching Brutus. "You are free! Free to go and return to your batey and cut cane."

Brutus had spent three days in prison, practically without eating. When the sunlight flooded his face, he reeled, in a half-stupor, so weak he thought he was going to fall.

He couldn't even walk any more.

And now, Estimé Mondestin was afraid. He felt an irrepressible and irrational anguish creep over him and grip his throat. He firmly gripped his machete, slipped between the swollen stalks that hemmed him in on all sides. Yellow and dry at the base, wider and green at the top, the cane curved over his head, forming an inextricable lattice work against the immaculate sky. Slender, upward-thrusting verticals, they oppressed him like the insurmountable bars of an interminable prison. He was surrounded by a jungle, far, far, very far from his companions and the camp.

The season was advancing, and henceforth the cutting began in the spot the farthest from the batey with the rainy season imminent; this way the cabrouet could avoid having to travel and get stuck on the sections of the roads already broken up by repeated trips and maneuvers.

Mondestin was working alone; he was discouraged. Isolated, alone in the cane, he was afraid of everything. Gérard André's disappearance, Brutus's departure had affected him. The incident the day before had definitively broken his morale.

When, as the months go by, the Haitians finally possess some money, won in the lottery, by chance, or saved, drop of sweat after drop of blood in the hell of the plantation, they keep it on them. But in the cane, they can be attacked by marauders.

Mondestin was really scared.

The first fly that had landed on him the day before had sort of pleased him. He stood still, and attentively examined the tiny, delicate folded-back wings and legs that were running over his skin but which procured him no sensation, his epidermis was so tortured. When this insect lands on you, he brings you luck. You're going to get some money. That was fine. He brushed it away with his forearm, advanced into the universe of salty sugar.

When you start cutting in a new section of the plantation, you have to penetrate into the interior in order to start the first pile and begin what is called the "cane sheep." Instead of cutting from the exterior towards the interior, you work your way out, going towards the road.

The next few dozen flies had surprised, then exasperated him. They were landing everywhere, especially on his face. The swarm and the smell had brutally stopped him. Especially the smell, an unbearable smell. A brutal anxiety made his blood run cold and he hesitated a long moment, time suspended in the putrid exhalation, before going over to the strange pile of leaves. He started to gingerly move the branches, stifled a cry of terror and backed away, his entire body trembling. The Haitian that was underneath there was in an advanced state of decomposition.

Now, he was in continuous fear, moving forward slowly, fists clenched, jaws tight, his eyes staring into space, just like a zombie. Dominicans were coming out of everywhere in the tangle of vegetation, and they wanted to kill him. He jumped, turned, crazed with anxiety, saw nothing but the boughs of cane swaying from his passage. He tried to reason with himself, talked about the object of his fright to an imaginary companion, hoping to exorcise it that way.

Sometimes you walk, you get the impression they were murdering Kongos all night. I've already seen corpses, even before yesterday. Some Kongos who just got here. I saw... One that they surrounded with machetes at six o'clock at night. They cut him in the back, then in the hand; he had time to get away. That's why he's not dead. He had a big wound on his arm. The Dominicans had surrounded him. If he hadn't had time to get away, they would have killed him.

And he, Estimé Mondestin, all alone in this immense vegetation that rustled at every step, insidiously hostile, and which was engulfing him... He let out a sob of terror, tried to get hold of himself, his eyes sought out the sunlight, so high up he could barely make it out.

They don't want to see us. We were sold, they bought us, it's to make us take it, because we're dogs. I don't know. Maybe it's because we've been sold that they treat us this way.

Fear was submerging him.

When later that same day a Company truck, surrounded by soldiers, disgorged its cargo of ebony, and he believed he recognized Brutus's familiar figure, Estimé Mondestin couldn't help quivering. It seemed to him like joy. He reproached himself bitterly, then declared that if he was happy, it was because he'd been afraid that Brutus was dead. He ran as fast as he could to the massive Kongo.

They embraced each other briefly. Brutus, reticent at first, later came out of it.

"I thought I had only one liberty left, but that it did exist, and that was to go home and refuse all this. I know now that I was wrong. We'll never see our country again unless they decide one day, you're going to see your country again." After casting a long look over the barracks, he held his head in his hands for a long time, then crouched down, mechancially tracing on the dusty ground signs that had meaning only for him. "And here," he resumed in a low voice, "how's life going?"

"As usual," said Mondestin wearily. "Plus, one Kongo that they murdered."

He told about his discovery of the day before.

"As usual," said Brutus, after having listened to him.

He got up, headed toward the shack.

"I thought a lot while they had me locked up in prison," he said to Mondestin. "I know one thing now. We are not here because of fate, or the Good Lord, by chance, or from destiny. We're not here because it was written. We're here because it's in the interests of two men and an entire big machine. The two men are Guzman and Duvalier. The big machine is the one they run, the big machine of exploitation."

He fell silent, felt himself penetrated by all the murmur and rumble of the batey. He let it build up, concentrated it in his very depths, then let out a long sigh. Mondestin thought he discerned an implacable determination in Brutus's eyes when he uttered in a silent voice, the silent voice of rebels, these words, which he still remembers today, and which, slowly, slowly, are making their way.

"Let our masters beware of the anger of the slaves!"

Brutus now burned with an interior fire, an unappeased rage that worried Estimé Mondestin at times. He slashed into the cane with big, reckless strokes, swinging his machete with an insane force, and you would have said that the blade, whistling over the stalks that it decapitated, was at the same time decapitating some secret enemy. Whack, Guzman, he hacked, putting all his weight behind the blow. And whack, Duvalier! He was sweating. Whack, Guzman and whack, Duvalier! At times he straightened up, wiping away the flood of sweat and the erosive, blinding cane dust with an enraged gesture. "We need a radio," he bawled to Mondestin, who, dubious, straightened up in turn. Brutus was already back at work. A radio. There were some in the batey, but only on the Dominican side. The Kongos heard no news from their country. Once, exceptionally, they'd listened to Radio-Sun, the station of "my father." It was at a Dominican's place after he had already listened to his own program.

Brutus stood up again, his whole body alert, on the *qui vive* in spite of this unbelievable weariness; he grabbed his chin with his hand free of the machete, and pondered. "We also have to find out who this nègre is," he said. "Absolutely must know. Ab-so-lute-ly."

You would never have thought he was Haitian, he was so healthy and well-fed. In any case, he wasn't a Kongo. They'd seen him arrive one morning, and take a nice long stroll through the batey; "*bonjour*, my friend" to the right; "*kouman ou yé*" to the left; he was friendly, garrulous, courteous. Too courteous to be honest, Brutus had immediately decreed, sure of himself.

To those who had tried to find out what he was doing there, and they had asked him, he replied in a confidential tone: "I'm passing through. I'm here to get an idea of the situation." Then, in even lower tones, taking special care not to be overheard: "It's a difficult situation, my friend, don't you agree?" The Kongos, almost without exception, did not answer. You don't discuss those things with a stranger. An old habit we got into in Haiti since the arrival of the Duvaliers. You don't discuss anything with a stranger. Nothing with your surest friend, either. Nothing with anyone.

The guy hardly insisted, seemed to understand why, glanced around with a look of complicity, and went to have a drink in the bodega. So, he had money, this guy who didn't work; he disappeared, came back dressed very nicely two days later, asking a million questions without really appearing to be doing so.

And sometimes, right in the middle of the day's cutting, Brutus stood up, and slowly shook his head, from left to right, from right to left. It is absolutely necessary to know who that nègre is.

Antoine the viejo very calmly suggested they go and make inquiries at the neighboring batey. "The batey next door!" started Brutus, interested. "Why, yes," explained Antoine the viejo. "When we want to communicate with the Haitians living in the other camps, we get up in the night to go and see friends, and we talk, exchange news, tell about our respective lives. Only, you have to be careful. If the police catch a Haitian who's walking, they throw him in prison." "Yes, I know," said Brutus. "I am well aware." Then: "When can we go?" he asked.

At seven o'clock, the night had already fallen, the sultry heat had melted into the ground, little by little making way for a lighter breeze. Antoine the viejo was at the head of the little group which was moving in Haitian file: Brutus, Petit Pierre Déroseaux, Estimé Mondestin, Déroseaux's viejo friend, another Kongo whose name we don't know; and without his experience, Antoine the viejo's experience, they would have never gotten there. To be sure, it was easy walking; there were no mornes, nothing but a plain, but a limitless plain, with no power lines, no distinctive signs, no apparent landmarks; and once past the immense, completely devastated expanse that had been cut, and where the new crop was already growing, you could see nothing but cane and more cane, the tops of the stalks illuminated by the moon, the pale and mysterious disc, silent witness to the world's misery. A faint trail ran through this enormous, black proliferating mass, barely discernible in the darkness, and the one who was setting the pace on this path had to know his way perfectly.

They were not surprised by the spectacle they discovered in the scintillating clarity of the starry night. One-room shacks, some barracones, evidently without water, without electricity, without hygiene, isolated from everything, surrounded by the plantations.

202

They headed directly across an open area sprinkled with huts and palm trees to the habitation of a viejo.

A young woman with a head full of pink plastic curlers, ill-concealed under a faded scarf, let them in. Estimé Mondestin blinked while his eyes became accustomed to the glow of the oil lamp facing him. Half the room was occupied by a metal double bed covered by a thin mattress and an old, faded, flowered cover. Some clothes were hanging on the scaling, pale green partition, and a few jerry-cans were under the cluttered table. Plus a few miserable odds and ends on the torn newspaper that served as a tablecloth. A few dishes on a corner shelf. On the ground, a miniscule charcoal stove glowed red under a dented pot. That was all.

The young woman had them sit down on the bed, and they squeezed up together. The Kongos were very ill at ease, their big, cracked hands lying flat on their knees; they had gotten out of the habit of life in society, felt very dirty, messy, in spite of their clean clothes. And this young woman was looking at them.

Antoine and Déroseaux's viejo friend greeted the two viejos who were already there when they arrived, made the introductions, perfectly at ease, almost as habitués of the house.

The young woman offered them coffee, and the Kongos felt a strange sensation sweep over them; painful, and at the same time marvelously reminiscent of times past. They almost felt like crying; thus, they were still men, a young woman was offering them coffee.

She wasn't rich, yet, with a sweet smile, she was offering them some coffee. They hesitated before accepting, then said yes with undisguised eagerness. They'd been right to put on their last clean shirt, old but worthy. They'd been right.

They drank slowly and silently out of chipped glasses, and it was a marvelous sensation. Antoine and the other viejos were talking about everything and nothing, about the sun, the cane, the rain, and the bad weather. There was a knock on the open door, and the massive build of a Dominican was immediately framed therein. The Kongos jumped, their faces suddenly tense. The man entered with a heavy step, his eyes hidden by the shadow which was accentuated by his visored blue cap. His clean shirt hung loosely on his wide shoulders. "Mario. . . *Qué tal?. . .Buenos, amigos,*" in a voice that was at once drawling and energetic. He sat down. The host made the introductions. "Mario, *wagonero.* Some Haitian *compañeros* from the neighboring batey." Mario greeted them again with a smile and a wave. Then he frankly relaxed and familiarly put his arm around the waist of the young girl, who was handing him a glass she'd just rinsed with clean water and half-filled with coffee. Laughing, she extricated herself, feigning to give him a not very serious slap.

"Put your dirty paws in your pocket, you old Dominican pig."

"Ay, Liliane..." He pronounced it Liliané, like in Spanish. "As beautiful as you are, you should have married a Dominican!"

"Never in my life," exclaimed Liliane, horrified. "You don't have any color, you're all white, and you smell like a corpse."

"You'd have made me coffee, and you'd have been happy your whole life making me coffee and watching me drink it."

"It's not coffee I would have made you, you old bastard, but a brew like we make them in Haiti!" She made a quick gesture with the side of her hand. Poof! The Dominican changed into a zombie!

They laughed, except perhaps the Kongos, who were still a little tense. Mario took off his cap, bent his head, showing his sparse brown hair in the thin beam of flickering light.

"Look at how sleek it is, it's smooth as silk to the touch."

Liliane hooted, then sobered.

"Piské sé Aisyin m'yé é ke man désandans Aisyin sé tèt grèn yo ginyn, m pito Aisyin ak tèt grèn!"

Then, at Mario's comic-questioning look, his whistle, eyes on the ceiling, she translated it into Spanish. "Since I am Haitian and the Haitians' ancestors have frizzy hair, I prefer Haitians with frizzy hair."

"Nasty tempers, these Haitian girls!" he grumbled, with a knowing wink at Estimé Mondestin.

The latter was observing the scene with great attention. He felt somewhat troubled, his certitude shaken; he was trying to take stock of the situation. That harmonious relationships developed between viejos and certain Dominicans, he already knew. And between a few viejos and them, sometimes. But practically never between Dominicans and Kongos. In this domain, the Kongos' opinion was unanimous and categorical. You don't have anything to do with the Dominicans because they are bad. They could cut off your head for no matter what. You can't trust them. Estimé Mondestin had observed the hundred or so Dominicans living in his batey a great deal, was beginning to form his own opinions anyway. They all didn't seem really bad. The majority of them showed the Haitians nothing more than a complete indifference at most, carried out unenthusiastically the more specialized tasks that had been allotted them—for they never cut the cane, that, never— and also seemed to have a very hard time making the two ends meet. The planet on which they were surviving didn't seem that distant. Even though you cannot seriously make a comparison between their life and that of the Kongos. But all things considered, perhaps what was lacking was time, a common language, a link.

"Too bad for you," clucked the viejo, head of the household, to his young wife. "You'll never be Dominican!"

"But she is!" exclaimed Mario. "She is, since she was born here!"

She burst out laughing, shook her head, leaning against the table on which she was precariously half-sitting.

"You know the old saying? Papers aren't for women. I was born here, but I have nothing, I'm nothing."

"By rights, you're Dominican!"

"I'm not Dominican because they never gave me any papers! Besides, even with papers, deep down in my heart, I'm Haitian."

"You were born here?" marveled Brutus, coming out of his long silence.

She nodded.

"I've never seen Haiti. But I am Haitian. I know deep down that I am Haitian." She contemplated the infinitely brown skin of her arm.

"*Vré nasyon an, sé noua an Ayti.* The real nation — it's the blacks in Haiti. It's not the same here in Dominicanie."

She spoke perfect Creole, the Creole learned in the batey, as well as fluent Spanish, as correctly as Mario, passing from one language to the other with great facility, mixing the two idioms in the same sentence without even realizing it.

"Won't you go to Haiti someday?"

She shrugged with fatality, her eyes lost in a somewhat complicated reverie.

"What am I going to do there? Starve to death? I am a foreigner here, I would be one there. I don't have any papers here, I don't think they would give me any there. I eat here, I live here. I'm at home. Some days I feel more Dominican than Haitian, and other days more Haitian than Dominican. But deep inside, I know that I am Haitian."

"Someone who is born here," said Antoine the viejo, "can no longer say that he is Haitian or Dominican. He's someone who lives in a batey."

The host agreed.

"Viejo," he added, "is almost a nationality in itself." Then, after a short silence: "But we are Haitian."

"The Haitian is the one who suffers," said Brutus gravely. "Born in Haiti or in Dominicanie, it's someone who suffers. When you see the Dominicans, you..."

He stopped abruptly, glancing with embarrassment at the man who just finished drinking his coffee. The latter put down his glass, looked up, and took up Brutus's sentence where he'd left off, faint gleam deep in his eyes.

"When you see the Dominicans...?"

"Nothing," said Brutus, his forehead lined with a big crease. "But a Haitian is a Haitian and a Dominican is a Dominican. That's what I think."

"Life is difficult for us, too."

"Not like for the Kongos."

"That's true."

"No, not like for the Kongos."

"But you Kongos, someday you will go back to your country. We..."

He gestured in the viejo's direction, indicated himself with his thumb.

"All of us, I do believe we are doomed to stay. That's worse, maybe. Especially for them." He indicated the viejos. "They can neither go forward nor backwards."

He looked down and gazed at his worn-out shoes. They could see the taut skin on the back of his powerful neck.

"Kongos, viejos, Dominicans," he resumed, softly... *"Como si fuera e maldad, nos han tirado a todos en este infierno.* They've thrown us all into this hell."

"How much do you earn?" asked Brutus, who was interested and always very practical.

"Three and a half pesos for an eight hour day! And all those kids to feed!"

It was little. Ridiculously little. Ninety pesos a month. But so much more than the richest of Kongos. And not cutting cane.

"But you are Dominican! Why do you stay if it's bad for you?"

The man started to laugh, not a burst of laughter, but a thin, bitter laugh, full of sadness and suffering; who could have believed that of a Dominican?

"In this country too, there are those who have, and those who have not. They told us that was going to change, but it hasn't."

He told his story. The Kongos listened in silence, and only an occasional, indistinct cry, swelling out of the batey night, disturbed the attentive silence of the little room.

"Before coming to rot here, I was a peasant in the community of Jarabacoa, in the Palo Blanco area. My family had been working there for more than fifty years and we were living, well, pretty badly, but we were living. One unlucky day, the *terrateniente* José Miguel Piña passed himself off as a friend, snowed us with a lot of fine words, asked us, as well as the whole community, to let him graze his considerable herd of livestock, and we, with the stupid naivety of decent folk, those who work to eat, let him do it."

Mario looked deep into Brutus's eyes.

"Well, hombre, we might just as well have killed ourselves that day, or at least held on to our britches. We thought he was just buttering us up, but in reality, he was screwing us! *Pura marica!* Listen to this. That man, who already possessed thousands and thousands of *taréas* of land, who eats whenever he's hungry, who goes to a doctor if he farts sideways, who owns everything that a son of a whore could ever dream of owning, then claimed that that land belonged to him, and the proof was that his livestock were grazing there. And the corrupt courts, because they are corrupt in this country, the corrupt courts said he was right. They evicted us all. Since that day, all my people live in vile *callejones*, reduced to appalling poverty. I came here to sell my strength to the company, in order not to starve to death. But I was wrong, it'll just be a slower death."

His whole body straightened up, his clenched fists thumping together, the only exterior sign of a great, suppressed anger.

"Don't ever think, compañeros...whether Haitian or Dominican, that it's a pleasure to end up in a batey."

His eyes caught a beam of light and shone hard and deep; an occasional sparkle reminiscent of a long-lost naivety and tenderness.

"It's the sugar that's devouring us," he said forcefully. "The sugar is devouring us in the batey and even out of the batey." He snickered. "You see, compañeros, a country's wealth can also be its misfortune."

Silence, time stopped still. No one felt like talking. He continued.

"I've got a friend...I've got a friend, Juan Nelascado, who lives over there, in La Loma. Well, do you know...In La Loma, thousands of acres of cane planted by the CEA haven't been cut for five years now because, due to the nature of the terrain, it is very difficult to bring in the company vehicles. For five years! Well, on this land which serves no purpose, the peasants are forbidden to sow for survival. If someone cuts the cane, he is put in prison. My friend Nelascado, with his ten children who help him work, has to sneak into La Loma by night to work the little plot of land he planted in secret. If they catch him, I don't know what will happen to him. All of that cane is left uncut just to prevent the peasants from planting. Meanwhile, they are starving to death."

Mario looked at them one by one, and sighed, disillusioned.

"Meanwhile, they claim the regime has changed. Well, I'll tell you something: for us as well as for you, nothing has changed. The PRD* took over the government, and nothing has changed for us." He calmed himself, and continued in a lower, almost inaudible

---

*PRD: The Dominican Revolutionary Party, affiliated with the Socialist International and in power since 1978.

voice. "They tell me that for the bourgeois in Santiago and Santo Domingo, life is better, that there is a so-called Democracy, and that they can even print whatever they like in their nice newspapers. They tell me that it's big progress. Maybe. For them, no doubt. But for us, compañeros, nothing has changed. *Como quieran en esta Republica el chiquito es el sufrido*. It's always the little guy that has a hard time of it in this Republic!"

"*Sé oun lavi ki rèd*," said Antoine the viejo to break the silence that had set in. "Life is hard."

They were all silent, each grappling with the present, the past, some hypothetical future.

"I will go back there," Mario went on suddenly. "I will return to Jarabacoa. I've already talked about it with the others. We are determined. We will occupy the land and we will work it."*

Brutus was mechanically playing with his big, misshapen fingers, his face fierce. Mario observed him a moment, then continued: "But in the meantime, here we are. Us, you, Haitians, Dominicans..."

"Yes," said Brutus. "But still...there are some very bad Dominicans here."

"Of course! They don't have much choice."

Mario was thinking. "It's this huge machine that twists men, wringing out their sweat and their blood and changing it into money that develops, amplifies, and multiplies their inherent badness, be it ever so little at the outset. If you don't want to croak yourself, exploit your neighbor.

"The pesador, the cabrouetier, the capataz, the majordomo, are all paid on what the Kongos produce! So they work the Kongos to the bone; what else can they do? If they don't, they get canned themselves, get replaced by others who know they, too, will be replaced in turn if they so much as appear human!"

"It's true," said Antoine the viejo; "it's the Machine that is crushing us, it's the Machine."

"Certain viejos," continued Mario, "manage to eventually become a capataz. They are just as hard as the others, even worse, for this favor bestowed upon them got them out of their abject poverty. They don't want to go back to it."

"It's true," agreed Antoine the viejo, and the other viejos concurred, "*es verdad*. It's the Machine that crushes us, it's the Machine that turns us bad! And those who pull the strings of the Machine, we

---

*That is, in fact, what happened. During the course of 1980, the despoiled peasants occupied the land. They were imprisoned in the fortress at La Vega and were brutally repressed.

never see them, but they are responsible, the only ones really responsible, the only ones really to blame."

"Yes, there are those who pull the strings," said Brutus. "That is true." Then he raised his voice. "I know who they are. It's Guzman and it's Duvalier."

"They just met, those two," said Mario, hearing the names of the two heads of state. "They get along fine."

"Who's that?" asked Petit Pierre Déroseaux. "Who just met?"

"Guzman and Duvalier, your president and ours."

"We didn't know," said Déroseaux.

"We need a radio," said Brutus.

"They met just recently, last 31 May, in Malpasse-Jimani, and they shook hands. They say that your president is a dictator and that our Guzman is democratic, belonging to a big socialist club, but they gave each other a good handshake. Meanwhile, you others, you are starving to death!"

"They must have had a nice big meal to our health," said Brutus. "With a nice, sweet dessert."

"And us, we can't even go back to our country," said one of the viejos in a sickened voice.

"Not even go back to your own country!" cried Petit Pierre Déroseaux. "Not even go back!"

"That's our life — the life of the viejos," said Antoine. "Many of those who are here illegally would like to go back, but they don't have the means. Some live with the vague hope they will someday win the jackpot."

"So here we are," continued the other viejo. "You arrive one fine day, you don't go back, you get buried, you stay. You wait. One day, you get tired. You feel the need to *coger el piso à la finca*. To find a woman, get her pregnant, or to drink rum your whole life."

"You've done all that?" asked Brutus softly.

"Yes, I've done all that. Except drink rum. It's too expensive for us."

Antoine the viejo bent forward, clinking his glass as he set it on the ground. He stared at it for an instant, as if hypnotized.

"My nephew," he said, after a moment of silence that all had respected, "my brother's son came two years ago, victimized by the propaganda, and thought he was going to earn enough money to go back home well off. For two years now, he's been complaining, griping, only lives in the hope of getting together enough to go back. Up to now, he hasn't succeeded. The trap shut on him."

From time to time, Liliane filled the glasses with water. There was no more coffee. Abruptly, she emerged from her silence, addressing her companion with vigor.

"Your nephew shouldn't have gone to the CEA, and neither should we! I've been telling you that for a long time, but you don't want to listen to me!" She pointed a menacing finger. "But I'm warning you, if it continues, this miserable poverty, one day I'll leave all by myself."

"Oh yes. . . and where would you go?"

"To the Americans!"

The man grimaced with an unconvinced look.

"The Americans. . . Some say it's better, but I really don't know."

"They pay more. They're rich. A whole lot richer than the Dominicans!"

"What Americans?" asked Petit Pierre Déroseaux, suddenly very interested.

"The Americans," said Liliane, all wrapped up in her train of thought. "*Tienen dinero, dinero! Mucha plata!* Those people have got money, they're the richest in the world!"

"Gulf & Western," pronounced Mario softly, equally doubtful. "Yes, they say it's better. Who knows! It's in La Romana."

"*Seguro* that it's better," flared up Liliane, "but this old mule doesn't want to budge. He claims he's too old to launch into the unknown."

She let her mind wander, glancing around at her loathsome, everyday decor. Anyway, it couldn't be worse with the Americans.

Estimé Mondestin was admiring this modest, border-line survival interior, comparing it to their ignoble shack. The viejos can save more than the Kongos. Since they are more experienced, they can cut a cabrouet in one day, and plus, they don't take out the taxes that are withheld from the Kongos.

Antoine the viejo was thinking about their situation and about their isolation. In these bateys they never saw a priest or an official, just the Administrators, the majordomos, and the police. He wondered why he was thinking about that.

Petit Pierre Déroseaux was totally absent, lost in the undulations of the sheet metal roof. An extreme concentration. As if he were preparing something very important. The girl had said it was better with the Americans. No one had really refuted the assertion.

Brutus was tapping the edge of the bed with the flat of his hand. It's absolutely necessary to find out who this guy is.

He broke the general silence, put the question on the carpet of hard-packed earth.

"Haven't you, in your batey, noticed a Haitian who. . ."

No need to go any further. For the viejos in this batey, that Haitian was a *calié*. Of course they'd noticed him. He spent a lot of time here, even has a room to stay in, with a bed, chairs, tables, facilities;

often went out to the other bateys in the vicinity, hanging around, talking, making the rounds, listening, maintaining good relations with certain Dominican capataces. He was a *calié*. They couldn't prove it, but for them, he was a *calié* without a doubt. They avoided him like the plague.

"Watch out," they told the Haitians from Batey 7A visiting them, "he's a *calié* for sure."

The Dominican Republic was occupied by the Haitians on two occasions. The Haitian Governors on the eastern part of the island had brought with them a whole string of individuals who acted as intelligence agents, watching the subversive and nationalistic activities of the Dominican patriots who wanted their independence. These paid agents went around with a notebook* in which they noted names and information about all suspicious individuals. The word *"cahier"* does not exist in Spanish, but "calié," as the Dominicans pronounced it, remained. It's somebody who walks around with a notebook. But especially a spy.

The cane cutters are terribly afraid of these *caliés* who watch them day and night in the barracks, in the bateys, in the cane fields. They decided to keep informed of this individual's activities, to pass on all the information gathered to one another. In the meantime, don't take any chances, you have to be careful.

Then they talked again about the good weather, about the rainy season soon to arrive, of the harvest, of life, of the bit of information that had reached them through "Radio Djol" (literally, Radio-mouth), the Haitian telephone which functions by word of mouth, *chita tandé*, mouth to ear. That is how the news gets around that sustains the resistance in Haiti and in the bateys.

In Zagua, a fight had broken out among Kongos because they were hungry, they were tearing each other to pieces. The police intervened, surrounded the batey; a Kongo was shot dead on the spot. A lot of others had been pushed around, mistreated.

Their host also related what he knew of a grim story. To tell the truth, he knew very little about this incident. It was just that the rumor had spread, and they knew it was true. A Kongo had had his two arms cut off by a Dominican. This is what happened. They cut off his arms. It was a guy who liked to talk, carry on discussions. He didn't die because he had a friend. This friend provided him with food. They took him to the hospital, they didn't give him anything. The Dominicans didn't give him five kobs. The Embassy didn't give him a cent. There's a law that says when the Haitians are injured they're supposed to get the *seguro*. Nothing. In this same batey,

---

*Notebook: *Cahier* in French. — TRANS.

moreover, two cane cutters died in a fire; a house had been totally destroyed. But what held everyone's attention, of course, was the drama of the bracero with his arms cut off.

Brutus persistently repeated the same phrase several times. "Certain men are bad," he said, "but the Machine makes them even worse." They talked a little more, and finally agreed on the subject of the guy with his arms cut off.

"It's horrible, my friend. But anything is possible in the bateys."

They had made him believe he was going to leave for 15 pesos a day. That was what interested Obénor Jean-Baptiste. A lot of money to go home, to get his big family out of their wretched poverty.

He was lucky to save his neck in the hiring operations; but when he arrived at the batey *San José* all he found was misery. In the hell of the plantations, you didn't often manage to make ends meet. It took three of them to fill up a container of cane the size of a train compartment and earn five dollars. Sometimes you didn't earn anything. There was no one to take the case into consideration, although apparently there were several Haitian inspectors monitoring the work. Such was the situation.

In spite of this, he continued to cut, for it was the only work available in Santo Domingo for those Haitians hired. Without that, you couldn't eat. He had come to take advantage of this opportunity because he was young and the father of two children. He wanted to provide for their needs.

Life was very hard for these poor ragged people whose only wealth was in their arms. In order to be able to resist, to feed and wash themselves, they sought the aid of viejos established in the country.

That was how Obénor Jean-Baptiste met Elvire Saint-Germain, a Haitian woman he'd known as a girl a few years before in the slums of Tokyo Alley in Port-au-Prince. He didn't know how she'd landed here. She now had three children of a Haitian immigrant, a certain Magistrat, who'd been living in the Dominican Republic for a long time, but not with her. Elvire Saint-Germain invited Obénor Jean-Baptiste and one of his companions, Jean Raynold, under her roof.

Thanks to this Haitian woman's kind cooperation, life began to be easier to bear for Obénor. The lady assured him that she had completely broken all ties binding her to this Magistrat, of whom she'd had three children. Of course, Magistrat claimed to whomever would listen that Elvire was still his wife, but for Obénor Jean-Baptiste, it was ridiculous and false. Considering her advanced age, she could have been his mother, but certainly not his wife.

The grave misfortune was that this Haitian couldn't swallow her repulsion for him. Of which Obénor Jean-Baptiste was quite simply unaware.

Upon learning that two Kongos were living under Elvire Saint-Germain's roof, Magistrat decided to have their heads cut off. A Dominican was paid to accomplish this task.

On 15 March, upon leaving work, Obénor Jean-Baptiste went to this lady's house, not knowing what he was in for, looking forward to the little dish she prepared for him as usual. Just as he was finishing, in the presence of Elvire Saint-Germain's son, Mira, Magistrat and the Dominican, each with a well-sharpened machete in hand, burst in with the intention of spilling some brains.

It was eight o'clock.

The Dominican rushed towards Obénor. Luckily, the lady, realizing what was happening, threw herself in front of the assailant with the idea of blocking his way. Three of her fingers were severed in a single blow.

The second blow was for Obénor Jean-Baptiste only.

When the machete whistled in the shadowy light, he instinctively raised his left arm to avoid being decapitated. And his left hand fell with a thud.

When the blood-smeared weapon whistled once again, he shielded himself with his other arm in a final desperate effort. Then he screamed in pain and horror. He no longer had a right hand either.

It was thanks to the darkness that his life was saved.

He escaped—but can one really say that he escaped—with gashes on his shoulder and his head, and both arms systematically amputated.

A friend devoted himself body and soul, had him driven to the hospital. He would stay there a month and a half. During his confinement, with the exception of Elvire Saint-Germain's little girl, he found no one to come to his aid.

He suffered a lot. He said to himself, "If I die, I die."

He didn't die.

When he was leaving, the Dominican doctors, who were very attentive, advised him to go to the Haitian Embassy. Another Dominican accompanied him in an automobile.

Someone told him: "If the Embassy takes your case into consideration, you can be awarded a good sum of money by the Company."

He went to the embassy every single day, walking an enormous distance, like from the National Palace in Port-au-Prince to the suburbs in Carrefour, an enormous distance every day, with his head bandaged and his amputated arms in a sling.

He spent days in the courtyard of the Embassy. The inspectors categorically refused to talk to him.

One day, he happened to hear that Cinéas, the new ambassador, was on the premises. He asked to speak to him. But every time this important personage swept by him, all he saw was his coattails.

So one day, when he was just about out of strength and hope, he began to rant and rave. The Ambassador did not receive him, but ordered that he be taken to see the District Chief, a Major in the Dominican army. When the latter finally received him, after making him come back several times, he made him understand that he could go back to Haiti. If they needed him one day, they would let him know.

He set off for his country on 24 June.

One of his sisters who'd been in the Dominican Republic before and Elvire Saint-Germain took care of his transportation expenses.

Upon arrival, he went before the Haitian authorities. They would do nothing for him.

He later learned that his Dominican assailant, who'd been incarcerated, bought his liberty for 200 dollars. At first, he thought that the authorities would give him something out of the 200 pesos paid by his torturers. He received nothing.

Not knowing what else to do, nor to which Saint he should make a vow in order to get a compensation, or some kind of help, he went and made his situation known to the independent press in Port-au-Prince, Radio Haiti Inter, Radio Cacique, Radio Progrès, and *Le Petit Samedi Soir*, who made a lot of noise about his situation.

Consequently, the Haitian officials let him know that, for having sought out the "media of opposition," they were dropping his case.

From then on, he would live in the vile Tokyo slum uniquely on the good will of this one or that one, in the charge of God and the People, to use his expression.

He had obtained the card that permitted him to cross the border. Like so many others, he'd bought himself a shirt, a pair of pants, and a pair of shoes to go "over there."

He came back without his arms.

But he was lucky. He came back. His friend, Jean Raynold, met his death the same week in the same circumstances.

A few days had gone by. It had been raining since the morning, that heavy tropical rain which, after a few hours in the plantation, left them trembling with cold despite the moderate temperature. It seemed as though it went right through their very skin, as it would an old, no-longer-waterproof raincoat. Convulsive, irrepressible chills rose in uncontrollable waves from their very depths, surfacing in a clammy tremor. Prolonged, disquieting coughing fits exploded in the alveoli of the barracks at regular intervals.

Nevertheless, the sky miraculously cleared as evening fell, and the infinite lights of the firmament bathed, in a limpid glow, the infinite shit of this concentration camp. They walked in the mud, trudged through the mud, sank in the mud, became inexorably covered with mud, had to take refuge inside their cells and try to light their meager fires, prepared the semblance of a meal that tasted like shit and mud. It was an evening just like so many others, and that's all there was to it.

All things considered, the news didn't surprise them any more than did the appearance of the soaked viejo who brought it. He'd just made the nocturnal trek across the plantation, dressed in a drop-cloth, drenched from all the dripping stalks along the way.

"Better watch out, you can't trust him," declared the messenger, without any preliminaries. "You better beware. That guy is a *calié*. He's a Tonton-Macoute!"

Brutus let fly a string of obscenities in lowered tones. Mondestin shook his head, rather saddened. He didn't even have a cup of coffee to offer this soaking wet viejo.

"He's a Tonton-Macoute!"

"A Tonton-Macoute," started Mondestin, alarmed, forgetting his dreams of coffee on the spot. "There are Tonton-Macoutes in Dominicanie?"

"They come from Haiti to spy on us."

"How did you find out?" asked Petit Pierre Déroseaux.

"Well, right from the start, this man asked many too many questions; at first, completely innocent, then less harmless, a whole lot of questions, in fact, and we started to get suspicious. Then, he insidiously spoke ill of Jean-Claude Duvalier, or rather, nothing really bad, but nothing really good, and this, without taking any precautions, without hiding it, in front of perfect strangers. But this character didn't fit in, a guy who lived without having to work, the batey gave him the cold shoulder. Nevertheless, he was there. Two days before, however, he changed his tune. Two Kongos were foolish enough to challenge the regime in front of him, two Kongos, one of whom was literally starving to death. The guy suddenly got very angry, apparently forgetting to control himself. He violently reviled them; taking to task all those *manfoubins*,* that category of Haitians who show their defiance right in the street, asked them if they weren't ashamed. Then he took their names; that, someone saw him do very discreetly. Then, he calmed down, told them not to mind him, that in the situation they were all in, everyone had his moments of irritability. Except that he, someone had remarked, didn't seem to be in a situation that was all that bad. The two Kongos had silently acquiesced, but since then, they seemed worried and said nothing more."

It was the next day, in fact, that the news broke with absolute certainty, thanks to the collaboration of Marta, a Dominican known for her big heart and her little virtue. For several days, at the viejo's instigation, she'd been doing her best to attract the Haitian's attention, and had done such a good job swaying her hips under the too-short skirt riding high on her muscular legs, that he'd finally noticed her. She then calmly aroused him with little flicks of her tongue, sensually moistening her lower lip, and by imperceptibly undulating her belly which she casually stroked with a seemingly unconscious movement of her hand.

The first time he'd invited her over to his place, she only put up the strictly minimum resistance. Then, after the thing was rapidly terminated, she dawdled, lolling on the bed, her legs half bent, her inert body nicely stretched out on the sheets, damp with perspiration. He was perspiring profusely as he discreetly checked out her anatomy, and hardly protested when she suggested that he go and buy two *refrescos* to quench their thirst before resuming, resuming what?, ah, ha!, she laughed and calmly rubbed herself in the spot well below where her unbelievably white skin made way for dark fleece. He slipped on a shirt and pants and was gone.

During his short absence, she had the time to take a quick look around.

The bodega was at the other end of the batey. This is what she discovered.

In a suitcase, stuck between two shirts, there was a loaded pistol. In addition, she'd also noticed a black apparatus with buttons, but wasn't capable of determining whether it was a machine for recording—a tape-recorder; or for sending communications—a transmitter. In any case, there was this apparatus, and it wasn't just a radio, of that she was certain.

"He's a Tonton-Macoute, you're going to have to be careful."

Mondestin found it hard to believe. Macoutes in Dominicanie!

---

manfoubin: derived from *"je m'en fous bien,"* *("Je m'en fous bien"* is the French equivalent of "I don't give a shit."—TRANS.

Nevertheless, there are.

By 24 March 1979, the Haitian patriots and their Dominican companions had established with certainty the presence of the following National Security Volunteers in the Dominican Republic: Gesner Laporte, 27, from Cap-Haitien; Alix Poulard, 21, domiciled Monseigneru Guillous St. in Port-au-Prince; Roland Duroseau, 25, from Carrefour; Jean Augustin, 24, from Jacmel; Mario Valentin, from Meaux St. in Port-au-Prince; Denise Tibili, from Carrefour; the officer Mayan, residing at the La Fama Hotel in Santo Domingo, and maintaining permanent contact with the new Haitian Ambassador, Frantz Cinéas; Mirabo, a boxer who occasionally serves as a trainer for Jean-Claude Duvalier. When, on 30 June 1979, Mr. Odius Lacroix, vice-president of the Jean-Jacques Dessalines Liberation Front (an anti-Duvalier organization founded two months earlier), would be brutally torn from his bed in the middle of the night, arrested without a warrant, and thrown in prison, the Dominican police would be accompanied by a Haitian Tonton-Macoute answering to the name of Dieusèl, residing at the Ozama Central in San Luis, thus openly and unequivocally marking the close collaboration of the repressive forces of both countries.

It is under the surveillance of the Tonton-Macoutes who cross the border to spy on them, to prevent any contact with revolutionaries, unions, committed priests, or ministers, be they Dominican or foreign, that the Haitians sink a little deeper each day into their misery. Anyone spotted has the proper authority's boot awaiting him at the Haitian border.

With Brutus in the lead, they made a tour of the barracks in order to warn the Haitians, particularly the Kongos. Without even realizing it, they were starting to organize.

Exclamations greeted the little group that darted from door to door, exposing the situation, commenting on it, before going on to another cell, its ranks swelled by one or two additional members. Attracted by the incipient rumblings, other Kongos emerged from the darkness, slow-moving viejos arrived; yes, my friend, as if all that weren't enough, there are Tonton-Macoutes!

Slowly, the anger began to rumble.

"We are beaten, mistreated and spied on," launched someone suddenly.

"I imagined that they owed us a little respect for sending us to work!"

"None at all! And if only they paid you when you cut cane, it wouldn't be so bad, since it's *la misère** back home."

---

*La misère: wretched poverty. — TRANS.

"Yes, it's *la misère* back home."

"*La misère*," chimed in Estimé Mondestin, and he must have been really exasperated, he wasn't by nature outspoken..."Me, I'm a driver. If there was anything in my country, I wouldn't have left it to come looking for a better life here!"

That was certainly true. The Kongos nodded. Brutus, Estimé Mondestin, and Petit Pierre Déroseaux were there. There was Antoine the viejo and some other viejos. There were some Kongos. There was a mechanic, another who had worked in a shop on the Cape, on Jean-Jacques Laroche St., another cabinetmaker who had also worked. Two from the Cape and another who'd been learning to drive in Port-au-Prince. There were many peasants.

"Me, up 'til now, I found nothing to do. I'm twenty, I was born on 29 January 1958. I came to Port-au-Prince in 1976. My aunt was there and I went to stay with her. My father and mother live in Mirebalais. They're old. They have six children. And I couldn't find anything to do."

They nodded, listened without listening, it was everyone's story, they knew it.

At this point, someone put forth an idea he would have never dared to express in Haiti. The guy was an intellectual, and he was pretty smart since he'd been all the way to the last year of Primary School. With a wave of his hand, he indicated the entire assembled group.

"If our government was capable of handling the reins of power, these trained people wouldn't need to come and cut cane!"

"Yeah, the Duvaliers," said a voice.

Then there was a silence and, alarmed, they looked at one another anxiously. Conscious, perhaps, of having already said too much. This type of comment...They shuddered. They weren't used to it.

"It's not Jean-Claude's fault," said someone, without much conviction, but just in case, so no one could claim someday that he had said what had just been said.

Strangely, this comment wasn't a big success.

"Yeah, the Duvaliers," said another voice, louder this time.

"Jean-Claude sells the Haitians," launched Brutus, and they all quivered. "He takes advantage of us to fatten up his Swiss bank account!"

And someone, hidden in an obscure corner, applauded. Then somebody else. Other somebodies.

"For twenty-two years now, we can't even live!" Brutus was already continuing. "It's the flatterers, they are getting rich, the others are starving to death!"

"He's right!" cried Déroseaux. "The Haitian president sold us like animals and already pocketed the bread, before we even got here."

"What makes things harder is that the President raises the prices of the Haitians," agreed an old Kongo whose limbs were scarred with souvenirs of past campaigns. "Before, the bosses paid us better, but this year the price went up and our wages are lower to make up for it."

He stopped, continued muttering under his breath, getting all worked up against that Duvalier. "All that I've seen!" he mumbled, "*mêm bagay!* Everywhere the same thing! Same old thing!" The first actual shout snapped him out of the middle of his reflection, and for an instant he was completely petrified. Something had just happened that floored him, and which floored them all, judging by the strange silence adrift. It was something that they couldn't even imagine.

"Down with Duvalier!" a Kongo had shouted. "Down with Duvalier!"

And the sky hadn't fallen on their heads. Suddenly, others recovered, filled with less and less contained excitement and fury.

"Down with Duvalier!"

The sky still didn't fall. Something had just happened which someday will have great repercussions in the history of Haiti. For the first time in a very long time, they dared to cry: Down with Duvalier!

A few Kongos voiced a sharp protest.

"Ah, no gentlemen, you mustn't overdo it!"

"No talking politics, huh!"

"We can't shout like that, do you want to get us killed?"

"Those who want to talk politics—out of the batey. We don't want to get ourselves murdered!"

"Eh, what?" Brutus, incensed, was the first to gather his wits. "It's not the truth?" Solitary and resolute, he shouted as loud as he could. "Down with Duvalier!" Then he raised both arms to dominate the crowd after his cry. "They're getting rich, they're getting rich, they're getting so rich that there's no more room in the coffers of their Swiss banks! While they are driving down the Haitian People who can't even eat. . ."

"It's not our place to straighten that out," protested an old Kongo, his face feverish, visibly worried.

"*Sé pa vouazin ka va ranjé sa pou nou*," retorted Brutus with determination. "It's not the guy next door who's going to fix things for us!"

"But it's not us. . ."

"What do you mean, it's not us?"

A powerful voice ripped out of the crowd, came to the aid of Brutus, who raised his fist to a hubbub of approval.

"*Sé nou ki pou mété lod lan sa!* It's up to us to straighten it out!"

Several Kongos moved away, stepped back from all these people who'd taken leave of their senses. "Shout 'Down with Duvalier!' I've got family in Haiti," apologized one of them, abandoning the group. "I've got family in Haiti. What you're doing is very dangerous—for us and for them!"

Trembling, he disappeared into the darkness. It was madness.

Some of the young people there don't want to ever go back. They've said some true things about the government. The inspectors, the supervisors, the Tonton-Macoutes, informed by squealers, have promised them that their names will be turned in, so that they can be stopped at the border in Malpasse as *kamokins*. This is the reason why many don't go back. Without even having decided of their own will, they swell the embittered ranks of exiles. They shout "Down with Duvalier"; it was madness.

And so very new.

They talked long into the evening. They realized that their situation wasn't at all due to fate, but to the flaws in an incompetent, reactionary, fascist regime.

In the evenings, on Saturdays and Sundays, some among them got in the habit of talking, of discreetly discussing what should be done to get rid of this guy that had sold them. There was talk; a rumor going around that in other bateys, the viejos even had "certain associations" in which they discussed the compatriots' problems in the Dominican Republic.

Brutus very quickly distinguished two categories of Kongos. The people from the capital, young boys who'd heard on "Radio National" that there's work for fifteen dollars a day and who'd said to themselves, "Great, we'll go there, we're going to make some money." The other category, made up of peasants, from Léogane, from Jacmel, etc., not used to cash, for whom the practically nothing was already a big deal.

There was conflict between the two groups.

The peasants kept quiet, were afraid, were content with very little. They'd left behind a little patch of land, a cow, a pig, so that their wife could eat. If they went back to Haiti with twenty dollars, they'd consider themselves satisfied.

But the guys from the capital, with no work, no lodgings, suffered enormously the implacable urban poverty, and were working to really make money. Among them had formed a genuine group of rebels. Jean-Claude sold them, he'd taken the bread, they'd have practically nothing to go back with. They were ready for anything.

A few of the youths from Port-au-Prince were saying that once returned, if they could find some weapons, they'd go right ahead and attack the Government, for Freedom. Tchak! Even if you had to die, it would be for a good cause.

Article 13: Fifteen (15) days before the expiration of the period for which the Haitian agricultural workers have been engaged, the State Sugar Council will notify the Haitian Embassy by letter of the repatriation date. The State Sugar Council agrees to repatriate, at the end of the sugar season, the 15,000 Haitian agricultural workers who must be the same individuals who were hired in the different hiring centers established in Haiti for this purpose. The Haitian Embassy will immediately inform the Haitian government. The Haitian agricultural workers will be repatriated at the expense of the State Sugar Council.

The transportation will be carried out in buses providing the same guarantees of comfort and security.

The State Sugar Council will pay the Haitian government the sum of eighty-five thousand dollars ($85,000) to cover the transportation expenses of the 15,000 Haitian workers from Malpasse to the centers in which they were hired.

Article 29: The Company agrees to pay the day laborer, concurrently with payment of the last fifteen days work's wages, the amount of the annual bonus provided for by the Work Code of the Dominican Republic.

Article 30: The State Sugar Council agrees to guarantee the conversion to American currency of the savings realized by the Haitian agricultural workers in the Dominican Republic at the time of their repatriation.

On 3 July 1979, the CEA began repatriating the 15,000 Haitians from the zafra.

No joy hung in the air, there was no inhabitual or spontaneous activity, no excitement. They had stripped the last acre of land, felled the final stalks of cane on the fringes of the batey, and now they were waiting, silently, for the end, absent from their own lives. At the gates to the barracks on the edge of the camp, the cane they had cut upon arriving was already half-grown, and implacably gathering momentum for the next zafra.

They showed no enthusiasm at the idea of packing their bags, taking off, and going back to Haiti. They knew they were going to starve there. They didn't give a shit. Starve here or starve there...A few of them had made a secret decision to stay in Dominicanie, come what may. "Me," announced Petit Pierre Déroseaux one night, "I'm not going back." They had looked up in silence, abandoning for an instant their meager portion of beans, badly cooked in water. "In Dominicanie you eat every day anyway, even if the work is no good. Even if cutting isn't paid, you find something to do. I'm staying," he'd said. Then he added: "But not here in this rotten batey. I'm going to the Americans. They pay well." Brutus had vaguely shrugged, made no comment, and started chewing, again making the lack of pleasure last. Estimé Mondestin said nothing, but he knew that he wouldn't be leaving either. Not this year anyway. Next year, he swore it to himself. When he will have made enough to pay back his debts. Just one year and he was going back. He had nothing to fear, he would never become a viejo, no way! Just one year, he repeated to himself. From time to time, Brutus stared at him as if he had guessed, shook his head and said: "We have to go back. Our place is there. We have to go back to smash Duvalier's face in!" "But when you have debts and nothing to pay them with, how can you go back?" Mondestin shook his head wearily, thought about his wife, his children, and a shooting pain began piercing his temples. He would rather stop thinking. He would ask another Kongo to go and explain the situation to them, and to give them his promise. Just one year. Then, head down, he walked aimlessly, listening to the muffled buzz floating over the batey. The Kongos were getting together their meager bundles. But it was no big event.

The time had come for them to go back, nothing more.

Brutus briefly embraced Déroseaux and Estimé Mondestin. They left to go and hide—nègres marrons. They were going to have to remain unnoticed for a week or two before surfacing. Antoine the viejo and Déroseaux's friend were going to help them stay out of sight for a while. Then, they would see. Déroseaux would leave for La Romana, the Americans' place. Mondestin didn't know yet.

An uninterrupted rumble of trucks was progressively rising from the four corners of all the plantations. At the last minute, those who were leaving felt a pang in spite of themselves. They could not have pinpointed why.

Installed in the back of the roaring vehicle into which they had been piled, Brutus gazed at the horizon of the *cañaveral*, his eyes lost in the monotonous undulations of the vast fertile land, enriched by the sweat and the blood of the Kongos. Then he plunged into a profound silence, agitated by the thousand confused thoughts clashing in his head.

Two Kongos standing next to him were talking, clinging to the railing so as not to be thrown by the jolting and unexpected swerving of the truck. The engine's irregular noise intermittently drowned out the dialog, then diminished on a sudden downgrade, letting their voices be heard. Brutus came out of his reverie and realized that he had unconsciously followed the beginning of their conversation. They had been involved in other zafras and seemed pessimistic about the repatriation operations.

"How was it last year?" he cried, forced to shout to drown out the engine noise.

One of them gestured abruptly, a vague gesture which needed no clarification. It meant: it went very badly. "Yeah?" said Brutus, moving closer as best he could in order to know more. "Oh yeah," said the Kongo. He added: "In fact, last year, I don't know, I wasn't there, but two years ago, it was no good at all." He hung on, shaken by the vehicle's vibration. Then he fell silent. The engine was screaming louder than he. They were crossing a green region and while the truck struggled up a sharp incline, Brutus saw supple forms of banana trees pass through his field of vision. Attentive, his mouth open, the Kongo waited for a more opportune moment to relate the following events as he had lived them.

In 1977, at the end of the zafra, the Balaguer government lost interest in the problem of the Haitians who were still in the Dominican Republic after finishing out their contract. Ten thousand of those waiting for transportation back to Haiti in a village called "El Manguito" remained in those narrow streets, under the stars, exposed to the ravages of rain, sun, and damp nights, with no sanitary comforts, without the slightest facilities for the physiological needs, without a drop of water to drink, and without food for twelve days, forced to spend their meager, painfully hard-earned savings.

The road was now downhill. The engine ran smoother and the Kongo could speak again.

"They made us gather at the corner of a street called Mango, or Manguito because there are mango trees, I imagine, until there were twelve thousand of us." "Twelve thousand," murmured someone, "But that's all of the Kongos!" The man nodded his head without interrupting his story: "We were close to being that many, but there still lacked a few, and we had to have the exact number. It started to rain. Each morning, the company gave us each two pieces of bread and a can of sardines, but you had to pay. We gave the money to one among us and he went to buy the food, to stand in line. There were several lines. We were living out in the open, under the mango trees; the sanitary conditions were disastrous, worse than in the batey." A gasp of stupefaction went through the truck, and this unbelievable fact passed from mouth to mouth: sanitary conditions worse than in the batey, but in this country you should expect anything — diseases broke out and epidemics started.

The Kongo broke off again. A cloud of dust engulfed the rear of the truck as it passed over a portion of unpaved road. He remembered it as if it had happened yesterday or the day before. "If we don't protest, they are going to leave us here at this intersection," the most exasperated among them had started to bellyache. "We have to do something." They had already been waiting for five days.

"Well, what happened?" prodded the voice of the robust Kongo next to whom he was being jostled about.

"Well, on the sixth day... You have to admit, we were living under the stars and the few odds and ends that we possessed, the bits of clothing that we had salvaged, were little by little destroyed by the rain. We began to protest. They sent the police to break up our demonstration of discontent. That made us very angry. After six months of forced labor and all that we endured, you can imagine — they could imagine, it was like today — we were at the end of our rope. We went into the offices in the factory and we wrecked everything. We wrecked all the houses in the vicinity" (a gasp in the truck — "they wrecked everything"); "we wanted to destroy the factory." "Yes, yes," shouted a Kongo, "you're right, that's what should be done, destroy the factory!" "We wanted to destroy the factory." A short silence. "A lot of police came." Another silence, eyes far away.

"So, then?" asked someone impatiently.

"So, then?" A big smile, the first in a very long time. "Well, my friend, five Dominican police officers were hospitalized!"

A hubbub of satisfaction rose in the heavy air, mixed with the engine's belches and the exhaust fumes. Five Dominican police got a working over. That must have been great.

"Afterwards, the Haitian Ambassador came."

"The Haitian Ambassador?"

"Yes, the Haitian Ambassador."

"Don't talk to me about these ambassadors," someone snorted

bitterly, upon hearing these words. "They're not in favor of the Haitians. We are dogs in their eyes."

"The Ambassador came."

"They don't bother about us..."

"Shut up and let him finish!"

"Well, he came! He never comes to the bateys, but that day he came. Ha, ha! When he got there, of course we didn't know who he was. We busted up his car!" Peals of joyous laughter rang out into the countryside that was flying by: "Smashed up the Ambassador's wheels!" "He got out, pulling his hair and trembling with fear. 'My beloved People, who are so dear to me,' he said, 'calm down, I beg you, calm down!' But we did not calm down. 'I've just talked with President Balaguer and he formally promised that they are going to repatriate you.' We continued the demonstrations anyway. We built small barricades with stones." "Barricades, they built barricades, barricades built by Haitians, they never told us about that in Haiti." "To prevent the cars from getting through, and the cars no longer got through."

"That was when they sent in the soldiers." "White soldiers," someone shuddered, "should have expected it, Dominican soldiers." "Well, as a matter of fact, no, the soldiers they sent were blacks, blacks just like us, physically." "Blacks..."

"Oh yes, blacks. The forces of the law were very violent."

"That doesn't surprise me, blacks are bad!".

"No worse than whites, moron," thundered Brutus, recoiling.

"Oh yes, he said so, these black soldiers were very violent with the Kongos!"

"Don't say things like that, you are black. They were violent because they're soldiers, not because they're black!"

Nègres against nègres, this repression had become a nègre affair, with possible excesses to be accounted for by the black's natural savagery. On this occasion of repression any chance that public opinion could have reared its ugly head and talked of anti-Haitian racism was short-circuited.

"The blacks are very brutal."

"When a black is clubbing and when a white gives the orders, who is more brutal, the black or the white?"

"The black, since he's the one clubbing!"

A sudden commotion sprang up in the truck. Interjections interrupted other interjections. Opinions differed. One Kongo's opinion was approved unanimously.

"Well, my friend, they are both just as brutal. The only difference is that in this business, one is a bastard and the other is an asshole."

"Big deal!"

"Exactly!"

"And when you get beat up, would you rather it be by a bastard or an asshole?"

"Bastards and assholes—the same damn thing!"

"Besides, as far as we're concerned, the bastards are the blacks."

"That's right, the same thing."

"Even so," remarked Brutus, "if the bastards were less bastardly, the assholes would surely be less asshole."

"What exactly does that mean?" asked a Kongo who was perplexed by this circumlocution.

"What that means is that the first thing to do is to get rid of the bastards, here as well as at home!"

Even though they were cautious enough to avoid talking about it further, this stance made a strong impression on the Kongos.

Then they asked the veteran to continue his story.

"The forces of repression were very violent," he went on immediately. The regular hum of the engine was no longer bothering them now, the road was descending in a gentle slope towards the clear light of the sea. "They beat us with rifle butts, forcing us to disperse. They herded us all in the same spot that they roped off to prevent us from getting out. The guards had us surrounded and had us covered with their guns. At that point they requisitioned all the existing buses in the vicinity. They promised they would give us something to eat on the way. Nothing. When we got to Jimani, they told us, 'you are going to get in line again.' We protested. We wanted to go home immediately. There were incidents. The Dominican police called the Haitian police, the army, the Tonton-Macoutes for help. They all arrived and beat us up, saying: we didn't send you to go on strikes. We sent you to work..."

"That's exactly it," mused Brutus, whose exacerbated consciousness was particularly aroused. " 'We sent you to work...' It's them that sent us! They are the ones to blame!" The other continued.

"They gave us a very violent thrashing. We tried to defend ourselves but took a severe punishment from both the Haitian and Dominican police. They got along really well beating us up, you would have thought they were from the same country. It caused a scandal in Dominicanie. Not in Haiti. But in Dominicanie the newspapers talked about the lot that was dealt us. So they stopped hitting us, they didn't give us any food, and they repatriated us."

An indignant outburst shook the little group as they discussed these events, then they fell silent at a signal from the Kongo. He had something to add.

"When we got to the other side of the border at home in Haiti, the leaders were arrested, the rest were dispatched to Croix-des-Bouquets. But above all, the leaders were arrested."

They fell silent. The popping cylinders under the hood alone punctuated their rapid advance. Now a fearful shadow hung over the truck. That of the Tonton-Macoutes and of Duvalier whom they were going to encounter again.

This year was a good year, as far as the return was concerned.* Except for Ofaniel Ceslum, which goes without saying. They were made to get out promptly when the truck stopped at the esplanade of the *Colonia Yaco*, where two big sheds had been erected and twelve latrines had been installed. This was incontestably progress. Groaning vehicles were arriving one after another, discharging their human cargo, which immediately scattered over the vast courtyard at the foot of the buildings. Each Haitian received his "dry ration," an eight-ounce loaf of bread and a can of sardines — their sole nourishment. Once that operation was taken care of, they were moved ed into a large room on the first floor where the parcels were marked and deposited to be sent by van to the border. A few Kongos dropped off cardboard cartons, bundles of clothes, a few scant objects. They saw several sewing machines go by, then nothing more except the fighting cocks that some had bought and were now holding firmly under their arms, completely enveloped in newspaper except their heads. But for the most part, this business of baggage wasn't much of a problem.

"When I left home," a Kongo unknown to Brutus told him, "I had eight pairs of pants, two pairs of shoes, a small trunk, eight shirts, two t-shirts and ten dollars."

Brutus gazed at him, not really surprised. The guy had nothing left. He looked just like the rest of them, his situation seemed so bad, he was walking barefoot. He went on.

"The pants that I'm wearing were given to me by a friend. A guy from the batey who saw I couldn't go home like that and gave me these pants that you see!"

"When we got there," another Kongo said darkly, casting a disgusted look at his own rags, "we all realized that we were in hell. We couldn't buy anything. It's lucky that we're not dead."

"Yes, it's lucky."

---

*In August of 1980, 5,000 Kongos would be stranded at the time of their return for several days under the same conditions.

In the same building, it was announced that they were going to carry out the currency exchange operation, to give them dollars for pesos. Hands dug into pockets, knotted handkerchiefs, bags, hiding places, and emerged, clutching meager bills. A sigh of disillusionment rose from the line of near cripples.

"In order to go back with money," launched Brutus, "you'd have to have been lucky enough to win at the *bolita*, the lottery. But as far as cutting sugar cane, no one will find a cent to bring back. We don't even have the money necessary to eat every day."

"That's for sure, brother. Someone who was lucky in the lottery, or who found a little sideline...but cutting, you can't. *Ou pa kapab!*"

"What happens is that we think we're leaving for a country like the United States, and when we get there, we find ourselves with that."

About thirty faded bills suddenly appeared in the Kongo's hand. Thirty pesos was all. He was going to add something when, at a wink from his neighbor, he chose to be quiet and became absorbed in attentively observing a crack running in the corner of the ceiling.

Haitian inspectors were walking from group to group, surreptitiously trying to hear the conversations. One of them was slowly passing near them, feigning an absent look.

A brief altercation that broke out near the table where a Dominican bureaucrat was conducting the currency exchange attracted everyone's attention and rid them of the eavesdropper.

"It's entirely out of the question," they heard, while a Kongo violently protested.

"You have to change it for me! There's no reason not to!"

"Sorry, but it's against the agreement."

"The agreement...What agreement?"

"The agreement signed between the two governments."

The bureaucrat called for the aid of other Dominican officials and the Haitian inspectors who were in the vicinity.

"What's going on?" asked a well-dressed inspector.

The bureaucrat said nothing, just indicated the pile of bills placed before him with a brief gesture. A nice pile. An unbelievable pile. Silence. The inspector turned toward the Kongo who was waiting feverishly.

"What's that?"

"Well, it's my money."

"But how much is it?" demanded the inspector with irritation, squinting suspiciously.

"It's 1,448 pesos, sir."

"He claims that he won it in the lottery," blurted the cashier.

Then, to the Kongo: "We change pesos for dollars up to the sum of two hundred."

"But why two hundred?" blurted the Kongo, torn between anger and utter dejection.

"The CEA experts estimate that's what a bracero can save in six months."

"But I didn't earn it by cutting cane, I won it in the lottery!"

"Cane or lottery, two hundred is two hundred."

"But the contract doesn't forbid winning the lottery!"

A Haitian inspector quickly made the Kongo shut up.

"What proves you really won the lottery? That you didn't steal this money?"

"But I . . ."

"Your story is very fishy, my friend! What's your name?"

"My name is Ofaniel Ceslum."

"And where do you come from?"

"The Catarey ingenio in Piedra Blanca."

"Very fishy, your story."

Haitian and Dominican officials consulted briefly. This clause, of course, was nowhere in the contract. But it existed tacitly. "More than two hundred pesos!" growled a Haitian inspector, "we've never seen that!" How could Kongos be authorized to gather in six months the equivalent of his monthly salary? It was their universe gone haywire. "Let's go see the Ambassador," he proposed amidst the flurry, "he'll tell us what he thinks, what we should do with this individual." Thus they learned that the Ambassador himself was present in the vicinity.

Brutus watched with disgust, as the inspectors passed their miserable line without a glance. "And why aren't the braceros themselves allowed to defend their own interests?" he asked himself angrily. "To organize themselves?" He thought for a second; and it wasn't hard to find the answer.

The unionization and organization of the Haitian workers interests neither the Haitian dominant classes nor the Dominican dominant classes. As for Duvalier, it would be a catastrophe for him to see workers return to Haiti having acquired the experience of the class struggle.

The officials returned, Haitians and Dominicans conferring placidly. After the consultation with the Ambassador, Ofaniel Ceslum was refused the exchange of more than two hundred pesos in dollars. As for the rest, 1,248 pesos absolutely unusable in Haiti, let him figure it out. And let him consider himself lucky that an investigation wasn't launched as to the origin of all this very likely illicitly gained money.

Thus, a new and revealing light was shed upon the slave trade in Haitians. Officials on both sides brazenly admit that after six months of work, a bracero cannot have saved more than two hundred pesos. In fact, this is strictly forbidden him.

So what Brutus and his companions were wondering was the following: Objectively speaking, in these conditions, are we to be considered men or slaves?

But it was a completely theoretical debate since, in reality, it was not even relevant to their situation. With average earnings of 40 pesos a month for a period of about seven months, that is, total earnings of 280 pesos, it is entirely out of the question to put aside two hundred pesos.

It has been calculated that the seasonal worker returns to Haiti with an average of 40 pesos a person. Seven months of work for forty pesos (forty dollars)! A little more, however, than in years past. According to an investigation carried out by the Haitian State Department of Labor, 710 braceros from the "Central Romana," the "Ozama," the "Angelina," and the "Sante Fe" brought back with them an average sum of 32 dollars at the end of the 1957 zafra. The figures at the return of the 1967 zafra, for which 16,300 picadors left, indicated a financial flow of almost $500,000, or 30 dollars per immigrant.

Brutus and all the Kongos were within six pesos of being at the same point in July 1979.

"And the bonus?" inquired an innocent suddenly, as he was about to pass the official. "They haven't given us the bonus yet!"

A brief instant of suspended animation held the line. What was this business about a bonus? Most of them had never even heard about it. Nevertheless, the Kongo was insisting, and after the first moment of surprise, the officials seemed to know what it was all about. The State Sugar Council agrees to pay the amount of the annual bonus provided for by the Dominican Republic's Work Code at the time of the payment of the last two week's wages . . .

"You'll get it in Haiti," an uppity official snapped curtly. "Come on, keep it moving!"

The cane harvest generally begins around November and ends in June or July, sometimes in August or September, but the norm is November to July. The bonus that the braceros are entitled to is drawn up and distributed after the harvest in December. The 14,000 Kongos are long gone. Where does the bonus go? It appears officially in the sugar industry's accounts. That being the case, two explanations are possible. Either they don't pay it and this sum is still deducted from their taxes, thus constituting a hidden profit, or they do pay it. But to whom?

A tumult of protest greeted the terse reply. The man paled and stubbornly repeated what they had already understood, which was why the uproar broke out in the first place.

"We told you, you'll get it in Haiti."

"In other words, never," the Kongos immediately translated.

"And the tax, the other tax, the one peso they take every two weeks that they're supposed to give us back at the end of the zafra! Where is all that?"

"Where is the money?" cried several Kongos, and the crowd surged in a swirl of dust and heat.

"It's been sent to the Haitian Ambassador in Santo Domingo, you'll get it in your country."

In other words, never, they had understood as well.

They were filing forward, they were parleying, they were protesting, thinking about it nonetheless, and muttering all the while as they moved.

During this time, in an unobtrusive corner, Ofaniel Ceslum was desperately negotiating the exchange of his 1,248 pesos with a Dominican official who, very discreetly, had come looking for him. He agreed to change them, but at fifty percent of their value, of course. Ceslum had no choice. With rage in his heart, he accepted.

Then, things began happening fast for all of them.

They were brought to Jimani by bus. When they arrived at the border, the *cédulas* handed in at their arrival were carefully verified. Those who were leaving had to be the same ones who came. The officials were comparing the photograph on the card with another one they had on file. An obvious means of preventing the illegal entry of a political opponent, an enemy of Duvalier.

Omnipresent, the army was keeping an eye on the area.

Then, they were made to walk, and in front of the police station at Malpasse, in the shadow of their first VSN, they awaited the vehicles that were to permanently repatriate them.

Between Wednesday the fourth and Saturday the seventh of July 1979, the first eight hundred cane cutters, bushy-haired, bearded, and unrecognizable, arrived in Léogane. Between the Kongo leaving full of hope seven months before and the one returning, a universe of desolation, misery and suffering had indelibly marked a profound difference.

There they were, bewildered, going round in circles, unable to separate. So they talked and talked, recounting as if to exorcize past and future. They could not stop talking. Slowly, the truth began to filter through.

"In March," one was saying, and his voice was distorted, "a Dominican machine-gunned eight Haitians. He wanted to avenge his wife who got her finger hurt during an argument with one of them. The bodies were taken to the San Pedro hospital in Macoris."

"I know something worse, myself," said another, wiping away the sweat that pearled on his forehead. "In March also, in the Byucal Consuel batey, twenty-two Haitians died from poisoned water from a well where a stone-dead dog was floating."

"Twenty-two Haitians?"

"That's right, twenty-two."

"No, twenty-three, with the dog!" corrected someone darkly.

"Yeah, right, like dogs!"

And somewhere deep down, they found the strength to smile.

"Like dogs," 37-year-old Durogène Xavier repeated slowly. He was moving from one group to another, unable to make up his mind whether to go home with empty pockets. His ravaged features still carried the mark of eighteen entire days of existing on nothing but a little cane with salt and lemon added. A Kongo jostled him. "Anybody heard anything about Ferrer Georges?" he cried at regular intervals as he combed the survivors. "Has anybody . . ." No one answered. "After an argument with a Dominican majordomo, Ferrer was deported to an unknown area in June," he continued. "When he left, his bags stayed locked up in the Moral batey." Then, taking up his cry once again: "Anybody have any news of Ferrer Georges?" And no one answered.

"I had eight pairs of pants and two pairs of shoes," Innocent Compère was stubbornly repeating amidst the cries. "Eight pairs of pants and two pairs of shoes! Look at me now!" And you could see very well that he had nothing left. Nor was anything left to Jean-Louis Josaphat but his still terribly painful scar.

"I spent two weeks with a deep gash in my arm," he said. "No one took care of me."

"In Dominicanie, no one ever takes care of you."

"The majordomo said that I was lazy, that I didn't deserve any care."

"He said that . . . It doesn't surprise me. My friend Gerson was tortured by a huge abcess on his lower belly for three months. Three months. It was only in April that a generous Dominican, not an official, took him to the hospital."

"Yes, there were some good Dominicans, but not where I was."

"In the capital there's some good ones."

"But in the batey, the Dominicans don't give us any consideration."

"Anyone heard anything about Ferrer Georges?" continued the

dogged Kongo's monotone in the distance. "Has anybody..."

"Many aren't coming back," observed a robust Kongo, a small suitcase in hand. "Alexis, for example, a young one who was arrested the same week we were supposed to come back, and whom we haven't seen since. Alexis Jean from the Cape. Seen no more. Put in prison 26 June 1979. He was arrested by the bosses then, I don't know why."

"And Lyvio Massena," said a voice, "and Victor Noure, arrested in a mango grove! They were so hungry they could no longer resist!"

On each side of the entrance to the police station two cannon stocks imperturbably stood guard. In the courtyard, you could see a magnificent mango tree whose lower trunk had been painted white. A handsome colonel, very handsome and very well-dressed, was standing framed in the doorway, staring scornfully at the motley crew parked there, a bedraggled insult to his handsome, well-dressed colonel spiffiness. He approached.

A Kongo was making conversation. His shoes were ripped old sandals that a Dominican had thrown out and he had retrieved. He didn't want to come back barefoot. His pants were ripped in back, and so was his shirt.

"When we arrived," the ragged man was saying, "there were a thousand of us. They separated us in three groups. Three hundred went one way and three hundred another. The batey where I went was bigger. Four hundred of us went there. Well, when it was time to go home, we were barely two hundred fifty! Of the rest, some had left, others were in prison or resold to the colonos,* others disappeared, who knew how...Only two hundred fifty of us left!"

Those who were listening to him in silence drew aside brusquely, and the handsome colonel planted himself facing him and observed him a moment in silence. What filth!

"But, my friend, where were you? In prison?"

Taken by surprise, he didn't know what to reply. The colonel assessed them one after another, and spat with disgust.

"How did you get yourself in this state?"

Someone stepped forward to answer. He didn't have a chance to.

"In my opinion, you are all lazy loafers!" Then, brutally: "Go on, get a move on! If you stay there I'll have you arrested!"

Brutus felt himself slowly suffused with a white rage. He got hold of himself. So, they'd come full circle. He slowly spun around. All these Kongos were telling their stories, they were only eight hundred, what an abyss of misfortune one would discover if fifteen thou-

*Colonos: The private sugar companies. — Trans.

sand could speak!

And there, in front of them, this all-powerful colonel was acting disgusted!

"It's for them that we suffered," thought he, filled with anger. "They profitted from our terrible poverty."

He would have liked to know just how much.

One million two hundred fifty thousand dollars, of which only a small amount, surely no more than $100,000, is utilized for the hiring operations; two dollars per employee paid to the Haitian Embassy as an immigration tax, a total of $30,000; the bimonthly deduction of one dollar taken from the Kongos' wages, or $210,000 for seven months; $32,000 a month, or $224,000 for the season allotted to pay the supervisors and inspectors whose number does not reach the figure announced — it's true you have to pay the Macoutes.

At the very least, one million five hundred thousand dollars of clear profit, which appears nowhere in the Haitian State's accounts.

In exchange for so much human misery . . .

A Kongo suddenly grabbed Brutus's arm. He was laughing and crying at the same time.

"I will never leave again," he declared with vehemence. "I'm happy to be back." His hand was trembling with retrospective fear. "I was afraid of getting sick, but there was no choice. I was afraid of never coming back to Haiti. I've come back. God was with me, that's why. But now, never again."

He fell silent. He gazed at Brutus without really seeing him, and thought with sudden dread of all the terrible poverty that was awaiting him in Haiti, and after having half closed his eyes, uttered the terrible words which already announced the next zafra. "Never again." But when you are starving to death, if your memory is weak, you will go back anyway.

"We'll have to be done with these Duvaliers," thought Brutus in a flash.

With a determined step, he cut through the crowd and headed for Port-au-Prince.

In witness whereof, the Plenipotentiaries have signed the present contract in two copies, one in French and the other in Spanish, the two texts having the same juridical value.
In Port-au-Prince, Haiti, 14 October 1978

For the Haitian Government   For the State Sugar Council

Achille Salvant,   *Dr. Milton Ray Guevara,*
Secretary of Social Affairs   *Secretary of State*

François Guillaume,   *Rafael Adrano Valdez*
Haitian Ambassador for   *Hilario,*
the Dominican Republic   *Secretary of State of the*
                            Dominican Armed Forces

                            Pedro Purcell Pena,
                            Secretary of State

                            Porfirio Brito,
                            Assistant Director of the CEA

                            Porfirio Basora Puello,
                            Executive Director of the
                            CEA

PART TWO:

**WHEN IT'S ALL OVER,
THERE'S STILL MORE...**

The consumer is probably unaware
of the role played by Gulf &
Western in helping build him
a simpler, more secure, and more
satisfying life.
(*G&W Annual Report,* 1972)

November 1979. Several months had thus gone by. A small red motorbike was laboring through the sprawling expanse of burgeoning cane. From the big factory of the La Romana ingenio, as far as the outskirts of El Seibo to the distant horizons of San Rafael de Yuma, the Gulf & Western Empire undulated for as far as the eye could see: 308,875 acres of North American cane, 18,000 permanently settled families in 125 bateys, 15,000 agricultural workers riveted to sugar, glued to sugar, stuck in sugar, of which 90% are Haitian. On the motorbike, a man. He'd already stopped in several bateys, each time heading for the shack of one, two, or sometimes three Dominican *compañeros*. Each time they had exchanged a fraternal *abrazo*. He'd drunk a glass of water to wash down the dust from the road (to wash down the cane stuck in his throat, he liked to say), joking with the women, running a vigorous hand through the children's bushy hair, taking the newest born in his arms — "*que bonito*," said he, and the baby laughed — then talked gravely with the man about the union's problems. They exchanged news, spoke in lowered tones about the struggle and about the hard times, and you could hear the woman sighing. Next, he took a few copies of the union paper out of his bag. "And what's new with Mario? Vicente, *como esta*? Ah! The son of a bitch!" He insisted again on a fundamental point — he repeated "fundamental," he really liked that word fundamental — of the action to come. Then he put on his cap, slung his bag across his shoulder, mounted his motorbike. "Talk about it with the *compañeros*, we'll bring it up at the next meeting!" Once again he took the hard dusty road, veering off on a faint trail along the railroad, then picking it up again a little further, sometimes on one side and sometimes on another. He had to keep a good grip on the handlebars.

Barefoot, or wearing shabby plastic sandals, their bodies covered in rags, the Haitians were coming out of the cane, moving slowly, blinking eyes assailed by the rediscovered light, then, with a still brisk step, starting up the few miles separating them from the batey. He overtook them, unintentionally spewing his dust in their faces as they silently returned from clearing the plantations, an empty *cambumbo* of water under the arm.

Four o'clock. He slowed down as he entered the last batey on his route. He smiled bitterly. The camp hardly resembled Higüeral, the model batey six miles from the city of La Romana, the one that Gulf has the visitors admire, explaining that if the Company doesn't raise the workers' wages, it's because it offers them the advantages of nature, lodgings, food, medicine, insurance, and education. But they forget to mention that Higüeral is an experimental finca, destined for raising livestock, and that the children bused to school every' day are the sons of the Company employees who live there, and that there are no cane cutters in the little village. No, it didn't look like one. Nor did it recall the few bateys that one can make out along the main road, rebuilt in conglomerate board, carefully painted (on the outside) and maintained in order to give credibility to the "Social Development" program, regularly praised to the skies in slick brochures destined for the press and propaganda. This batey didn't resemble that either. It was incontestably the carbon copy of dozens of human sewers: Magdalena, Palo-Blanco, Cuya, Bejucal, Campina, Lima, and many others, a jumble of wooden tumbledowns, sordid slums, Kongos' barracones, carefully hidden, cautiously forbidden, well off the beaten track. The man smiled bitterly. In their infamy, the Gulf bateys still proved to be a little less infamous than those of the CEA.

He drove a few hundred yards at low speed, up to the shack of the companion that he had come to visit. He didn't find him. He plunged into the batey on foot. Little shacks built of pale green boards mounted on low pilings were scattered in the most perfect anarchy over the vast expanse of land dotted with scraggy weeds and briars, and broken up here and there by a few limp-looking palm trees. Near the water faucet in this part of the camp, a woman was washing, observed by the absent-minded eye of an old woman whose emaciated cheeks hollowed to the point of no longer existing as she drew on her pipe with rapid little puffs.

He went a bit further, passing a Haitian with white hair sitting in front of a shack who seemed not to notice him at all. At the intersection of two paths, a group of Haitians was discussing the situation. Recognizing Maximin, Ramon smiled. A hell of a viejo! The latter noticed him almost simultaneously, raising his arm with a friendly, if weary, smile.

"*Salud, Ramon! Qué hay de nuevo?*"

"*A la lucha, siempre!* Still fighting!"

"Ah, yes, Ramon, as usual."

"*Como no, hombre! Luchando.* Here's to the struggle. And you?"

A bright gleam in the almost vacant eyes.

"Nothing new, except that it's even worse. We're still starving to death."

Maximin's three companions nodded sadly. "We're starving to death," they repeated in a broken voice. They fell silent. Then one spoke again. "We're starving to death."

The cane cutting had stopped three months before. Since then, they were once again experiencing a time of inexpressible anguish. Their wages no longer assured, each one had to go in quest of a means of survival.

Between the two zafras, the viejos undertake secondary tasks. The sowing is still done by hand, and the introduction of herbicides has not yet made the exhausting and primitive work of cleaning the cane fields obsolete.

"You have to get yourself organized," said Ramon. Mechanically, he half raised his clenched right fist. "You have to organize."

He stared at them one after another. Maximin. Two other viejos, one of whom was wearing a shirt so unbelievably torn that it was difficult to still consider it a shirt. Another Haitian, younger, skin and bones, whom he'd never seen in the batey, but there were many he'd never seen.

"You have to get yourselves organized," he began again. "Take a united stand with your Dominican fellow workers against this fucking company that's breaking our back."

It was time to begin some serious organizing work with these immigrant workers. The Haitian sectors of the bateys, he mused, constituted a key element of the political and trade union organization of the entire Dominican workers' movement.

"It's been a long time since you've come here," said Maximin briefly.

"I did come," said Ramon, a little overcome by the immensity of the task, which he knew, wishing that the guys themselves would carry the ball. "I came several times, but you were in the cane."

"We don't see you any more, huh, you're abandoning us!"

And Maximin laughed. He didn't really think it.

"You were in the plantations, I'm telling you."

"Fucking plantations," spat a viejo, and Ramon thought he was going to add something, but he said no more.

"And what's the word in the plantations?" he asked after a moment, seeing that nothing was forthcoming.

"The word is that they are going to devour us."

"They paid us the bonus last week," said Maximin. Then, after a look from Ramon: "The 29th of October they paid us the bonus."

"So! You're rich now," joked Ramon, but behind his heavy glasses, his eyes flashed without illusions.

A chorus of guffaws was his reply. That said all there really was to say.

"I've seen Haitians cry," resumed Maximin. "For eight months of work, we got bonuses worth between 8 and 10 pesos 18 centavos!"

"The sons of bitches," Ramon swore under his breath.

The viejo with the shredded shirt intervened in a very calm, very measured voice, without raising his tone, but without succeeding in dissimulating his bitterness either.

"That makes nineteen years that I've been paying one peso a month to the Central Romana United Union. They gave me seven pesos for a bonus. And I don't even get any help from them to speak up about a case like that!"

"It's a scab union," said Ramon tersely, "you know that very well."

"Nothing from the Company, nothing from the union."

"You know what I told you. Maximin knows it. The workers' union is the CGT."

The other one shrugged. "What good is it? The union does nothing."

Ramon was going to reply, but kept quiet. Maximin grabbed his arm, pointed to a viejo who was approaching them with a slow, slow step.

"There's Santana. Take a good look at him. He's the strongest among us, the bravest, the toughest. He works all day long. He doesn't even earn a peso a day."

The new arrival had stopped, was listening to the end of the tirade. Sighing, he contemplated the dusty ground.

"Tell him, Santana!"

He looked up, hesitated, staring at Ramon with a certain wariness.

"You can talk, he's a friend. He's from the CGT."

"The CGT," repeated the viejo slowly. "That's the union that..."

"*Exacto*," said Ramon. "The worker's union."

"Tell him," insisted Maximin. "how much do you make?"

"When I work all day," he said, "from dawn in the morning until twilight in the evening, without stopping, I don't even earn a peso."

"He weeds the cane," clarified Maximin. "He's the strongest among us. Not even one peso!"

"You can't," said the other.

"Each *tarea* cultivated pays 83 centavos," Maximin went on. "That means that the worker who weeds the cane is paid less than 83 centavos for twelve hours, because it's impossible to work such a surface area in this time span."

"You can't," repeated Santana. "Even all day, you can't."

"The viejos who weed the cane are in bad shape," said one of the Haitians, silent up until now. "They are given a little rice, a little oil. We never eat meat. We have no money. We are destitute. It's a miserable existence."

"In bad shape," agreed Maximin. He raised his eyes heavenward. "But in better shape than those who have no work at all. In La Higuera there are five old-timers who are literally starving to death. Someone told us. They are actually dying. And you see that everywhere."

Ramon was listening in silence. He knew the situation. From 1976 until 1979, the ton was paid 1 peso 42. But once the deductions are taken out—8 centavos a ton for social security, one peso a month for the scab union, the life insurance, 8 more pesos a month for the *cedula* (identity card), or government license to cut cane*—the actual pay works out to 1 peso 27 centavos. These deductions reduce the pay to two pesos a day during the zafra. Twenty-four pesos every two weeks? Not even. An investigative team from The National Council of Churches states in July of 1979 that the majority of Gulf and Western cane cutters received between 30 and 50 pesos monthly. Less than half the wage cited by the multinational in its official 1978 report on the Dominican Republic.

Ramon sighed. That wasn't even the worst of it, because ten thousand workers remain unemployed during the off-season—the awful time of inexpressible anguish. It was that time now.

"You've got to get yourselves organized," said Ramon. "You're not going to spend your whole life starving to death! You have to fight for the enforcement of the law. It's a minimum and it's a right."

"The law?"

"Law #45 of 25 May 1979," said Ramon, who knew it by heart. "The wages of an agricultural worker cannot be less than 3 pesos 50

---

*Plus, for the Kongos, immigration costs of 60 pesos for six months, or 40 "cheles" a day, paid to the Haitian and Dominican governments while Gulf & Western claims not to import manpower nor to employ Kongos, which is of course completely false.

for an eight hour day."

"That's a law?"

"Yes, that's the law. And it applies to everyone, for Gulf as well as for the CEA, for the Dominican workers as well as the Haitians."

"Here there is really bad repression," said the man with the ragged shirt.

"There's repression everywhere," retorted Ramon. "It's to make you keep your heads down. And you keep them down! You have to fight!"

"You don't fight against those people... They are too strong."

Ramon suppressed an impatient gesture, bent over brusquely, pulled his pants leg up to his knee, revealing a puffy scar embedded in the flesh of his calf.

"Take a look! The 'Yankees' shot me with a *balazo* during the Revolution in '65. But we fought. The People of Santo Domingo held off 35,000 Marines!"

"The American Marines?" asked the Haitian, whom Ramon had never before noticed.

"Yes, the Yankee imperialism."

"What were they doing here?"

Ramon grimaced, laughed briefly — what were they doing here — and the entire history of the Dominican People flashed through his head.

"On many occasions, the Yankees had to resort to military intervention in our country in order to protect their interests by force and to prevent the self-determination of our People. The last time they landed was in '65."

He ran his finger slowly over the cruelly swollen skin of the old injury, and felt the painful weight of all the oppression in his very flesh.

The assassination of Trujillo in 1961 officially marked the end of the dictatorship. It became difficult for the United States to continue to openly or covertly support the Trujillo clan trying to hang on to power. The December 1962 elections, supervised by the Organization of American States (OAS), were, in the opinion of domestic and foreign observers, the most free and the most democratic ever known since the beginning of the century in the Dominican Republic. Juan Bosch of the Dominican Revolutionary Party (PRD) — the party that he founded in exile in Havana in 1943 — a partisan of democracy imbued with the precepts of liberalism, anti-communism, and anti-Castroism, was elected to the highest office. He barely had the time to speak about the Constitution and social reforms. That was already too much. Seven months after the elections, in September '63, Bosch was overturned by a coup d'etat. The very next day, one of the figureheads of the sedition, Wessin y Wessin, proclaimed himself General.

In 1965, sickened by the too-visible corruption of the high-ranking Army officers and by their brazen collusion with the oligarchy, a core of young colonels rose up and distributed arms to the People.

Four days of popular insurrection in the capital. The entire city was armed. The big stronghold of the forces of repression fell. The people demanded the reinstatement of the Constitution.* On 28 April, Wessin y Wessin's tanks were repulsed, while a young black, Francisco Peña Gomez, President of the Dominican Revolutionary Party's Youth Movement, drew attention through his pugnacity and drive.

The loss of control of the military situation by the most conservative faction of the army generated the military occupation of the country that was launched by Johnson on 28 April 1965 — the sole objective of which was to protect the lives of American nationals, it goes without saying. All the Latin American dictatorships supported the invasion. The 82nd Airborne Division's parachutists landed in rapid succession in the runways of the San Isidro base — Wessin y Wessin's headquarters, situated nine miles from Santo Domingo. Over a period of five days, starting on 29 April, there were 1,539 landings at San Isidro, the biggest airlift in the world since the Berlin blockade.

After the foreign intervention, the "Constitutionalists," an armed movement headed by Colonel Caamaño Deño, withdrew, holing up in the capital's lower-town. The "Zone" set up its own government, with the leftist militants naturally playing an important role. The combatants were soon short of food supplies, and were no longer able to communicate with the exterior.

Nevertheless, cloistered in the hideout, faced with 35,000 American soldiers — more than were in Vietnam at the time — plus Wessin y Wessin's crack troops, the heroic People's resistance lasted six months.

Then the Americans entered the zone. A provisional government, named the "Government of National Reconciliation," was set up. In fact, after organizing new "elections," the Americans handed over the power to Balaguer, a former Trujillo lieutenant, and let him take care of unleashing a terrible repression, a veritable rebel hunt, during which all the organizations, unions and parties were

---

*An informative source concerning this episode in Dominican history is *La Revolution de Saint-Domingue*, by Marcel Niedergang (Editions Plon and "Circle Noveau du livre d'Histoire").

decimated. The Trujillo legacy returned to the few hundred families who constitute the core of the oligarchy, and all's well that ends well. The American nationals were protected.

Ramon was watching them; they were there and weren't saying anything, full of good will, even admiration, perhaps, yet overcome with incredulity. Ramon lost himself in a train of thought brought on by their lukewarm reaction. The great majority of workers in our country are not organized. This is basically due to the employers' repression and the right accorded them by capitalist law, the law of the employers, to fire any worker without having to justify the cause. The fact that there exists a large mass of unemployed workers ready to sell their labor power at any price is, of course, much to their advantage. Not to mention the specific problem posed by the Haitian cane cutters in the bateys. It is almost impossible to get in touch with the Kongos working for the CEA. They come for six months, leave immediately thereafter, are replaced by others the following year, don't speak the language, and in any case, live completely terrorized by all the repression constantly beating them down. With Gulf, and with the viejos, the situation is a little different. The population, installed in camps, is more stable. It is possible to tackle the task of organization.

Ramon broke off his reflection. Santana was addressing him, his voice full of fatalism.

"Struggle, sure!" the viejo was saying, "but we are Haitian!"

"So what!" replied Ramon sharply...

Seventy percent of the Haitian workers in the Romana Central living permanently in company bateys possess a temporary residency permit which is renewed every year for the zafra. This regular renewal, and its counterpart — the threat of nonrenewal — keep them literally tied hand and foot, from season to season, from year to year.

"So what? So that means that we are Haitians and we have no rights. The minute we lift up our heads, they make us lower them."

"For cutting the cane, you are Dominican," said Ramon, thinking aloud, "but when you complain, you are Haitian again!"

"That's exactly it," agreed Santana.

"People have been living here for generations," said Maximin, "but because of widespread racial segregation they are refused legalization of their status."

"We have to put an end to that," said Ramon. "They owe you some respect."

"Hah! Respect!" laughed Santana, weakly. "Respect for Haitians!" It was certainly the first time he'd heard that.

"Yes, respect. Without Haitians, there is no cane; without cane, no sugar; and without sugar, no currency! You are the main support of the Dominican economy."

Maximin slowly nodded in agreement. He'd been working in this country for twenty-three years.

"Without us," he began bitterly, "the administration, the Company bureaucrats, the employees, all the fancy, well-dressed directors couldn't live. We have the same right as they do. We have the right to eat, to clothe ourselves, to support our families."

Ramon half turned toward the others.

"Do you hear what he said? He's right. You have the right, and if you have the right, you have to struggle to get this right respected."

"Struggle," snorted one of the viejos, with an ill-tempered gesture…"Struggle how? The Dominicans repress us, humiliate us, walk all over us!"

"Not the Dominicans," countered Ramon, stung to his very depths. "The Dominican state! The Dominican *terratenientes!*"

The man grunted, hardly convinced. The Dominicans walked all over them, and that was all there was to it. Ramon interrupted him with irritation.

"Don't say the Dominicans! I'm Dominican, and I'm here, with you, today, and to prepare for tomorrow. For the CGT, you are all, Dominican and Haitian, above all, workers."

"And what do you do there in your CGT? Make nice speeches? Talk about politics?"

"We are getting ourselves organized and we've already worked out a specific project for a collective agreement for the workers in the factory."

"The factory workers…That's still Dominicans!"

"Son of a…" Ramon forced himself to stay calm and burst out laughing. Then, more seriously, emphasizing each word, he took up a few fundamental notions again. "The CGT is not a scab union reserved for one race or nationality, but a class union; see, friends, this is fundamental, a class union."

The young Haitian who had, without taking part, been following the conversation with a great deal of attention, sometimes with difficulty due to the rapidity of the exchange—all these old Haitians spoke Spanish like real Dominicans—emerged from his silence and asked earnestly what a class union was. In his country, they didn't talk about this sort of thing. Ramon explained clearly to him. "In the Dominican Republic, society is divided into classes." "Yes, but…" "Wait, I'm explaining it! In other words, there are groups of people who control the means of production, the factories, the enterprises, the plantation services, and who are called capitalists. The bosses, if you prefer. While the others'—the majority's—only wealth is the strength of their backs, which they sell in exchange for wages. So, while the Dominicans or foreign owners make themselves the masters of our country's wealth, and our sweat, we who produce this wealth live a little poorer each day. And that is what we are starting to fight against."

Ramon broke off. The young kid gestured that he'd understood. He was thinking intensely, brows knit.

"I can tell you one thing... This business about classes, it's the same story in Haiti!"

Ramon burst out laughing. Discovery! He got serious again. Twenty-two years of dictatorship leaves its mark, but the reflexes come back fast, and, one day, these guys would fight in Haiti too.

"*Exacto*," he said. "Duvalier and Guzman, it's the same system; Haitian and Dominican workers, the same combat."

"What I really don't understand," suddenly said Maximin, whose mind was elsewhere, "is that the Dominicans don't cut cane, but agree to do other work, such as crushing stone—I've seen them—which is a really tough, dangerous job, where they get hurt a lot, and which is much harder than cane."

Ramon digested all this, and took his time answering.

"The Dominican is here with his whole family. It's rare, as you know, that the day worker's wages reach two pesos" (a pained murmur—oh yes, they knew). "All these Dominicans know," continued Ramon, "is that, with two pesos, it's impossible to make ends meet and to feed a family. They refuse this work."

"But we, too, are here with our families!"guffawed one of the viejos.

"We have no choice," put in Maximin. "Here, we don't have the papers to do anything else. In Haiti, it's wretched poverty and it's the Duvaliers."

A hubbub rose, going further than the limits of the little group. "First of all, if the Dominicans respected us..."

"We can't expect the Dominicans to respect us," said the young guy, "when Jean-Claude himself doesn't respect us!"

"Quit making me sick with 'the Dominicans,'" sighed Ramon, who was hurt at the mention of this word each time he heard it pronounced in this tone. (But in spite of his good will, his great honesty, he'd never live what they had lived.) "The ones that exploit you are Jean-Claude, Guzman, and Gulf! Gulf! Besides, this Company isn't even Dominican, it's American. Gulf, shit! You've already heard of Gulf." (And in his own way, he was right anyway.)

Since the Cuban Revolution, the biggest North American cane-cultivating and sugar-producing enterprise, the South Puerto Rico Sugar Company, has produced two thirds of its sugar in the Dominican Republic, in the Central Romana Inc. plantations. On 12 July 1967, Gulf & Western,* a fast expanding American conglomerate, and the South Puerto Rico Sugar Co. merged. Central Romana Inc., the most productive sugar maker in the Dominican Republic, with 276,218 acres of land, passed into the hands of Gulf & Western. For the record, the operation took place a year after this same Gulf bought Paramount's *Love Story*, filmed in '71 for 2.5 million dollars, which yielded a profit of roughly 80 million dollars. At the end of '73 and the beginning of '74, the second part of *The Godfather* would be filmed in the streets of Santo Domingo, which resembles Havana, where the scene is supposed to take place.

At the time of the merger, the assets of the South Puerto Rico Sugar Company were overevaluated in order to make things difficult for a Dominican government which might one day want to nationalize the installations of the enterprise. Many Cubans who left their country when Castro arrived joined the new staff, thanks to their know-how in this field of production and their absolute political reliability. As an initial condition for the increase of the production and productivity, they considered it indispensable that the workers' movement at La Romana be disrupted. In the wake of the repression launched against the progressive sectors since 1966, the fighting *Sindicato Unido de la Romana* was dismantled. It was replaced by the *Sindicato Libre de Trabajadores del Central Romana*, completely subject to the multinational. The possibility of free unions disappeared. The Company wouldn't tolerate any union not directly dependent upon itself. The local authorities obeyed orders.

The octopus spread its tentacles. In 1967, Gulf & Western had begun its operations with an investment of 61 million dollars. By the end of '78, its investments in the Dominican Republic surpassed 300 million dollars.

On 9 March 1969, a thirty-year contract was signed between the Dominican State and Gulf, in order to install and administrate a free trade zone in the Romana Central. Since then, the Company spread to the following sectors: construction, through the *Banque Hypothécaire de la Constuction;* finance, through the *Corporación Financiera Asociada;* tourism, through *Dominicus American*

*Part of the information which follows has been taken from *La Gulf and Western en Republica Dominicana* (Editora de la Universidad Autonoma de Santo Domingo — Republica Dominicana).

Development, *Costasur Dominicana* and *Corporación de Hoteles S.A.*; manufacturing industry, within the enclave of the Romana free trade zone where, among others, were established the *Tanna Dominicana*, *Textiles Internationales, Inc.*, *Consolidated Cigar*, *Delta Brush Manufacturing Co.*, *Consolidated Co.*, etc., etc. . . . Gulf owns or has major interests in: *Fertilizantes Santo-Domingo* (fertilizer), *Matadero Industrial del Este* (slaughter houses), *Fabrica de Ron Siboney* (rum), *Expresos Dominicanos* (buses), *Banco de los Trabajadores* (bank), *Cementos Nacionales* and *Cemento Haina* (cement); in agriculture, Gulf exports through *Farmer Producted*, etc. . . .

Through Gulf and Western's La Romana interests, the Dominican Republic is second only to the United States in the world production of "furfural," and first in exportation. Furfural is the oil obtained from the *bagasse*, the cane residue. Used during the fifties in the manufacture of nylon, it has since become valuable as a selective solvent and as an intermediary product in chemistry, utilized in the space industry among others. But the Dominican Republic's position — as the biggest exporter worldwide — doesn't benefit the country a whole lot. The contract signed on 31 October 1953 between the Central Romana Corporation and the Dominican government, and renewed in 1973 for twenty years, exempts the Company from all taxes, on profit or duties, past, present and future, including on the importation of machinery, all types of equipment, vehicles and replacement parts, materials, accessories, gadgets, oil and other combustibles, etc. . . . according to the established formula.

Balaguer's government has never refused anything to the multinational. The complicity between Gulf and the Dominican government is so brazen that in January 1974 the American Ambassador himself, Robert A. Hurwicht, had to send a communication to the local administrator of the Company, Téobaldo Rosell, disapproving of his participation in political meetings in favor of the reelection of Doctor Balaguer. Smokescreen. The close ties of the economic sectors of the South Puerto Rico Sugar Company with President Johnson, who ordered the landing of the Marines in 1965, under the pretext of crushing a Communist insurrection in a country where he and his protégés possessed important interests, is well known. George A. Smathers, ex-governor of Florida, member of the Board of Directors of Gulf & Western, maintained close relations with the Du Pont interests, the principal buyers of the furfural produced by the Romana Central, and close personal ties with the ex-presidents Johnson, until his death, and Nixon. He obtained his appointment as a member of the Board of Directors of Gulf & Western in acknowledgement of the pressure he exerted on President Johnson to decide rapidly on the 28

April 1965 military intervention. Smathers's brother is married to the daughter of Charles S. Lowry, ex-Secretary of the Board of Directors of . . . South Puerto Rico Sugar Co. The world is certainly very small. And if the American nationals to protect didn't exist, it would be necessary to invent them very quickly.

The Gulf & Western Consortium comprises more than one hundred industrial installations in the United States and in ten foreign countries, in branches as diverse as the production of automobile parts, military instruments and materials, the manufacture of paper, cigars, etc., etc. . . . It owns, among others, 49 percent of the "Richards Group," which devotes itself to "urban development projects" in the United States and Puerto Rico, where it is associated with International Telephone and Telegraph (ITT), the philanthropic enterprise well known to Pinochet and to his friends in Chile. The conglomerate increased its assets from 5 million dollars in 1958 to . . . 3,300 million dollars in 1978.

Gulf & Western presently owes 38 million dollars to the Dominican State. This debt was acquired by the multinational at the time of transactions in futures on the sugar market, which took place in 1975 with the Dominican sugar production. The commercial operation brought in approximately $64,535,226 to Gulf, of which 38 million should, according to the past agreement, have gone to the Dominican State. Gulf has turned a deaf ear to the repeated demands of the social-democratic government in power in Santo Domingo since 1978.* At the same time, the multinational's propaganda arm has made a lot of noise about the Company's social welfare accomplishments and made a lot of promises. But always for the future.†

Questioned about the Company's investments in the construction of a center promoting tourism in New York, an artists' village in Alto de Chavon, near La Romana, and a baseball stadium in the Dominican Republic, Charles Bludhorn, President of the multinational, became very angry.

"Maybe you don't like baseball! As for us, we think it is preferable to see the people playing baseball than playing with guns!"

Over the period of 1970-1976, Gulf & Western realized a profit of 253 million dollars on its sugar operations alone — the toil of the

---

*It would be necessary to wait until September 1980 for Gulf & Western to agree to pay the 38 million dollars to the Santo Domingo government over seven years.

†The president of G&W announced on 30 April 1980 that the enterprise would invest 100 million dollars over the next 10 years to ameliorate and raise the living conditions for the Romana Central workers.

Dominican laborers, the viejos, and the Haitian Kongos. This profit on the sugar produced in the Dominican Republic is equivalent to four times the 62 million dollars borrowed for the purchase of the *Central Romana*.

In the bateys...

Ramon kept repeating to them that they had to fight, that they had to organize, and they themselves knew it was true, but they had been crushed too long. They were inert, run aground in the combat zone of the bateys like the *bagasse*, the refuse which lies inert after the sweet sugar is wrung from the cane and then flung away — contemptible remains. They walked a few steps in silence. Ramon thrust both hands in his pockets, and two Haitians joined them without saying a word, a youth with a determined air, and another, quite old, dressed in a shirt made of holes surrounded by shreds of fabric. Ramon mechanically consulted his watch.

"It's five o'clock," he stated. "Have you eaten today?"

A silence, punctuated by embarrassed laughs, was his reply, as if they were ashamed, and all shook their heads no. They had not.

"He's the strongest," said Maximin once again, indicating Santana, "and he doesn't earn one peso a day. Can you feed a family?"

Ramon shuddered. In 1978 it was calculated that the minimum monthly wages — minimum, that is, for simple survival — of a worker with a family of six would have to be at least 205 pesos, 120 pesos of which would go solely for the cost of their meager diet. They were earning 50, and not even all year long.

They stopped in front of a shack made of boards. A woman was hanging a few rags on a string strung between two stakes. "Isabela!" shouted Ramon, leaving the road and coming closer. She looked up and, recognizing him, smiled. He pressed her in his arms. "Ah, Isabela," he said laughing, "you get more and more beautiful." "That's right, Ramon," she replied, laughing also, "and you, more and more of a fool!"

The ritual over, they could go on to more serious things. "How's it going, Isabela?" A shrug. "And the children?" A veiled look in eyes that no longer had the strength to shine.

"They are hungry."

"Yes, they must be hungry," sighed Ramon.

He saw two kids in the dust a little way off. "There are so many of them," said Isabela, thinking of the whole tribe in the camp. "Why do you all make so many?" asked Ramon, smiling. "When it's night in the batey," sighed Maximin, "what else do you want us to do? No radio, no television, no diversions, no money, no books, no newspapers, no horizons. . ." He indicated the woman with his chin. "It's the only sport we have here!"

She shrugged, irritated. Her own man, the one who regularly moved between her legs, she couldn't ask anything of him. He didn't have anything. What could she have hoped for? Nothing. Nothing but one or two more kids to get through life, the long life of Haitians in the bateys. An entire existence: overcrowding, the fallout of wretched poverty, up to eight children in a family, broken or extended families, children of the same father, same mother, brothers by the same father, or by the same mother, or even distant "brothers" taken in after tragedy of death.

"You send them to school?" asked Ramon.

Generally there is a class in the Gulf bateys to teach the children to read and write. There are practically none in those of the CEA. The result is hardly different. Isabela gestured very vaguely in the warm, humid air.

"They spend more time cutting cane than studying."

"Cutting cane," said Ramon, who knew.

"Yes, cutting."

"How old are they now anyway?" inquired the Dominican.

"The two big ones are eleven and thirteen."

"And how much do they pay them when they cut?"

Isabela let out a strange noise. It wasn't a laugh, because it was without joy. "You won't believe it." "Tell me anyway; in this country, nothing more could surprise me." "You won't believe." "Tell."

"They cut every morning, all morning. The pesador pays them directly two and a half pesos". . . a silence. . . "every two weeks!"

The men murmured, their heads bobbing, not wanting to believe it, and believing it nonetheless. Any means to bring in ready cash, be it twenty cents, must be utilized. It wasn't a matter of choice, but of implacable necessity. If you don't want the children to die, it is necessary — as soon as they have enough strength to hold a machete — that they start working.

"The children are hungry." Isabela's voice got hoarser, her features sadder, madonna of the bateys. "And we, we have nothing to give them."

Ramon saw the figures of the two children running in the distance. All the viejos' kids were wasting away, gnawed by under-nourishment. Ramon couldn't manage to get used to this idea, to this terrible reality. The insidious, undermining work, day after day, in the deadened silence, the guilty indifference, was consuming itself. The kids' bones decalcified a little more each hour, each day more of their brain cells were dying off, never to regenerate. Situation defined by the ruling classes in a stock lapidary judgment: these people get uglier and stupider each day. Fortunately we're here to run the country.

"A baby died over there last week."

"Huh!" Ramon jumped, brutally drawn from his despondency.

"A baby died last week," repeated Maximin.

"Died of what?"

"We don't know. From the belly or from a disease. The diarrhea emptied him out."

"You couldn't see a doctor?"

"It's ten pesos for a doctor," said a voice, and it was useless to say any more.

It was an all too usual occurrence. They quickly spoke of something else. A little later Ramon came back to his first idea. "You've got to get organized for chrissake!" He turned to Maximin. "You understand? You've got to move your ass! Your future is in your hands!" Then, when they didn't reply: "Do you know how Guzman and Jean-Claude Duvalier work?"

Without giving them a chance to answer, he laced the fingers on both hands together and showed them. "Like that!"

"Yes, they work together," said the young Haitian.

"So, we, we should also work like that, be like that." Ramon once again presented them his interlaced hands.

Maximin and the young guy agreed, without saying a word.

"During the revolution of '65, the Haitians fought right alongside us," added Ramon.

He could still see the band of young guys from the neighboring country, the majority political exiles, raring to go, rallied around camouflage-outfitted François Andre Rivière, *El Francès*, and fighting like devils for the freedom of the Dominican People, in other words, for the freedom of the entire island. A fair turnabout, besides. During his short mandate, Bosch had greatly aided the Haitian opposition that was gathered in his territory and driven by the will to invade and liberate Haiti. Ramon smiled to himself at the memory of the lean figure of Gerard Lafontant, thin as a rail, the official interpreter in spite of himself, then a highly skilled combatant, putting all his energies* in the twenty *cuadras* going from Rio Ozama to Cuidad Nueva, the heart of Santo Domingo and of the rebellion. Yes, those Haitians well merited the help of the Dominican People.

"Bah," snorted a viejo, fatalistically, "when Guzman's gone all that's going to change!"

---

*After a long exile in France, Gerard Lafontant returned to Santo Domingo, where, with little means and a lot of will, he runs a center for Haitian refugees, the "Centre Henri Dunant."

Ramon shook his head in derision, running his hand over his neck to dispel the day's fatigue. He called Maximin to witness.

"Remember what they said in the Balaguer days?"

"Oh yes," laughed Maximin. "They said, after Balaguer, it's going to be better!"

"And is it better?"

"It's not better," replied the viejo. "It's even worse."

Ramon spun around on his heel, gestured his disagreement.

"No, it's not worse. I'm among you today and we're talking about the union. In Balaguer's days, they would have already blasted me in the back."

In those days, not so far off, Gulf & Western could take the liberty to do anything it pleased. Ramon was thinking of union leader Guildo Gil, assassinated in 1966 at the time of the destruction of the United Union of La Romana. And of the murders of the unionists Rafael Limonal Vargas and Miguel Fortuna, found riddled with bullets near the ingenio in 1969. Of the journalist Abraham Rodriguez, correspondent for the *Nacional* in Santo Domingo, who made public the death threats he received to prevent him from publishing his information on the treatment of Gulf workers, and who mysteriously disappeared in 1969. He was thinking about all that, and about his own headlong flight a few years before, to escape the Balaguer police hot on his heels. "No," he murmured once again, "it's not worse. I'm here today, we've built the union, we can meet, we can talk." He contemplated the camp of extreme poverty for a long moment. "But that's not enough."

May 1978. After a long night of dictatorship and oppression, the Dominican Revolutionary Party (PRD) affiliated with the Socialist International, running on a populist and reformist platform tinged with shades of nationalism, beat Joaquin Balaguer's Reformist Party and came to power, thanks to the very great popularity of José Francisco Peña Gomez, one of the heroes of the 1965 Revolution. Thanks also to the Dominican People's continuing struggle, outgoing President Balaguer, controlling the machinery and the funds of the State, never for one moment envisaged his defeat. The same day, in keeping with a classic maneuver in this region, the defeated government, challenging the election returns, attempted a coup d'etat. To his great frustration, neither the bourgeoisie, nor the Church, nor even the White House came to his defense.

The PRD, popular among the Dominican working class because of its tradition and its history of struggle against the dictatorship and the American invasion, realized as early as 1965 that it could not

259

come to power without any "rough stuff" unless it toned down its anti-imperialist position. Thus, long before election day, José Francisco Peña Gomez was careful to give guarantees to the liberal sectors in Washington, the party drew closer to the German Social-Democrats, and became a possible and acceptable Balaguer replacement for the Americans.

Don Silvestre Antonio Guzman, rich landowner, former Minister of Agriculture in the Juan Bosch government, took up residence in the National Palace and formed a Social-Democratic government. A general amnesty allowed for the liberation of some two hundred political prisoners, emergency legislation was lifted, and formal liberties reestablished: opposition parties enjoy all constitutional guarantees, activity of Communists is allowed, the majority of the political exiles return, and union organizations — of which the CGT is one — are created.

An invigorating breath of fresh air blew over the Dominican Republic for a few months.

Soon after, however, the illusion, or at least the hope, was succeeded by disillusion, and for some, despair.

Members of the military continued to occupy important government posts (Ramon Emilio Jimenez, vice-admiral of the Navy: minister of foreign affairs). To be sure, one of the new president's first measures was to send fifty or so generals and colonels off to retirement or on a foreign mission. With the armed forces marked by more than forty years of dictatorship, it was more a symbolic than a really effective measure. To get back to those in power, one also notes the presence of personages notoriously linked to the North American capital (Sacha Volman, an employee of the American multinational Falcombridge, the president's personal advisor; Gaetan Bucher, ex-president of Falcombridge, administrator of the CEA; Eduardo Fernandez, former local president of Gulf & Western, President of the Central Bank). Moreover, even though the PRD controlled the Parliament, Balaguer's party kept the Senate, and the former ministers remained at their posts. As for the Vice-Presidency of the Republic, that post fell to a grand gentleman of private finance, the *licienado* Jacobo Majluta.

Sole concrete measures: an increase in the minimum salary to 125 pesos a month was granted; a 10% increase to workers and employees who earn less than 300 pesos a month; an increase in minimum day wage for agricultural workers to 3 pesos 50. As for the rest, as soon as the new government arrived, it addressed itself to the workers, asking for an "indefinite truce" until the regime could manage to reorganize the economy. A few days after having won the elections, the leaders of the PRD created their own union organism,

260

the UGTD, an obvious maneuver attempting to put a freeze on demands. At the same time, in order to stave off the "organizing fever," the employers fired thousands of workers with the support of the government, through indifference if not through complicity. President Guzman's regime manifested a growing hostility toward the working class and even toward pro-union members of the PRD, pursuing the same policies as its predecessor Balaguer. It made no serious effort to change the fundamental ownership structure, nor the relations between classes, nor the relations with the State, which perpetuates the inequalities. On the other hand, the Armed Forces' '79 budget was doubled. The right to strike, formally granted, was violated through bans and dispersal tactics, in the same way that meetings and demonstrations were banned and dispersed. There was brutal police intervention. In August 1979, five persons were killed in the course of a demonstration supporting striking public transportation drivers. As for the problem of the bateys, it was purely, simply, deliberately, and scandalously ignored and left exactly as it stood. The only thing quite clear was the will to obscure the matter. It is true that any intervention in this crucial domain would require radical measures, involving a head-on conflict with existing structures, the institutionalized corruption, the established privileges. Guzman wasn't about to take the step; his Social-Democratic government claimed to be making an omelette, but refused to break any eggs. Or rather, agreed to break some eggs as long as they weren't theirs. The internal exigencies of the workers who were demanding a redistribution of the wealth clashed with the basic exigencies of the finance capital and the great Metropolis of the North.

Intergovernment relations with Haiti were excellent, to the great displeasure of the anti-Duvalierists, who were hoping for at least a certain neutrality *vis-à-vis* the Haitian democratic forces. During the elections Duvalier had invested nearly nine million dollars to support Balaguer. He neither envisaged nor wished a PRD victory, considering their long history of struggle against the Trujillo-Balaguer fascism, objectively a loyal ally of the Duvalier tyranny. In fact, one witnessed an increasingly frank entente between the two governments. Guzman needed Haitian cane cutters. The authorities of both countries have big stakes in the commerce of this labor force. Furthermore, Guzman wanted to open the Haitian market to Dominican industrials and merchants, a market all the more reasonable since products made in Haiti with lower wages brought in a better price than those imported from Santo Domingo. The Haitian investors, rapacious *nouveaux riches* (having murdered the "old guard"), weren't playing for medium- or long-term gains, but preferred the quick turnover of cash, depositing a maximum of liquid assets in a minimum of time safely in Miami. The Haitian government was ready to open the frontiers in both domains, but in opposite directions: men from west to east, and merchandise from east to west, if that would allow it to "cash in" in passing. Moreover, sending braceros to the Dominican Republic constitutes a safety valve in a country where famine and unemployment are endemic. Frantz Cinéas, Haitian ambassador in Santo Domingo, veteran diplomat, Papa-Doc's private secretary for two years, Jean-Claude's confidence man, undertook a series of contacts with industrialists, merchants, and political men influential in diverse sectors of the Dominican government and public life. In the course of 1980, he would be introduced to the most representative businessmen in Santiago, the country's second city and Guzman's stronghold, by a high level industrialist who would arrange private meetings in his secondary residence in Sosua.

Guzman was the first Dominican President to meet with the Haitian president so much, and in so short a time span — twice in nine months. On 31 May 1979, the two chiefs of state met at the border between Malpasse and Jimani. In his speech, Guzman talked about "the strict respect for the principle of self-determination of Peoples and the nonintervention in internal affairs." As if the Haitian People, saddled with a president-for-life against their will, had any such possibility of self-determination. Agreements were signed, including secret clauses and lists of names. Anti-Duvalierists living in the Dominican Republic were not long in bearing the brunt of it.

By February '79, Dominican authorities had already tried to deport to Haiti three exiles, Antonio, Masil, and Jerome, who were living, respectively, in bateys "Juan Sanchez," "Las Yaguitas," and "Montellano." The vigorous protests of Dominican democrats were successful in making the authorities reconsider their decision, as well as in April of the same year, when two exiles, Estenio Toussaint and Eliasin Jean-Baptiste, narrowly escaped deportation.

On 10 April 1979, a communique was issued by the Secretary of the Interior and Police forbidding Haitian immigrants in the Dominican Republic to participate in any anti-Duvalier political activity.

From that moment on, the hunt was on.

In May, Mr. René Théodore, Secretary-General of the United Party of Haitian Communists (PUCH), who was to attend a Communist Party congress in Santo Domingo, was expelled.

In June, the same fate befell Mr. Dorcival Dolciné, president of the Jean-Jacques Dessalines Liberation Front, a recently created anti-Duvalier movement.

On the 30th of the same month, Mr. Odius Lacroix, vice-president of the same organization, was arrested in the middle of the night in the presence of a Tonton-Macoute and thrown in prison.

During July and August, three Haitian citizens — Mr. Félix Alexandre, an ex-officer in the Haitian Army; Miss Yona Sorel, a student in Paris; and Mr. Guy Gilbert, known for his anti-Duvalier positions; all carrying entry visas — were turned back at the Santo Domingo international airport after undergoing interrogations in the course of which the question of anti-Duvalierism invariably came up.

In January '80, proceedings were undertaken against Louis Eugène Athis, general coordinator of the Democratic Movement for the Liberation of Haiti (MODELH), a resident of the Dominican Republic for seventeen years. His expulsion was avoided thanks to public outcry and the stand taken by José Francisco Peña Gomez, the secretary-general of the PRD, who declared: "The deportation of Athis would be catastrophic for the image of the Dominican Republic abroad. The government should permit Haitians living in the country to engage in lawful political activities."

But starting in August, with the bomb dropped by the London Anti-Slavery Society — which denounced the conditions of slavery prevailing in the Dominican plantations before a UN commission in Geneva — Haitians in the country who were struggling to make known, in Santo Domingo and abroad, the intolerable and scandalous situation of their compatriots would become the object of systematic persecution. The Dominican government intended to erect a barricade of silence around the Haitian camps.

On 27 February 1980, two Haitian exiles, Paul Denis and Robert Moise, were deported to Curaçao by Santo Domingo authorities, who accused them of attempting to incite the Haitian cane cutters to revolt against the Jean-Claude Duvalier regime. Once again, PRD Secretary-General Peña Gomez intervened, but in vain. A judgement was made forbidding their expulsion and restoring their liberty. Nevertheless, they were driven to the airport by imperial fiat, and the judge who handed down the verdict, Ramon Horacio Gonzales Perez, was removed from office within three days. In an editorial published Tuesday, 26 February 1980, the newspaper *El Sol* made the following comment: "The Dominican government's deportation of Haitian exiles Paul Denis and Robert Moise two days ago is a shameful act which offends the Dominican democratic sensibility and sense of solidarity. . . No one is unaware that the motivations [for these deportations] are not of a legal nature, but rather are perfectly political, and are not dissimilar to those which brought about the persecution of Haitian exile Louis Eugène Athis last month, and the deportation of Dorcival Dolciné in January '79. It is a matter of a governmental trend rooted in the extreme right-wing sectors which aims to close the doors to Haitian exiles in order to please Dictator Duvalier."

In May 1980, Jean-Claude Bajeux, a Haitian exile known for his work in Caribbean literature (like many others, he had been horribly marked by Francois Duvalier's dictatorship: part of his family was massacred with clubs by Tonton-Macoutes), would be denied residency. He was founding an Ecumenical Center for the Rights of Man in Santo Domingo, born of the existing concern over the absence of legal protection which the members of the Haitian community in the Dominican Republic endure, and he was devoted to gathering and diffusing information about the problem of the bateys.

Finally, in '80, his wife Sylvie Bajeaux, appearing at the Santo Domingo international airport in the company of French volunteer physicians desirous of working for a month to improve sanitary conditions in the bateys, found herself denied entry into the country.

The continuity with the preceeding regimes is obvious. One of the first gestures of the triumvirate which came into power on 23 September 1963, after the overthrow of Juan Bosch, was to expel the Haitian exiles who had attracted attention by their anti-Duvalier activities.

This, to the great satisfaction of the Port-au-Prince regime who thus sees its propaganda efforts aimed at giving credibility to the idea of a democratization of the regime legitimatized on an international plane. Coming from the president of a social-democratic country, Guzman's endorsement constitutes a precious trump. It is well known that friends of democrats are democrats!

To the great satisfaction of the army as well. In 1977, under Balaguer, General Jean René Beauchamp Javier, secretary of the Dominican armed forces, declared: "If the Dominican Republic becomes communist, the same thing would soon happen in Haiti. If Haiti fell victim to bolshevism, the same thing would also befall the Dominican People." To the great satisfaction, finally, of Washington, extremely uneasy about possible successors to the Duvalier regime in Haiti and quite determined to prevent any haven for "destabilization" in the Caribbean. In February '80, Major General Schweitzer, strategic planning bureau chief in the American armed forces, paid a visit to Presidents Guzman and Duvalier, with whom he discussed the communist menace in the Caribbean and Central American countries and to whom he offered military aid to withstand it.*

---

*Last but not least... alas! From 26 through 28 March 1980, the International Socialist Committee on Latin America and the Caribbean met in Santo Domingo, eighteen miles

On the international level, the Dominican president made it clearly known that his government had no intention of reestablishing diplomatic relations with Havana. During the Nicaraguan crisis, the Government refused to break off relations with the Somoza dictatorship in spite of internal pressure. The Dominican Minister of Foreign Affairs played a leading role in the mediation carried out by Washington in a desperate effort to avoid the total collapse of Somoza. Lastly, President Guzman's regime was one of the last to recognize the Sandinista National Reconstruction Government— several days after he came to power.

In the Dominican Republic, taking into account the social class and categories of their respective supporters, it was quickly perceived that the difference between Balaguer and Guzman was one not of kind, but of degree. Balaguer was supported by Santo Domingo's upper class, Guzman by that of Santiago; the interest lying in different sectors but remaining the same.

From that time on, sharp differences began to appear between the machinery of state and that of the party, which was in direct contact with the duped and disappointed masses. "The PRD is in the government," noted the disillusioned militants, "but certainly not in power!" Friction erupted between Guzman and Peña Gomez, incontestably the party leader and architect of its affiliation with the Socialist International in 1976.

Peña Gomez is black, of Haitian descent, from a family whose members were massacred in 1937. Due to his widely known origins, he categorically refused to get involved in the problem of the bateys, confining his position to one of stubborn silence in order not to be accused of being both judge and judged, and of compromising Dominican economic interests in order to "favorize" those of the Haitian community. "If Peña touches this business," say his friends, "he'll be signing his political death. Maybe even his death itself."

Peña Gomez is black, as we said, and commands an in-

from the nearest batey, in the presence of Willy Brandt; Bernt Carlson, Secretary-General of the IS; Carlos Andres Perez (Venezuela); and François Mitterand. If, in the corridors of the conference, everyone touched upon the matter without spelling anything out (denunciation of the batey scandal by the Anti-Slavery Society shortly before), no one would officially bring up the problem, were it not so much as to ask the Guzman government for an explanation. This, in order not to embarrass the Dominican Republic in its effort to reestablish the "formal" democracy. In the course of the talks, the principal leaders would manifest their solidarity with the Nicaraguan revolution and would acknowledge the necessity of the People's taking up arms to overturn a dictatorial regime when no other solution exists. But the "Declaration of Santo Domingo" would carefully forget to make any reference to Haiti and her President-for-Life.

disputable and almost charismatic popularity among the common people of the Dominican Republic. As such, he is the sworn enemy of the entire racist and reactionary Right and of all the forces of the status quo, which, due to their "distance from the power through legal channels," were not broken up. In this way, the position of the democratic forces in power in Santo Domingo was closer to the Chilean situation before Pinochet than that of the Sandinistas* in Nicaragua. Short of having actually beaten the enemy in combat and having put the forces of repression out of the contest, they knew just how far not to go in order to avoid their return to power: choosing to let lie status quo positions which made it impossible to implement their programs or to conserve their broad popular support, thereby losing political power. Unless they compromised themselves more and more with the conservative and reactionary sectors. Peña Gomez was never pardoned for having become one of the symbols of the 1965 resistance. That he knew. But on the other hand, the only thing really revolutionary remaining about Peña is his past. If, among other things, he maintains that agrarian reform is happening too slowly, he doesn't condemn the land takeovers any less, and claims that the leftist as well as the rightist groups cause trouble in the countryside. If he dispenses certain criticisms about the works of Antonio Guzman's "perrédiste" government, he also declares without batting an eyelash that "the Dominican Republic is one of the rare countries which offers security to millionaires just as well as to revolutionaries!"

The PRD of 1978 is no longer the same party which in 1965 took up arms to defend the constitutionalist uprising of Colonel Caamaño against the American Marines and the archaic sectors of the oligarchy.

To be sure, the Dominican Republic today is a nation where political crime and brutal repression have disappeared.

For some, that's a lot. For many, for the immense majority of those exploited, it is not yet enough.

The Dominican People have not yet really made themselves heard.

---

*Sandinista: from Sandino, the man who swore to expel the North Americans from his country at the time of the Marine occupation of Nicaragua. His flag was red and black, his motto "Fatherland and Liberty." All his official documents carried a seal which showed a peasant decapitating a Yankee soldier with a machete. He got together a troop of peasants, laborers, Indians, students, and children that he baptised the "Army for the Defense of the National Sovereignty of Nicaragua." Between 1926 and 1932, this "crazy little army" invented the modern guerrilla and inflicted upon the United States their first Vietnam. But after the victory, the "Director-in-Chief" of the National Guard formed by the Yankees had assassinated he who Henri Barbusse had called "General of Free Men." (Excerpt from *Muchachos — Nicaragua journal d'un témoin de la Révolution Sandiniste* by Frances Pisani, same editor, same collection.)

With lowered heads and furrowed brows, the silent little group once again walked on a bit further. "Guzman, Duvalier, Gulf, the Americans," mused Ramon, "all the same interests." The old man with the holey t-shirt took advantage of Ramon's moment of distraction to ask Maximin who was this Dominican who seemed to be his friend. "He's a union man from the CGT," answered Maximin. "A union man," the old man repeated slowly. "And what is he doing here?" he demanded in a livelier tone. Maximin placed his hand on Ramon's shoulder and raised his voice in explanation for the benefit of the few newcomers. Without even realizing it, he began speaking in Creole, even though everyone understood Spanish perfectly— there weren't any Kongos present, except perhaps the youth who'd recently arrived at the batey. *"Lifé on apèl a tout travayé sikrié ké sé travayé faktori o sé koupé kann an nou apiyé a CGT nan lit pou révandikasion nou-yo.* He's making an appeal to all the sugar workers, whether they work in the factories or cut cane, to support the CGT in its struggle to support our demands!"

The old man was listening, keenly interested. He moved closer to Ramon.

"I'd really like a union to really defend us! I'll be going down to La Romana."

He opened his remains-of-a-shirt, revealing a skinny torso and protruding ribs.

"I've got something in my chest that wants to explode," he went on, his throat thick with bitterness. "I've worked sixty-three years for the Company..."

"Sixty-three years!" sputtered Ramon. "But how old *are* you?"

"I'm seventy-four."

Ramon fell into step with the man, walking side by side, full of respect for this old worker.

"I'm seventy-four years old," he went on, and in spite of the fatigue, he held himself very straight. "I was over to the office for my pension. They asked me: 'You are Dominican?' I said 'no, but I spent my whole life here.' 'But are you Dominican?' 'No, I am Haitian.' 'Ah, you're Haitian...Fine, well, we'll see.'" The old man stopped suddenly, grabbed Ramon by the arm. "I don't know who they gave my pension to, but I never got anything."

Once again he opened the rag on his emaciated torso.

"This Company *chupa sudor,* these blood-sucking vultures got everything out of me. I'm nothing more than an empty carcass. They took my youth, they took my life. And from this compañero also..."

He pointed a finger in the direction of one of the shacks in front of which an old man with a vacant air sat solemnly. Ramon recognized the white-haired viejo who'd seemed not to notice him when he passed him upon arriving.

"This old man is blind," said Maximin. "He's been blind for some time. He can never pick up a machete again."

"It's the dust," said Santana.

"The dust?" repeated Ramon.

"Yes, the cane dust. It hurts the eyes and sometimes winds up killing them."

"Imagine," Maximin stopped, addressing Ramon . . . "He put in thirty-five years of labor, he's exhausted, can't see any more, was forced to retire. The Company settled his pension. All he got in all — and for life — was 85 pesos!" (That's 85 dollars.)

"It's an insult!" growled Ramon. "It's an insult to this old man! It's an insult to all the workers!" Then he called on all of them to testify. "Are you going to take this much longer?"

"I'm going to stand up for my rights," said the old-timer who'd been refused his pension. "And if necessary, I'll write to President Guzman! I'll do it, I'll do it for sure! I'll write!"

"You don't know how to write," said Maximin sadly.

"I'll write anyway! My anger is too great!"

"It's an insult!" Ramon continued. "Did you know that on 22 November 1974, Gulf & Western sold 50,000 tons of sugar at 65.20 centavos a pound and that this sale, considered the biggest ever, was concluded at the highest price ever realized by a company in the history of the market of this product? Did you know that? And where do you come in in all this?"

He turned toward one of the old-timers, who had said nothing up until now.

"Huh? And you? Where do you stand?"

"Oh, me," said the other modestly, "I was lucky. I am one of the fortunate ones." A weak smile lit up his face. "The Company gave me my pension."

"How much do you get?" asked Ramon.

"I spent my whole life here. I get 8 pesos a month."

An unbelievable weariness on his face and in his legs.

"An insult," exploded Ramon, "an insult! It took the sacrifice of thousands of workers, from the cane fields to the factories, to raise the production of the zafra to the peaks attained in 1975, when world sugar prices were the highest ever in recent years. Between 1970 and 1976, Gulf & Western paid its employees at the Romana Central 29.6 million dollars — less than 12% of the ingenio's profits. All this profit made by the capitalists," continued Ramon, carried away by his anger, "is gained on the workers' backs, with your sweat! And during this time, what? Your situation isn't even getting any better."

"It isn't even that it's not getting any better," thought Maximin, "you can say it's getting worse." He calculated. "In 1963-1964, I remember, the cane cutters received a daily wage of 1 peso 83."

"That was when the Romana Central belonged to South Puerto Rico," confirmed the other old-timer.

"Exacto," said Maximin. "Today, cutting, you can make two pesos a day. But it's worse. You can't buy anything any more with two pesos."

"Exacto," agreed the old man in turn.

Ramon shook his head. Since that time, the cost of living had increased by 113%. With a wage practically the same, the ability to survive has diminished by half. The workers are twice as poor under Gulf. They are croaking from hunger.

"Do you understand?" he said. "Do you understand why you have to get organized?"

One of the youngest took a step forward, a gleam in the depths of his eyes.

"Hombre, the day there's a change, we are all ready! We're going to fight with you!"

"Carajo!" exclaimed Ramon, incensed. "What do you think — the change is going to fall from the sky?"

Vaguely embarrassed, they looked at him in silence.

"It's you that must make this change — here, in your place of work."

"Here, we can't do anything," sighed one among them.

"Yes, you can!" Ramon almost cried. "You are the strongest! It's you who cut the cane! It's you who make their living! Without you, they are nothing."

He turned aside and held out his hand in the direction of the old blind man.

"See what awaits you, compañeros, if you do nothing! Look at your children! Look at this old-timer!"

They wavered, hesitated before his eyes — struggle, sure, of course they all agreed, but they were no longer used to it — well of course they all agreed, but can you, just like that...

"What do you have to lose? Tell me! What do you have to lose?"

"Nothing," said Maximin.

"Nothing really."

"Yes," said someone.

"Yes? What?"

"*La mala vida*. The bad life."

"It isn't even one," said Maximin. "No, it isn't even a life."

"And your children?" Ramon shouted at them. "What's going to become of your children? Cut cane at eleven years old for those who make it that far? Starve to death?"

The silence had become heavier, harder, thicker. One guy turned his head. He had tears in his eyes.

"Do it for your children!" implored Ramon. "If you do nothing, they are condemned to forced labor for life!"

The batey's stranglehold was loosening. A few Haitians slowly stood up.

"We have to get organized," said Maximin the first.

"Yes, we have to," took up another viejo. "It will be long, it will be hard, but we have to."

"Me, I'm with you," said the young guy who Maximin hadn't noticed before. "I'd rather die with a gun in hand that continue to die from hunger."

"Well, for the moment, we're not quite there yet," smiled Ramon, who wasn't asking that much. "But that's good. You are determined." Then, eyebrows raised: "What's your name?"

"Petit Pierre Déroseaux," answered the Haitian. "Before, I was a Kongo in a CEA batey."

"Well, Déroseaux," and Ramon gave him a satisfied wink, "to work, old man. Because don't kid yourself. We're not there yet. There'll still be a lot of hard times on the road ahead."

He left — dead tired and satisfied.

We are witnessing today the beginning of the Haitian workers' consciousness, of both their government and that of the Dominican Republic. Conscious of the injustices of which they are victim, they are turning more and more toward their natural allies in the struggle — the Dominican workers, and in particular those in the CGT.

Ramon retraced the immense plantation road in the opposite direction. At times the motorbike's handlebars shook nastily, his back hurt, fatigue was overcoming him. "It's a gigantic task," he sighed. And he continued. After a moment, he thought of all the thousands of workers who he visited regularly, parked in the bateys of the American octopus. His sarcastic laugh veered him momentarily off the path. The worst of the matter just occurred to him. As a matter of fact, those guys were the privileged.

The wages paid by Gulf & Western are 25% higher than those of the CEA.

The conditions of the sugar cane cutters are clearly improved. For us intellectuals, they have not yet reached the idea dreamed for by all those liberal minds imbued with humanism, but this year's contract, in the light of our information, seems better than last year's. And we at the university know that efforts are being made to ameliorate conditions even more in the contracts to come. In this light, we cannot honestly call these conditions slavery and quibble about a traffic, for the workers are free to leave the centrals and the fields when they are no longer satisfied.

> Dr. Bienvenido Valerio Lopez
> de Saint-Augin, Professor of
> French at the North East
> University of San Francisco
> at Macouris.

It is our judgment that in no way are the Haitians victims of real slavery, since we see them living in the country without papers.

> Conference of the Dominican
> Episcopat

Last year, after the return of the cane cutters, a group of young people were there awaiting the arrival of the peasants, their brothers, and their friends, to ask for information concerning the working conditions, remuneration, etc. It was a way to find out if they should try their luck. They were amazed to see a considerable number of injured, crippled, men in very bad shape. They were able to reach the conclusion that the Dominicans had mistreated the Haitians. Thus they started up a sort of information campaign in the cities, just to keep the people from repeating this bad experience. "The conditions are not good, the climate is not favorable, you musn't go." That was the word they spread in the streets of Port-au-Prince and elsewhere.

The local authorities started yet another hiring campaign for the following season, the 1980 zafra. When the two governments signed the contract for the hiring of 14,000 workers, the Dominicans had asked that the operation be carried out in less than fifteen days. Considering the hullabaloo caused by the denunciation of the Anti-Slavery Society, everyone wanted a maximum of discretion.

But all these young people had talked, a part of the independent press had courageously succeeded in relaying the information, and the Haitians were in no hurry to leave any more, compared to previous years. If they had to starve, at least starve at home. The truth was starting to be known. Encountering the peasants' indifference, indifference caused by the "consciousness-raising" campaign, they arrested the young people who were spreading the news, accusing them of being opponents, *kamokins*. Their panic-stricken parents had to pay a considerable amount of money — $35 each — to the magistrate and to the section head in order to lighten the charges, in other words, to prevent their transfer to Port-au-Prince as political prisoners.

Some heard the Minister for Social Affairs and the high-ranking representatives of this Department saying: "You shouldn't pay attention to what they say on the independent radio! You shouldn't follow these people! The President is asking you to go!"

The local authorities were relentless in spreading terror in the Northwest at that time. They wanted to create a climate of fear within the population in order to incite the youth to leave for Dominicanie. "You don't want to go and cut the cane? You don't like your country? You don't like Jean-Claude?" These young people were obliged to practice "marronage." They fled and took refuge in the woods. They were designated as opponents because they didn't want to leave for the bateys.

People were coaxed, they were stroked. They were "advised" to leave. And in spite of everything, in the enrollments two to three thousand didn't show up, which delayed the operations. They were fetched by force.

Duvalier and Guzman were accomplices in selling the Haitians for next to nothing. The Guzman Government said that if things didn't go fine, Duvalier would lose power. The Haitian Government benefited from the protection of the Dominican Army because the exiles were agitating, were organizing. So, in exchange, they endeavored to promote the hiring.

That's the rumor.

Ten days before the beginning of the '80 zafra, the CEA hadn't yet been able to obtain the 14,000 Haitian braceros needed for the harvest. The Secretary of State without portfolio, Milton Ray Guevara, went to Port-au-Prince. The negotiations had become very discreet since the international denunciation. The Haitians, embarrassed by these revelations, acted with great hesitation in the discussion of the new agreement. As far as the CEA was concerned, they were ready for the zafra. Only this "minor" problem was still pending.

11 December 1979. President Guzman declares that in the next few hours, an agreement will be reached with the Haitian Government for the voluntary entry of the braceros who wish to participate in the zafra. He specifies that talks are being held toward this aim, "government to government."

17 December 1979. An announcement is made, saying that the contract will be signed during the week. It confirms that the matter is being dealt with at the highest levels. Milton Ray Guevara is the only person besides President Guzman who knows the details of the negotiations. Gaetan Bucher himself, director of the CEA, doesn't know its developments. It is necessary to act fast. The national market could find itself without refined sugar if the zafra didn't start right away.

18 December 1979. Nothing to report. Considering the delay of the Haitian Government in signing the contract, a veritable hunt for Haitian manpower is organized on Dominican territory. In Enriquillo, Oviedo, Paraiso in the south, toward Mao in the north, the Dominican militaries make roundups. Bullets are shot up in the air and blows are dealt.

19 December 1979. Nothing to report. More than two hundred Haitians are jailed by the military forces in the province of Valverde, in the villages of Amira, Pueblo Nuevo, and Boca de Mao. Those who flee are shot. In Santiago, all the Haitians found in the street are forced to get on military trucks. They are taken to the Fernando Valerio fortress. The prisoners are then sent to the bateys where they are penned up like animals and obliged to work against their will. (In 1969, in the CEA alone, the lack of braceros occasioned a loss of 360,000 tons of cane.)

20 December 1979. The contract is signed for 14,000 braceros. Last year's agreement stipulated the amount of the transaction: $1,225,000 paid to the Haitian Government. This piece of information had created a very bad impression on international public opinion. It disappeared. But the payment remained. Only the amount would not be made public. Other changes: The sum paid to the bracero between his arrival at the batey and the effective start of his job went from 75 centavos to one peso. The ton of cane which was paid 1 peso 35 the previous season would be paid 1 peso 50 this year. The only fact that was really new, but important — these raises aren't real ones, the cost of living rises just as fast — was that in the 1980 contract, the International Labor Organization (ILO) was involved in the deal. According to article 14, the office of Secretary of Social Affairs of the Haitian Republic is entitled to appoint five Haitian civil servants and one representative of the ILO to see to the correct implementation of the terms of the contract.

21 December 1979. According to the commander of the Santiago police, the police raids on Haitians in the north are not made following a decision of the police. The orders were given by the army.

25 December 1979. President Guzman in Santo Domingo and president-for-life Duvalier in Port-au-Prince attend the midnight mass. Christmas hymns rise in the warm and starlit night. "J'ai bien mangé, j'ai bien bu ... J'ai la peau du ventre bien tendu... Merciiii, petit Jesus!..."*

25 December 1979. —P.S. And peace on earth to men of good will. Amen.

28 December 1979. Frantz Cinéas, Duvalier's ambassador in Santo Domingo, confirms to his country's press that ILO has been invited to carry out on-the-spot inspection of the current conditions, according to the agricultural workers' contract.

1 January 1980. Happy New Year, hugs and kisses. Since the Dominican Republic is considered an exporting nation, it obtains an increase in its export quota, which reaches 1,200,000 tons. According to experts, sugar prospects are improving. For the 1979-1980 campaign, a world production of 90 million tons and a demand of 93.4 million are foreseen. Prices are starting to climb to an average of 13 cents a pound.† For the Dominican Republic that means an opportunity to sell a big part of its production at a very good price. There is a possibility of big losses if the CEA could not supply the expected

---

*Well known French children's rhyme: "How well I've eaten, how well I've drunk... The skin on my belly is nice and tight... Thank you, little Jesus..." — TRANS.

†They would go much higher, exceeding $25 per hundred pounds in May '80.

quantities. It would be catastrophic for the country at a time when the foreign currencies brought by the sugar hardly cover the oil imports ($450 million) and when it owes $1,577.2 million to foreign lenders. Moreover, the 31 August 1979 hurricane had considerably worsened the economic situation.

3 January 1980. The first 5,000 Kongos arrive in the Dominican Republic. The CEA has requisitioned more than ninety "guaguas" (buses) for the transportation. These have been parked for more than two days in the Province of Jimani. On the other hand, now that the Kongos are starting to arrive, we can stop talking bullshit. About the International Labor Organization, Doctor César Estrella Sadhalâ, Dominican State Secretary for Labor, declares: "No international organism has asked to supervise the working conditions of the braceros in the Dominican ingenios... Also, this intervention was not requested by anybody."

The matter is closed. Nothing will be undertaken to organize the visit of a supposed ILO Commission which, in fact, was never considered. This clause was only aimed at putting international opinion to sleep and deceiving the future slaves thrown by the thousands into the plantations.

In the distance, the high chimney of the Ozama plant was belching dense black smoke. A truck slowly cut through the swell of cane, leaving behind it a long, rectangular wake of soft tar. In a few moments, it would reach the San Isidro junction. There, it would turn to the right, continue a bit further through the two walls of the *cañaveral* and then along a long forbidding wire fence, would rumble without slowing down in front of the military-guarded concrete gate. The driver might have a lump in his throat, or might not. If he knows, he would think to himself — move on fast — and he would unconsciously accelerate. In the Trujillo times, those who walked through the doors of this military base rarely had a return ticket. It presented an appreciable advantage for the police interrogations. Located more than fifteen kilometers away from the capital, nobody heard the cries that escaped it.

Through the windshield, covered by a thick film of grey dust, the driver sees the T of the junction. Suddenly, from the little wooden house nestled at right angles to the intersection, plunged in the dark shadows of a mango tree, a guy comes out, calmly plants himself in the trajectory of the truck and raises his hand. In his other hand, he is holding a gun. Sharp braking. A storm of vehement protests rises from the rear of the truck, from the group of passengers knocked about by the sudden stop. The guy approaches the cab and talks for a while with the driver. You can't hear a word of what they are saying, then you can hear a snatch of a sentence, then the driver with his metallic voice, "Do what you want, man, but hurry up!"

The unknown walks around to the rear of the truck, carefully looking over the passengers. He is black, wearing a cotton hat slightly tilted back on his head, a light shirt, a watch on his wrist, pressed pants held up by a real belt, shoes that are a little worn but not too much. He's gripping his gun by the barrel. As soon as he opens his mouth, you can tell he is Haitian. Twelve different faces are silently watching him, and the weapon in his hand seems at first glance more like a hunting weapon than one of war, but still a weapon. He rapidly inspects all the faces, eliminating nine of them right away, pale complexions of genuine Dominicans, selects three. No need to be a physiognomist to guess their nationality. Haitians. "Gentlemen, show me your identification!"

Not even nice, not even polite, just sure of himself. You can read visible distress, some secret fear, on the faces of the two youngest of those questioned. On the face of Raymond, the third and oldest, a certain hardness is slowly suffused. This guy asking for their identification, this Haitian, except for his gun wears no distinctive sign, no outer appearance of authority.

"Our identification! By what right?"

The man calmly stares at him. You can make out the cold glint of insensitivity in his little eyes.

"It's the administrator of the ingenio who hired me to watch the Kongos, so that they don't flee to the private *colonos*."

"But you are a Haitian yourself!"

"Yes," the other says, embarrassed and falling silent.

Sylvain won't tell them anything more. He is getting paid four pesos a day to do this job; he's paid for it and he does it. With a brisk gesture of his hand, he repeats his invitation to the two other suspects. They have not budged, paralyzed as they are. "*Ba'm cédula*," he says to the first one. The guy sighs, visibly ill at ease.

It is a disastrous zafra. Cutting the cane has been delayed in most of the ingenios of the country. As of today, 16 April 1980, the CEA is 30,000 tons short compared to the previous year, but this figure could increase as well. According to official reports, the enterprise could finish the year with a deficit oscillating between 150,000 and 200,000 tons below the 900,000 expected tons for the CEA alone. And this during a year when the price situation on the market appears favorable for exporting countries! Something needs to be done.

The two Haitians possess no identification whatsoever, are not Kongos, arrived in Dominicanie surreptitiously, crossed the border in complete illegality. Sylvain orders them to get off the bus, and the two guys hesitate to get off, and the Dominicans tell them to get off, and they have nothing to do but get off the bus since they have no identification. To hell with the Haitians. The man by the name of Raymond, however, doesn't let himself be intimidated, addresses Sylvain.

"You say you have to arrest the Kongos who came with a contract..."

"Exactly," Sylvain says.

"But these two aren't included in that batch! They came *an ba fil*, through the border! That's none of your business."

"They carry no identification."

"So what! You are not a policeman, you work for the factory, from what you say! They don't belong to the ingenio, you have to let them go."

"I have to arrest them," snaps Sylvain—hasn't this pain in the ass understood yet that he, Sylvain, Haitian auxiliary agent, was put there to stop anybody that looks like a nègre!

"What are you going to do with them?" Raymond asks nervously.

"They're going to work, that's what they're here for."

Then, sharply addressing the one who questioned him: "You too—get off the bus!"

"Oh no," Raymond says with a start, "I'm not getting off."

"You get off; I'm telling you, you too are Haitian, even though you talk loud."

A sun beam grazes the dull gun barrel, bounces, and is lost in the hot cane- and dust-saturated air. A few exasperated sighs burst forth from the Dominicans. "Let this old man obey, and let's get it over with!"

"No way," Raymond protests, "I am not a slave, I'm a political exile."

"Exile or not, get off the bus," Sylvain dryly orders; and, "Yes, you get off," a Dominican says; "Yes, absolutely, get off," another Dominican says.

Raymond stands rooted where he is, looking for something in his pocket, takes out a *cédula*, shows his residency permit, and as an exile is perfectly legal with the authorities, there's nothing to add, nothing.

"I have my political exile documents," he says calmly, but a Dominican swears and spits, "You might be an exile, but you are Haitian, and Haitians are here to cut the cane," and to Sylvain: "Go and arrest him, that's what you're paid for," and then a few other Dominicans protest, "You can't do this, he's an exile, nothing can be done to him." "Besides, I have been here for sixteen years," Raymond says, "and I work in the factory," and at this point it would have been better for him to keep quiet for he just triggered off a tempest. A Dominican explodes, "You are not entitled to work in the factory, that's a job reserved for Dominicans; get off and go cut the cane." "Oh no, señor, as an exile he is entitled to, besides, I";"the son of a whore"; "but if you consider it that way"; "ah no, but besides. . ."

Raymond clenches his fists. It's the same old story over and over again. There's already problems with the person in charge of the Central Ozama ingenio, a bad sort. He says that the Haitians came to cut the cane, and that they have no damn business in the factory. He wants to kick out all the foreigners who became integrated as workers because this isn't what they came for, and the zafra is already late. He forbids the Haitians to take even a piece of cane when it comes to the factory. The Haitians protest and appeal to the local Secretary General of the PRD, so that he would apply pressure and have this guy removed from the position of boss of the factory; they've been here for years, they have slowly worked their way up, they escaped the curse of the bateys, workers today just like the others, Haitians or not. It is the Ozama factory, in the town of San Luis, a former batey that grew to the size of a Haitian town, where more than sixty percent of the population are Haitians. Creole is spoken much more than Spanish. Before, they used to have an inferiority complex; people would endeavor to speak Spanish, but now they are not ashamed to express themselves in Creole any more, and Raymond clenches his fists. It's the same old story again, and it's the same old story, over and over again.

Sylvain, finally fed up with this business about papers in order, drops it. He's got two of them, will catch others before the day is over, let this pain in the ass go to the devil. He motions to his two prisoners and escorts them — they walk with their heads held down — as far as the mango tree which is loaded, the fruit hanging on its stems between the stiff and slender leaves. Tonight he will take them to the San Isidro base, they will be thrown in a cell, and as soon as enough of them are caught, en route for the cane!

It won't kill them.

The truck started up again, and was soon under way on the perfectly straight highway. A heavy atmosphere now hangs over the passengers. They look at the Haitian, a few of them with antipathy, and Raymond knows for sure that they are staring at him, he is a Haitian who got out of the bateys, Dominicans generally don't like that. He recalls for instance this compatriot who had. . .

There was a Haitian who had found a little job in Consuelo, he was starting to make *un ti kob*, a little money, he had bought a refrigerator and even a television set. The Dominican bosses arrested him. They had seen that this young man was managing on his own.

He was making at least two hundred pesos. A Haitian is not entitled to earn so much money, they told him. They confiscated all he had and threw him in jail. His name was Daniel Plaisir, born in Gonaïves, and he had been living in Port-au-Prince, Fort National. He was nineteen years old. He was in jail for eight days. After these eight days he was in such bad shape he was ashen. They sent him to a batey to cut cane. He was very intelligent. But of course they do not want a Haitian to earn too much money. He has to cut the cane.

In a cloud of exhaust, the truck leaves the route leading to the international airport and enters the suburbs. Meanwhile Raymond is thinking of the two guys that they left on the road, and about this big Haitian hunt, unleashed since the beginning of this year, but which has always existed. The Haitians are so afraid of the army that, during the hurricane last August, they fled while the army was coming to protect them, yes sir, while it was coming to protect them. In the Esperanza area, flooded by the Rio Yaque del Norte, a lot of immigrants drowned because they were more afraid of the soldiers than of the hurricane.

The truck crosses the Duarte bridge, arching high over the Rio Ozama, and noisily enters the noisy heart of Santo Domingo.

Later, Raymond takes off on foot, intoxicated by the animation in the streets — Mella, 30 de Marzo, and Amado Garcia — and all the streets just as lively, and all the Haitian women shopkeepers on the Avenida Duarte. And at the very same moment, throughout the country, strange things continue to happen, even in the capital, strange things for a civilized country. He walks past Benito Gonzalez street without paying attention to it, and in this street, in front of the Concha Hotel, there is a cafeteria, Cafeteria Citera, a big room with a greasy floor littered with papers and surrounded by insipid green walls, with two ceiling fans wheezing uselessly, not even stirring the thick and stinky air; a long counter, a few high wobbly stools, on the counter an NCR cash register, and in the vast space behind it, shelves with red and white cans of milk, and a washed-out, dog-eared, torn poster, on which was distinguishable — but only if one really cared to look — a fat radiant fellow: "I sold cash," and a desperate skinny one: "I sold on credit," and through the perpetually open door erupts the infernal noise from the street.

Cafeteria Citera. A Haitian — another one! — takes one, two steps; he is skinny and timid, and poorly dressed and very black and very Haitian. He mechanically heads for the far end of the room, towards the wall bearing an opening which must lead to the kitchen, you can tell from the smell, and where there is a greasy red door, that must be the toilet, one can also tell from the smell. A girl is pushing a dripping broom. The Haitian stops, quite lost, walks towards the

279

counter — a sort of cluttered bar . He has left his batey, batey Hoyo Indio of the Central Rio Haina, a few kilometers away from the capital. He'd had it, he had already had it; there had been that business of the cabrouet falling off the bridge taking eight Kongos with it and two of them drowned, and then the companions wandering off, one with a butchered foot, the other with a broken collarbone, whom nobody treated, who slowly perish in the big hellfire of the batey, all this misery, all this despair, just the same as last year, nothing had changed. The Kongo decided that it was enough, he left the batey. Now, bewildered in this cafeteria in the big capital, he's really lost. He looks up at the list of daily fare, particularly considering the prices. *Mondongo: 1 peso 50 — Cocido de pollo: 1 peso 25 — Cocido de res: 1 peso.* The dialogue that he's trying to start with the waitress comes to a brisk end, and everybody is watching him, he sighs, everybody is watching him, a few of them laugh, and in this idiom that he doesn't understand, he understands only the laughter, and he can tell they are making fun of his awkwardness. A muffled voice coming from the stool nearby draws his attention. *"Res sé viann béf,"* says a compatriot (probably) whom he had not noticed, white hair over a lined face and heavyset, *"Res,* that is beef and it's one peso." Then he loses interest in the poor slob, furious for having to express himself in Creole, but on the other hand he could not just let him flounder. When one has had the good fortune of successfully breaking away, managing to fit in, of being less and less Haitian in this Dominican society, one doesn't feel like attracting attention, slipping down a rung. The Kongo understands, thanks him in silence, resumes his interrupted dialogue with the waitress as he very slowly and carefully unfolds a one peso note washed-out and worn by centuries of sweat.

The man nearby has put down his glass, has paid and is leaving.

It's later now, and the man is still walking in the city. A sidewalk, another block without thinking, and this patrol of soldiers . . . or police? Police, who motion to him to come closer. A little crowd of nègres nearby, with arms dangling abject.

Of course, he has no papers. But he's got a job, *si señor,* he's got a job. He's been a tailor for three years, *si señor,* three years, in the El Ensanchito district, near the national cemetery, *seguro señor, El Ensanchito.*

"But you have no papers!"

"I work, señor, I'm working in the city and . . . !"

The answer cracks, as sharp as the breech of a rifle.

"Haitians go for 80 pesos nowadays! At this price you are not entitled to walk on the streets of the capital! How did you come into this country!

The Haitian is silent, he has already understood that he is trapped. The border, the wandering, the long, angry months of beans, a little something here and an odd job there, this tailor's job one day in a Dominican guy's shop, the tiny room where he works and where he sleeps.

"The Haitians who get across, when we catch them, we should shoot them!"

"And then beat them for a month with a club," adds a mirthful sergeant with malicious eyes, just for good measure.

"What are you going to do with me?" asks their anguished victim, who has not heard them raving.

An imperious finger is levelled at the group of silent captives.

"We are acting in compliance with Law 95 regarding entry of these foreigners in this country," the chief of the detachment specifies, emphasizing his tirade with a toss of his head. "You entered this country illegally, you are arrested."

The Haitian understands and lowers his head. They are going to send him back to Haiti. His universe collapses brutally. Months, years. . . of pain, of relentless work, the pride of succeeding, of managing to do it, to have it all end up like this, this pitiful end. A bitter sob rises up in his throat, salty tears burn his eyes. All there is for him to do now is save what can be saved.

"I have nothing with me," he says to the chief who is staring at him unkindly, "but I've got my things, some shirts, you have to let me go get them."

The burst of vicious laughter cracks like a whip. In this very second, there is something rotten in Dominicanie.

"Haitiano!" the chief roars. "When you left Haiti, you had nothing! There's no reason why you should return with something."

"But, I . . ."

An out-and-out shove propels him toward the group, where a helpful arm catches him, keeps him from falling.

Staring at all his compatriots, he reads in their eyes what he still refuses to believe. He is losing his bed, a wardrobe, a stove, his savings hidden under the bed, his clothes, still other things, including hope and dignity. Especially hope. The dignity, too.

He turns in distress to one of the other prisoners who fatalistically shrugs his shoulders. "The capital is not for us," he says.

"When are they going to repatriate us to Haiti?" the new arrival wonders aloud.

One of the captives bursts into a painful laugh. His name is José Pié and he bursts into a painful laugh.

"They aren't going to take us to Haiti, but to the bateys."

A few pairs of eyes turn their gaze towards him.

"That can't be," says the guy who was just arrested. "The chief said to me that he was arresting me because I came into this country illegally. They're going to send us back."

"Listen," José Pié says, "I have already been arrested for the same reason. They didn't take me to the border. They need cane cutters in a few CEA ingenios, especially in Montellano and in Catarey, because of a drop in production. They threw me in a batey. I worked for four days in Catarey. During this time I got a salary of one peso fifty! I escaped." A disenchanted glance around him, and he bites his lips, his features tense. "Unfortunately, they busted me again."

They take them away. They tell them — they have to face it — that tomorrow morning they will leave for the batey. Somebody protests, the last who got busted shouts that they must either release him or take him back to Haiti if law means something. The chief becomes really angry. He doesn't give a damn about the law. He turns to his men, pointing at the miserable herd.

"The zafra isn't progressing, the country's getting poorer, while scattered over the fields and towns in this country are thousands, tens of thousands of nègres doing all sorts of jobs, and who left the work for which they were hired and who are walking around without any residency permit! And that, Gentlemen, is the situation!"

He slowly comes back toward the prisoners, advancing in particular on the one who had dared protest.

"Listen to me, you bunch of rotten Haitians! If you don't want to cut sugar cane, we'll encourage you with clubs. Understand me?"

You could read in their pupils, dilated with rage and fear, that they had understood.

They throw them into a cell and forget to give them anything to eat. The next morning, they throw them in a truck, and again forget to give them anything to eat. Afterwards, they throw them in a batey, they don't give them any bedding, and nothing to eat. It's not even that they forgot.

At the first word of protest, a *guarda-campestrë*, club in hand, came and planted himself in front of them. "If you don't walk like I want," he spat in their faces, "I'll break your heads." And as an indeterminate murmur persisted, he brandished his whirling bludgeon, sending a tremor through the warm sweet air. "If you don't want to cut cane like Duvalier ordered you to, your life is on the line." He rested his club, snickered between his very rotten, broken teeth. "If I do something to you, no one will say anything to me." He swung around violently, legs spread, and as if they were no more than stray dogs in the night, began to piss at length, eyes lost in the infinite infinity of the plantations.

In these tormented times, the shame raining down silently over the warm earth of the Dominican Republic is disturbed now and then only by the desperate cry of a slave less discreet than the others. And if they all don't die from it, they are all affected.

In his little shack in the batey Palavé, Andrès is quietly heating up a little coffee, letting his sixty-odd-year-old bones wake up slowly. He is unaware of all this commotion; he lives far from all that. He's been working in Dominicanie for close to thirty years, and now he's found a nicely paying little job — not a fortune, not at all — but work, with better pay than cutting, and a little less exhausting labor. He is padding about the room, the wife is already up and about, ready to leave for the river and the children's children. A brutal thump makes them both jump, cleaving the whispering silence and making the door shake. "At this hour," murmurs the astonished woman. Andrès has already moved forward, circles the little table, opens the door. The daylight flooding in through the screen door is immediately obscured by four men, two of whom are carrying guns. Andrès closes his eyes, caught off guard by the bright light, opens them, recognizing with difficulty two capataces — one named Cristobal, the name quickly came to him — and there behind a *guarda-campestre* was Tomas maybe, that's it, Tomas, and the massive frame of a boxer, the guy they call the boxer. Flabbergasted, his eyes opened wide, "and to what do I owe the honor of your visit"; well, he didn't say that, but what he did say meant just about that.

"Is that you, Andrès?" "Yes, it's him." "The zafra's late, come and cut cane!"

And that's all there is to it. They come and surprise him at dawn and want to force him to go and work. But he, he has other things to do, isn't that right, he has other things to do. And their ass, he has other things to do? No, what he meant was that another task is awaiting him, and besides, he hasn't cut cane in a long time. Sorry, but all the Haitians in the ingenio have to go and cut. If not, it's the police and prison; illegals who don't work get sent back home.

The woman wrings her hands, she shouldn't, there's nothing to fear; the kids are frightened and crouch in a dark corner.

"OK, fine, there's no problem, my friend." If Andrès were illegal, like so many of his compatriots, it's true, he didn't deny it — he would have been stricken with worry. But Andrès's papers are in order. He's managed to master the language, vanished in the masses, escaped the hell of cane, and most of all, a rarity worthy of note, he possesses a piece of identity which is going to protect him. A *cédula*, Dominican identification papers, a residency permit.

The one named Cristobal can't keep from spitting, and winks slyly at the boxer who chuckles moronically. "Papers! What do you mean? Can we see them?" "Certainly, Gentlemen!" A few seconds later, Andrés is back with the documents. He is a legal citizen and perfectly protected by the laws. At his age, he's surely not going to go back to cutting cane.

A cry-plea, two outstretched hands, it's already too late. While he was soliloquizing, Cristobal has just calmly ripped up the document with a nasty sneer. Andrès no longer has a *cédula*. One by one, the capataz throws the pieces on the muddy ground, and the pieces stick, and the ink runs and smears, and it's in the mud.

"Well Haitian, still consider yourself a Dominican?"

At first Andrès doesn't answer, his heart seems to let go for an instant, then he rushes forward. Poor old man. He only has time to glimpse the boxer's nasty smile, Tomas's hate-charged look. He topples forward, the breath knocked out of him by the punch. Groaning, he takes a blow in the head and is hurt. His mouth opens in an inarticulate cry, his eyes become strangely glazed, and he's nothing more than someone to hit. He gets up. They throw him back on the ground in a chaos of nasty laughter, the wife's cries, and the children's tears. They force him to his knees. "Pick up your nice identity card, Haitian; hah, hah!" He refuses, he's no animal. And they beat him in front of his whole family: "hah, hah, since you don't want to!" And he's bleeding from the mouth and the nostrils. And—face crushed into the ground—they make him suck his own blood. They pick him up. "And now, to the cane, son of a Haitian whore!" Once again he takes a punch that hurts him, and the *guarda-campestre* screeches in his ear, "take that one too, bastard, it's for Peña Gomez! That dirty nègre bastard Peña Gomez!" And this is the blow that half knocks him out, and he has only time to wonder, why, why, why?

The news from London indicates that the world sugar shortage is becoming more and more imminent. It's time to produce.

"Three thousand braceros abandoned the CEA camps," proclaim the authorities under pressure, "three thousand Haitians running loose..."

At the same moment, in the CEA batey Consuelo, several Gulf & Western employees are caught recruiting Kongos bought by the consortium from Duvalier in order to take them to cut cane in the plantations of the multinational, which raised the price of a cut ton to 1 peso 70, in other words 20 *cheles* over that paid by the CEA.

The military, police, *guarda-campestres*, private militias, and traffickers are unleashed. In Tierra Fria, Bimbe, Abina, La Jagua, Alejandro, Caimita, Estrella, Chicharron, China, Haitians living outside the bateys are pursued, hunted, imprisoned. Anyone could be picked up. They arrest Dominicans who have the physique of a Haitian—blacks—and throw them into the bateys, who often from that moment on refuse to continue to consider themselves Dominican, tear up their *cédulas* themselves, begin to speak Creole, become Haitians since they are treated like Haitians. They understand. Being Dominican comes out only second to being black. Nothing but batey meat.

Thousands of illegal Haitians are hunted down throughout the territory. Some attempt to legitimize themselves in the eyes of the law. Didn't the Director of Immigration declare: "I am at the disposal of any foreigner at all to legalize his papers"? They appear before the concerned authorities. They are asked their names and addresses and they are told: "We'll look into your case." And there they are, on file. Not only is their case never looked into, but as soon as some manpower is needed, the Haitian who six months before had taken these steps is astonished to find the police knocking at his door. "You are illegal. You have a choice: cane or prison."

April '80, still...

Mao, in the northwest of the country. Two men are walking down the street. Suddenly they turn around and one lets fly an exclamation. A military truck passes them, jostling them in its draught, and the sonorous roar echoes between the double row of low-lying houses. They only have time to catch a glimpse of the captives crammed in the back—shaggy, weary *nègre* heads. One is bloodied.

"That's the second truck today," says one of the Dominicans, aghast.

"Last week, six hundred!"

"Six hundred...?"

"They arrested six hundred."

They hear the roar of the motor. The truck turns right at the next intersection, undoubtedly headed for Fort General Benito Moncion. The two men fall silent. The big round-up is in full swing. Dominican army troops are imprisoning Haitians found in the city and in the rural communities of the province. They are *nègres*, easy to identify—peddlers, lottery ticket hawkers, peons, agricultural workers, laborers in the fruit concerns and the private *fincas* owned by the well known *terretenientes* of the province. They are taken unawares; they must abandon wives, children, jobs; climb aboard vehicles without seeing their loved ones again.

One of the Dominicans tugs gently on his tie, which is interfering with his breathing.

"After all, let them quit invading us."

His friend frowns, says nothing.

"It isn't really necessary to recruit 15,000 braceros in Haiti," continues the one with the tie, "there are more than 250,000, maybe

300,000 Haitians that congregate in this country from year to year, whose natural work is to cut cane."

"Is that any reason to treat them that way?" A less than agreeable glance.

"What . . . the Haitian people and their government make a big mistake now and in the past to think that the Dominican Republic has to take over their population overflow, with all the defects and degenerates that that brings! If the Haitian Government doesn't take an interest in the lot of its nationals who break the Dominican Republic's laws, it can't complain about what might happen in the future."

The man thought of the historic bloodbath of 1937, which caused so much pain and sorrow, and said to himself, "well, . . . there certainly had to be a reason. Or then, if they can't stay at home, let them seek the aid of the United Nations and set up refugee camps under international supervision!"

"I agree," puts in his companion, visibly ill at ease, "we should prevent illegal entry into the country, but the authorities don't have the right to imprison just anyone to send him to work in any old *cañaveral* or *finca* whatsoever!"

The other one grunts, unconvinced. "No right, no right. . . These guys come to this country illegally or under contract, but break the contracts, abandon their place of work, and shamelessly, surreptitiously insinuate themselves into the Dominican population. You see them reappear in construction, in the sewers, begging in the streets and the squares — to see the amount of Creole manpower taking over jobs in agriculture! A lot of them harvest rice in the Cotui and Angelina regions. They are in Nagua, Factor, Mao. The coffee in Villa Trinay is harvested by them. They've eliminated native manpower in construction."

"It's time to put a stop to it! Their presence outside of the bateys is a detriment to the national labor force. It all goes to show that the public authorities are too lenient, if not criminally negligent, not to mention the Haitians' abuse of our tolerant attitude."

They don't give a backward glance as a sudden drone once again looms at their backs, surging past them. No surprise. A new cargo of captives rumbles past.

"Three truckloads of them!"

"They must have gotten between two-fifty and three hundred of them! What an invasion! Hup, hup! To the cane! That'll teach them!"

"No!" This time it's absolute disagreement. "There's something rotten in your reasoning. We can't turn the cane fields into forced labor camps under the pretext that these men are illegal!"

"What can you do? They come despite the fact it's forbidden, get around all the measures taken to prevent them from getting in!"

The other one sighs, not really knowing what to think. It's true that when these guys elude the vigilance of the border guards they put themselves in the wrong. But on the other hand. . .

What should be known, in fact, is just exactly what happens at the border.

The more than two hundred miles of border separating the two countries, Haiti to the west and the Dominican Republic to the east, are sprinkled with a few privileged passing points. In a manner of speaking, for outside of the great Kongo migration the border is practically closed. The only connection between Santo Domingo and Port-au-Prince is by plane, but border towns exist. In the north, Dajabon faces its Haitian counterpart Ouaniminthe; then Pedro Santana on the Artibonite River, an arid mountain, a vast no man's land* and "no one's land"; then halfway between the north and the south, Elias Piñas faces Belladère on the Haitian side; further still, near Lake Enriquillo, Malpasse and Jimani, the official passage points of the Kongos; Pédernales at the southern extremity; plus a multitude of intermediate points.

Victor Larose decided to go by way of Ouaniminthe. He got there at four o'clock on national route number one, entirely rebuilt and repaired by His Excellency President-for-Life Jean Claude Duvalier's government. He didn't push on as far as the bridge over the Massacre River, from which he could have viewed directly the neighboring town Dajabon, asphalt roads, cars, and trucks. He didn't feel like getting himself noticed. Around seven o'clock he crossed the border. This was relatively easy for him since he was well informed. The Haitian patrol, as well as the Dominican, is comprised of two men. That means that they have to cover about five miles each way, coming and going. They start out at six o'clock from mile marker number zero headed for mile marker number five. As soon as they've passed, you can go. Consequently, at seven o'clock, Victor Larose makes a dash for it. You have to find a spot to ford the River Massacre. He tries to ease himself in, in a spot where the water doesn't appear too deep. Halfway across the river, he loses his footing and has to swim. It is seven thirty-two. For him, all is well.

At Belladère, the situation doesn't seem so good. Agonized, Elder Jacquelin turns toward his companion.

"Labonté, what are we going to do now? We don't know anyone

---

*In English in the original — Trans.

here."

"No problem," said Labonté. "We're going to sleep just the same. Follow me."

The problem is that he, apparently undecided, hasn't made a move. Elder Jacquelin nervously grips his little suitcase. Labonté motions to him. Moving further away, the narrow streets become deserted, the hum of the center fades. Once again they stop. Labonté cocks an ear. Drifting from a church — or chapel, who knows — comes the sound of a hymn, pure and indescribably beautiful; it rises, soars, and dies. A slight movement of the head. "Let's go." They watch from afar. There, a Protestant service is in progress.

"Let's go into this church," says Labonté.

Which they do. It's a building under construction which doesn't even have doors yet. When the service is over all the faithful leave, Jacquelin and Labonté as well. They are noticed a little because of the suitcase and the gym bag, but they don't stick around. They quickly melt into the night. A little later, they return discreetly, slip silently into the shadowy room, and each stretches out on a bench.

Elder Jacquelin is daydreaming, at times struck with sudden trembling when he thinks too carefully about the great unknown. He would have never dreamed he would leave for Dominicanie one day. Even in the heat of the heaviest hiring periods, when the whole country talked of the big exodus, it never occurred to him. He was living at his mother's. His aunt in New York sent money to raise the children — $100 a month, sometimes $150 for the whole family. There were the four young ones in school, a sister working on her diploma, plus himself, who was doing what he could. He learned mechanics and electronic soldering, but had never found any work in this field. He was working in a factory in the industrial park in Port-au-Prince, where shirts were manufactured for a North American concern. Elder was in charge of the second operation — the shirt collars. He was making eleven *gourdes* a day. That made $25.30 every two weeks. The cost of living is high in Haiti. It wasn't enough. He's young, he likes to go to the movies, he likes girls, all that. Twenty-five dollars is nothing. One day he met Labonté. That one could talk. He asked him.

"You work here in Port-au-Prince?"

"Yes, I work here."

"How much do you make a day?"

"Eleven *gourdes*."

"But that's nothing! That's ridiculous! Did you know that in Dominicanie you can make seven or eight pesos a day in a factory?"

"Really?"

"Seven or eight pesos. Why should I lie? That's how it is, I know.

If you want, come with me when I go. You'll see."

Elder says to himself, "why not?" Then, to Labonté: "If you want, I'll leave with you."

"No problem, old man, but I don't think you dare."

"Yes, yes, I want to make it! I'll leave when you want."

"Fine. But you have to pay for my trip, I haven't got a cent."

Elder had fifty-eight dollars in the Bank of Canada, the money from seven months of working on shirt collars. He withdrew it yesterday and they left this morning. The bus left Port-au-Prince at noon and arrived in Belladère at seven o'clock. And now, there they are on the wooden benches. Elder surmises Labonté's regular breathing in his immediate proximity.

"We should have gone through Jimani," says he.

A muffled grunt responds. He turns his head, glimpsing the clear blue night through the gaping opening in the wall, the luminous rays of darkness hanging there over the high wooden cross.

"Or by Pédernales. Why didn't we go by Pédernales?"

A movement on his right. Labonté is propped up on his elbow.

"I think this way is easier. I don't know anything about how things are in Pédernales or in Jimani." Then, in a commanding voice: "Go to sleep! Tomorrow you'll need your strength."

Elder Jacquelin gives in, conscientiously stretching out on the uncomfortable bench, imagining these towns he doesn't know. Pédernales, Jimani. . .

Jimani. It's rush hour. The unceasing tide of Haitians has just turned. They arrived in the morning, as usual, to sell their labor power in the border region, were returning home the very same evening, across the strange swamp-covered country, bringing a little money to the family living on the other side, only to reappear at dawn the next morning.

The Dominican town of Pédernales. Half the town speaks Creole. All the domestics are Haitian. Employers obtain them by slipping a little something to a few Tonton-Macoutes of their acquaintance. But now it's evening. All the visitors from the neighboring country have left with their little business trades—sugar, flour, spaghetti—piled in the crate that in the morning brought fruit, grapefruit, oranges, yucca. Also a strange atmosphere, one of latent fear, a heavy dread among the shadows, and the shadows are going to know why.

Long and cold is the night.

Since he didn't know the region, Victor Larose, chilled to the bone from his swim the day before, chose to head directly for the first Dominican town, Dajabon. A few hundred yards before the first houses, he was stopped. The customs post was manned by only a minor detachment. They took him to the regional headquarters. They threw him in prison. "I blew it," he raged inwardly, prostrate with disillusionment. "They are going to send me back to Haiti."

As for Labonté and Elder Jacquelin, they were up at five o'clock and left Belladère, headed in the direction of the border at Elias Piñas, the nearest Dominican town. They walked quickly and silently, both thinking of the possible encounter, they went on more quickly and more silently still, even more quickly and silently. It was useless. Silence and speed didn't spare them the danger. The first one they saw was a section chief. There was the Macoute, sitting on the railing in front of his house, and he saw them pass, so he calls them. Just what they were afraid of.

"Where are you going, gentlemen?"

"No, no," blurts Elder, with an utterly botched, completely suspect nonchalance: "We're not going! We're from here!"

The VSN gazes at them ironically. Elder Jacquelin lowers his eyes. The great enormous weight of his small suitcase is burning his hand.

"You aren't from here, I don't know you. You are going to Dominicanie."

"No, no," gushes Elder again. "Not to Dominicanie at all!"

That's the end of their escapade. Labonté had explained it to him the day before. "You have to leave very early to avoid the VSN. If they catch us, they'll take us to Belladère, then to the casern. After that, the gendarmes will transfer us to Mirebalais, and from there, to Port-au-Prince to be locked up and forgotten in the National Penitentiary where we'll spend a year or two in prison!"

And there they were, good and caught. Elder sees that it is serious.

"Very well," says the Macoute, after their long silence. "We're going to Mirebalais."

"Listen," launches Labonté, less sure of himself than usual. "You know that life is tough in Haiti. We can't find anything to do there, that's why we're going — to look for a living."

The other one is there listening, head slightly bent to one side, eyes half closed, fingers fidgeting lightly.

"You can understand that because you have children, you are the father of a family! You can't just..."

"Duty is duty. If I had to let by all the bums who wanted to cross the border!"

"Listen," attempts Elder Jacquelin...He is racked with fear, but makes a desperate effort to appear sure of himself. "I'm a man from Port-au-Prince, I know how things are. You don't need to talk. Here!"

He holds out his hand. The other holds out his too. He grabs the fifteen gourdes without a word, and lets them go.

A little further, they encounter another one. Same deal. They cross the *mornes*. Having left Belladère early in the morning, they reach the border around seven o'clock at night and step foot on Dominican ground. Then stop there. Labonté appears worried. "You have to be very careful. When Dominicans find Haitians on the border, they kill them. Because when the Haitians have nothing more to live on in their country they come and raid the Dominican's gardens or steal their horses. It'll be very rough for us if they catch us."

But for the time being, the night swallows them up.

Once again, day breaks over Pédernales. Heads loaded with heavy baskets of oranges, pineapples, and beans, the first have arrived. The crossing of the border is a daily affair, tolerated from time immemorial. The Haitians come to trade, to work as peons in the coffee plantations, the small agricultural enterprises. Some come for a week, for *cualquier cosa*, a little something.

Télémaque Jacques comes over often. An ear of boiled corn in his pocket for the trip, he slept where night had found him. Now clear-eyed and wide awake, he advances slowly in his superb *pachangas*, plastic sandals that his last trip here had brought him. He was coming back for a few days again, to labor for a bed, a meal, a few meager cents to bring back to his family for food. It is lucky for the Haitians that in Pédernales the weeds grow fast. The fincas must be continually cleaned. That's why they always need Haitians. For example, he works here often, does odd jobs.

"Give me two pesos and I'll cut all the grass?" And they haggle a bit, more for the principle, and "OK, for a peso!" Télémaque Jacques sets to work. He's satisfied.

Not so jolly, the two accomplices in Elias Piñas. They haven't managed to get by. Each time they get up, make a few hundred yards headway, they hear noises, voices, back down in all haste, lie low in the woods, and they can't manage to get through. They have already spent the night, and after the night, half the day.

Menos mal, as they say. Lesser evil.

In Pédernales, Télémaque Jacques didn't understand a thing, didn't have time to understand, understood nothing. It's already hell. The Company had telephoned. They call regularly, pick up all the Haitians! It's already hell. They bag them in the *conucos*, in the fields, anywhere, wherever they are, they cart them away by force.

Military patrols swoop down on Mencia, Altagracia, Aguas Negras, Los Arroyos, covering the rural zones, launching the big manhunt, beating those who don't want to get in the trucks, and they do that every day.

Télémaque Jacques is slowly walking along a hillside while the blazing sun beats down on him. He stumbles; he is suffering terribly. It was the blow of the rifle butt that hurt him. He feels a trickle running slowly down his head, drying immediately, an obscene mixture of dust, sweat and blood. He is the first in line; the rope is brutally cutting at his wrists. He moans, everything is whirling around him.

Five Haitians tied together with a thick rope are walking in single file, pulled by a soldier on horseback.

The scene is not happening in Africa at the time of the slave trade. It's the Dominican Republic. Today.

A few miles away, a small group of captives and soldiers and guns. A massive sergeant approaches the jeep and grabs the microphone of the radio transmitter. A few crackles, a whistling, a distant voice, but loud and clear.

"*Verde de Rojo...Verde de Rojo...Digale al colonel que y tenemos los que nos pidio y que ven para alla!* Tell the Colonel that we've caught what he told us to, and we're bringing them in."

It's still eleven pesos a head for Haitians.

Elsewhere. When they were arrested in the village of Elias Piñas, everything happened very simply. Together, Elder Jacquelin and Labonté noticed the two policemen, who called out to them.

"You are Haitians!"

It wasn't even a question.

"Follow us!"

The men in uniforms brought them to the Elias Piñas jail without talking to them further, without asking them any questions.

Neither was sent back to Haiti, turned over to the authorities for "illegal entry."

Elder Jacquelin and Labonté spent three days in jail. There were no beds. There was a bench that people sat on all day long. At night, some lay down on this same bench, the others on the cement ground. There were also two basins in this big room. One was to urinate in, the other served as a toilet. While they were sleeping, they smelled the rising odor of fecal matter. In the morning a bucket of water was thrown in it to flush all that.

There were around 100 persons there when they arrived. Three days later, there were 250. Company trucks were then sent to pick them up. They were piled in like slaves in the slave ships.

Télémaque Jacques was brought to Oviedo. He doesn't know how many were taken with him. "Very many," he says. They were made to sleep at the police station. Outside. In the courtyard. On the bare wet ground. The next morning, stomachs empty, they began the long journey.

292

They said that three days later, in Pédernales, a woman came down from the mornes. A *moreña*. A very dark, very black one, all dishevelled, in a frenzy. She was looking for her husband. She walked round and round, she asked, she wrung her hands, and she searched feverishly. "Télémaque Jacques," she said. "Télémaque Jacques is my husband's name."

It was only the next day that a woman decided to speak to her. "Go back to your country," the Dominican woman said to her, and her voice was trembling. "Go back to your country, your husband is gone. You won't see him again. *Se lo llevaron para la caña*. They took him for the cane."

She wept, she went crying and walking back toward the country of Haiti. "*Kité mwin sèl, mwin ginyin la pèn . . .*"

"He left me alone, and I have so much grief . . ."

So the Haitians arrested are not sent back to their country for "illegal entry," but are dispatched by force to the cane fields. Curious practice from the point of view of international law. But a logical practice if one examines the rather particular context of the Dominican sugar industry. It is a matter of necessity there, especially for the CEA, which as we know is state-controlled. At Trujillo's death, the dictator's estate, as immense as Somoza's, was nationalized. Its management was entrusted by Balaguer, as a priority, to the faithful generals and colonels, an entire clique of not particularly disinterested political friends. The pursuit of profit by any means and corruption at every level won out over the interests of the workers and the Nation as far as these custodians of the wealth were concerned. If it is true that a good part of the CEA's profits — when there are any — is reinvested in the agricultural sector through the "Bank of Agriculture," the dividends paid by this institution are rarely distributed to their natural beneficiaries, but are more often funneled into commercial and speculative activities — construction, commerce, tourism. In any case, no investments of a technological order permitting the augmentation of work-productivity, or the diminution of its arduousness. The low wages notwithstanding (and it is a euphemism to speak of wages), the sugar companies prefer the harvest by hand to mechanization.

Corruption and technological retardation are thus the lifeblood of the CEA.

Corruption . . . a few examples. The Dominican press recently revealed that certain individuals possess thousands of *tareas* of CEA and Dominican state land in the bateys of the Barahona ingenio and in the Independencia and Bahoruco provinces. Thus it is learned that retired General Robinson Brea Garo has appropriated 10,000 tareas — one tarea equals 1,367 sq. ft. — in Tabila; retired Colonel Léandro Modina owns 800 tareas within the Barahona ingenio; CEA bureaucrat Roberto Payano confiscated 2,000 tareas of batey number eight in Guaraguao; agronomist Jorge Larraudi, ex-bureaucrat in the Department of Agriculture, 1,300 tareas of the same batey; Alberto Suarez, 300 tareas in Altamaria; and Juan Bautista Rivera, 1,000 tareas in the same spot; Francisco Gonzalez Tapia and Manuel Antonio Santana, together, 20,000 tareas in the vicinity of Mena in the Tamayo region. With whose complicity, these appropriations?

Another notoriously known fact: before the start of the zafra, the order is officially given to carry out the weeding and cleaning in several successive operations, so that the cutting can take place in ideal conditions. Those in charge receive the money for these operations, but have only one operation done, spreading only a portion of the herbicide envisaged, pocketing the difference. Result: the viejos work less, because the number of operations is reduced. They starve. When the cutting begins, the cane area is overgrown with briars and thorns. Cruel working conditions are disastrous for the braceros. This is reflected in their productivity.

Undoubtedly the same problem exists in the private "colonos," since CEA director Gaetan Bucher reminds them on 24 April 1980 that "they must use the resources put at their disposal in a more efficient manner in order to ameliorate the levels of productivity in their plantations."

Thus, corruption and waste. The CEA spends $15,000 a month in vehicle rentals for the bureaucrats in its hierarchy, for their private as well as professional needs. This corruption, and the ensuing technological retardation, obviously leads to a rather feeble productivity. The net cost of a pound of cane is lower than its selling price on an already rather perturbed world market.[*] During the past three fiscal years, the CEA has accumulated a loss of around $98 million (1977, $26; 1978, $42; 1979, $30). In his analysis of the origins of the CEA's loss of capital, Gaetan Bucher cited three causes: the low price of sugar on the world market in '77, '78, and '79; sales on the domestic market below the production costs; and production costs (!) in the 12 ingenios.

---

[*]The United States, leading member of GEPLACEA (a group of 21 Latin American and Caribbean sugar exporting countries), which imports 50% of its sugar requirements, causes the market to fluctuate through the play of supply and demand. The United States's sugar production is insufficient for its domestic consumption...is more expensive than its importation. (*Information Caraibes*, June '80).

At the same time, Gulf & Western, which pays its braceros 25 percent more, realizes profit.

In these conditions, the sole solution consists of superexploiting the manpower to the point where it approaches and ends up becoming slavery, just as it was done before to increase profits. One can easily understand the extra profit margin provided by the Haitian immigrants for those in power who use them, be they private or state. In the CEA's case, the profits pass into the hands of the state, then to the local ruling class through the machinery of the state which is controlled and manipulated by this class.

The best way for this superexploitation to become an institution is to dispose of a mass of workers who are excluded from the normal processes of negotiation and organization existing in the Dominican Republic. Thus, a clandestine labor force, whose illegality is maintained to permit low wages and insecurity, is tolerated, implied, and provoked. This illegality is essential to the role of the Haitian manpower. Often entering the Dominican Republic with the complicity of the Dominican army—when they are not purely and simply abducted—the Haitian workers are practically transformed into the property of the ingenios. The illegality of their status explains why, subject to the extra economic pressures which the Dominican worker escapes, they are forced to accept whatever working conditions befall them. The legal recruitment of 15,000 supplementary braceros constitutes nothing more than the institutionalized continuation of this process for the periods of maximum need. Moreover, it exerts additional pressure on the illegal workers. It utilizes a series of intermediate Haitians, buys their silence and the complicity of the mafia in power in that country. This is the reason why the Haitian government advocates and insists upon writing up a contract which may be presented to the public as a measure defending the national interest and the Haitian citizen.

We will not go back over the problems of the conditions of existence of these 15,000 victims of the new Slavery again.

But if one day, under the pressure of national and international public opinion, Duvalier stops signing the contract, officially selling his 15,000 countrymen—the visible part of the scandal of the bateys—the problem will nonetheless remain unsolved. The Dominican Republic needs around 45,000 cane cutters a year.* If

_____

*Total production of the Dominican Republic: 1,200,000 tons of sugar, or about 12,000,000 tons of sugar cane. Production/day for 6 months: $12,000,000 \div 180 = 66,666$ tons. Average amount cut per individual per day: 1.5 tons so $66,666 \div 1.5 =$ about 45,000 cane cutters.

It is worthwhile noting that Mr. Vicini, of the Vicini family which already owned an

15,000 are eliminated, it will be necessary to find them elsewhere. And what better hunting grounds than in the Dominican Republic, among the 250,000 Haitians residing there, veritable hostages of sugar cane! These forays — unless there is a radical change — may very well take on horrifying dimensions.

Meanwhile, awaiting possible developments, viejos and Kongos are neither free nor equal under the law. The issue of race aside, they are still not respected. They have no freedom of association whatsoever. They have at their disposal no protection from unemployment, sickness, or inequity. Their children have no access to education. The fruit of their labor isn't even enough to allow them to rebuild their strength to work. The article which suspends their freedom of movement by confiscating their identity card, or the practice of purposely maintaining their illegality, turns them into prisoners condemned to forced labor. They are kept in servitude officially.

That is precisely what slavery is.

The evening is closing in around people and objects, but it is still daylight — that diffuse light full of the sounds of the coming night which makes one almost forget how hard the times are. The newcomers are getting out of the trucks. They barely arouse the tired curiosity of the viejos and Kongos who are walking slowly through the batey, heads plunged into a turmoil of misery, hands placed painfully on the stomach or belly. Barely.

Further, in the distance, on the straight dusty road that extends all the way from the plantations, you can see two tiny figures, imperceptible dots. But it's not time for contemplation. The slaver which vomited its cargo is already gone. They are darting worried, feverish glances around them. They are getting organized: each one is given 75 centavos for food — they've gotten so hungry since the time of the capture and imprisonment — you can buy a pot to cook it in, they were told, and they wondered what the hell with.

There, closer, on the dusty road, the two men have made some progress, little elongated geometric figures on which you can begin to distinguish arms and legs.

They regroup themselves in twos and threes to buy a couple of pounds of rice, or something else, no meat, with their seventy-five centavos.

A group of very excited women rush out of the batey squealing.

ingenio in the country in 1882, and who consequently knows what he's talking about, estimates himself the average cut per day per individual at 1.25 tons. If this hypothesis is to be considered, the figure 45,000 would be largely surpassed.

The newcomers discover almost simultaneously that the barra-cones are made for Kongos.

The Dominican and the Haitian, there we are, the two figures—are tranquilly coming back up the road, with a good, rhythmic step—the bracero and the wagonero, one from the cane and the other from the railroad. Talking about everything and about nothing. Also talking—and in modulated tones—about the hard labor and the repression, the Dominican laborers, the Haitian braceros, about Guzman and Duvalier. Who they are is of little importance; their names, the name of the batey don't matter, you will not know them, but they are there, I guarantee it.

In this place, they are two; elsewhere, there are more and more like them. The Haitian stops—his companion waits for him—and looks piercingly, one might construe sorrowfully, but it is not—into the forest of cane, the immense green carpet that unrolls endlessly to the limits until you can see no more, but where the cane nonetheless continues to spew forth. "Sugar cane," he murmurs, fascinated... "Sugar cane!" He smiles. "The Caribbean's great wealth." Then his face hardens. "From it we extract the sugar that sweetens foreign coffee, and makes our lives bitter!" His Dominican companion nods his head. He says: "That's going to change."

They start to walk again, slowly approaching the batey. Between the camp and themselves, they make out what looks like a whirlwind coming, but not really moving; they hear shouts; "it sounds like women," observes the Dominican with interest. "Yes, it sounds like women. Wonder if by any chance it is." "Change," the Haitian is still murmuring, unruffled. "Ah, yes, change..." After a silence. "Us too." His companion gives him a questioning look. "While you must work here, the solution to *our* problems lies at the source." And as the other redoubles his look of interrogation: "In Haiti. We must fight with you here, but we must get rid of what makes us have to leave our country. Miserable poverty, oppression." His eyes light up, sweeping over the plain, the rolling hills, he walks in great strides, his soft voice rings in prophetic tones. "We will remake our country. We will reinvent Haiti. We will work there. We won't come here any more, but we will be closer as brothers than we are today." He smiles. "We won't undercut your wages any more. You will make the living conditions better in the plantations. The Dominican *compañeros* will go back to the cane. You will mechanize." He extends his outstretched hand, and the shadow of his finger cast in the slanting light loses itself in the cane fields. He dreams, but the Dominican doesn't smile, he knows it's not a dream, he does the same thing himself all the time. "The preparation of the ground for the cane will be entirely mechanized." The Haitian has raised his voice. "Every day the country will see more machinery to plow, to seed, to fertilize, to irrigate, to harvest the fields of cane." "Yes," continues the Dominican, won over with enthusiasm, "the labor which through the centuries has been synonymous with slavery, poverty, humiliation, exhaustion, will be a worthy participant in the economic development of the country, the elevation of the standard of living of all the People."

"Sugar will no longer be bitter," says the Haitian.

"Sugar will no longer be bitter."

"But for us," the Haitian suddenly says gravely, "this vast program begins over there."

He falls silent, thinking in a flash of the immense force compressed here, in the entrails of the bateys, and of the slow fermentation of the anger, of the fantastic accumulated pressure, year after year, in this gigantic furnace . . . 250,000 desperadoes, infuriated with their destitution, who could very well sweep through Haiti someday. A feeling of calm but intense elation sustains him. One of the keys to the great refusal — one of the levers of the great protest — is situated here, he knew, locked up in these vile camps in the same way that things were beginning to seethe in the country itself. "It's up to us to make the bread rise," he murmurs with determination and a fully lucid awareness. "Our turn."

A nudge brings him back to the reality around him. "It *is* the women," chuckles the Dominican with an amused look, "look, it's for you!" The Haitian comes to a halt as if petrified, can't believe it, bursts out laughing, and laughs again, "Do you think that's it?" "I think so," says the Dominican, and they both laugh with pleasure.

Marta, Philomène, Claude-Marie, in their modest dress, but radiant. Little Héléna. And there's laughter, and there's shouts.

"Well?" cries the Haitian, having understood, "Well?"

Old Marta, running as fast as she can. Old Marta.

"It's a boy, my friend! It's a boy!"

"A boy!" bounds the Haitian. "Is he beautiful? Is my boy a beauty?"

"Ah, is he ever . . ."

She holds her tongue, fearing to have said too much, but keeps laughing, when a baby is born, you have to be careful not to say he is pretty so as not to give him bad luck.

"It's Wednesday today," she shouts. For her, that says it all. Children born on Wednesday are normally safe from supernatural dangers, protected from sickness, from spells, from misfortune.

"And how is . . ."

"She's fine! Just fine."

The labor had been short. The baby had come when they were

not expecting it. The women had quickly cut the umbilical cord with a scissors, an old scissors, a little rusty, but sterilized with rum. Then, Marta herself had bathed the baby with warm water while the mother was kept warm.

"We didn't let him cry for long," says another woman proudly.

"That's good," says the father, with a vague seriousness.

Marta shrugs. "Men don't know anything about these things. You try not to let the newborns cry too long so they won't have a big navel. He's a beauty, your little one," she says. Then after a moment: "*pitit sé richès!* A child is a blessing." The Haitian agrees. Yes, they are the future. A different future. But a question is burning on old Marta's lips. A burning question. Oh yes, a question.

"What are you going to call him?"

"*Monpremier*," suggests one of the women.

The young father smiles, and shakes his head no. "Even though it is *Monpremier!*"*

"If he were mine," says Marta, "I'd call him Clermeil!"

"But he's not yours," laughs the Haitian mischievously. "He's mine."

"Dieudonné," says little Héléna.

And it's still no.

"Well, what then? What?"

The man took a deep breath of the twilight air; a son, his son, he'd already thought about it long before the birth and he knows. He knows.

"Eugene," tries Marta again, because she knows that the maternal grandfather . . .

"No," says the papa. Oh yes, he knows and has known for a long time. His features stiffen, a slight tension amidst the joy. He gazes far away, yet nearby into his universe of plantations, the insane inferno, that inhuman trap into which they've been thrown. He gazes, straightens up, thinking of his country over there, the high and wild land of Haiti, and places his hand on his Dominican *compañero*'s shoulder.

"He will be called Sandino," he says gravely.

Old Marta is silent because she doesn't understand. The Dominican clasps his hand. The Haitian is silent for a long moment, then smiles slowly. He suddenly has a thought. The People of Haiti would surely not wait until the little one grew up.

Port-au-Prince
Santo Domingo . . .
. . . Bateys
February-May, 1980

Monpremier: My first — TRANS.

Appendix

Contract

In accordance with the agreement on the airing in Haiti and entry in the Dominican Republic of the Haitian temporary day laborers, agreement reached on 14 November 1966 between the Governments of the two countries in order to determine the financial clauses of the implementation of the above-mentioned agreement related to the hiring operations of the Haitian day laborers entering the Dominican Republic for the 1978-1979 sugar season:

Article 1: The "State Sugar Council" (CEA) solicits from the Haitian Government for the 1978-1979 sugar harvest, by letter addressed to the Haitian Embassy in Santo Domingo, the hiring of 15,000 (fifteen thousand) day laborers for the needs of the sugar factories of the Dominican State.

Article 2: The State Sugar Council (CEA) agrees:

a) To recruit the 15,000 Haitian day laborers according to the current Haitian laws. The recruiting operations will take place in Haiti, by agents of the State Sugar Council (CEA) in the hiring centers established for this purpose by the concerned services of the Haitian government. The duration of these operations will not exceed 30 (thirty) days.

b) To provide transportation for the Haitian agricultural workers from Malpasse (Republic of Haiti) — Jimani (Dominican Republic) to the work centers in the Dominican Republic, in fully comfortable and safe buses. It is understood that the transportation from the hiring centers to Malpasse will be provided by the Haitian Government.

c) To cover the food and lodging expenses for the duration of the trip from the hiring centers to Malpasse, as well as during the trip from Malpasse to the work centers in the Dominican Republic.

d) To pay the Haitian agricultural workers wages equal to those paid to the Dominican workers for work of the same kind.

e) To put at the disposal of the Haitian agricultural workers and their families, from the date of their arrival in Dominican territory, during their stay in the different work centers, and up until the date of their departure from the Dominican Republic, dwelling units or communal apartments providing all the conditions of hygiene and sanitation required by law, as well as furnishings (table, chairs, beds). The roof of these habitations must be covered in order that the workers not be exposed to inclement weather.

f) To permit the Supervisors and Inspectors of the Haitian Embassy in Santo Domingo to visit the premises where the Haitian agricultural workers will live before the arrival of the latter in the Dominican Republic. Moreover, the dwelling units must be equipped with metal beds and mattresses, provided with drinking water and proper facilities for baths and other conveniences of the above-mentioned workers. The installation of decent, hygienic dining halls is compulsory, so that the workers will have at their disposal suitable places for their daily meal.

g) To extend to the Haitian agricultural workers during their stay in the Dominican Republic the benefit of the Dominican Social Security laws, the compulsory health insurance, social assistance, insurance covering work-related accidents, weekly time off, maternity insurance, the annual bonus, etc. It is understood that a worker injured in a work-related accident, who had not been given permission to leave, will be entitled to all the expenses needed for his treatment and also to the legal benefits at the time of his repatriation.

h) To cover the expense of the Immigration Tax in the Dominican Republic and the registration fee at the Haitian Embassy. The latter fee shall be set at two dollars per worker registered at this Embassy.

i) To repatriate them at the end of the harvest for which they have been hired, and to pay for their food and transportation expenses from their place of work to Malpasse. A preliminary notice will be given to the Haitian Embassy at least fifteen days before the date when the repatriation will start.

Article 3: The State Sugar Council (CEA) agrees to cover, by an insurance policy valued at at least $1,000 (one thousand dollars), travel accidents incurred by any and all Haitian agricultural workers during the journey from Jimani to the work centers and, similarly, during the repatriation trip from the work center to Jimani, including eventual hospitalization expenses, doctors' fees, etc., and any other compensation provided for by the laws dealing with this subject. These dispositions will also apply to the Supervisors and Inspectors of the Embassy who will accompany the agricultural workers in the buses.

Article 4: The State Sugar Council (CEA) agrees to pay the Haitian agricultural worker the sum of D.R. $0.75 a day from the day of his arrival in the Dominican Republic until the date when work for which he has been hired begins.

Article 5: The State Sugar Council (CEA) will transmit to the Haitian Embassy in Santo Domingo the list of all the Haitian agricultural workers hired for each Dominican state sugar factory, as well as their travel documents within eight (8) days after the end of the hiring operations. The above-mentioned travel documents will be returned to the concerned workers at their repatriation.

Article 6: The State Sugar Council (CEA) agrees to report to the Haitian Embassy in Santo Domingo and to the Dominican Institute of Social Insurance of the Dominican Republic, any accident befalling the Haitian agricultural worker in his work center or in the course of his duties.

In the event of a work-related accident leading to the death of an agricultural worker, the CEA formally agrees to cover any expenses and damages resulting from it in accordance with the legal provisions. Any death of a Haitian agricultural worker must be reported the same day, in a detailed report, to the Haitian Embassy in Santo Domingo and also to the Dominican civilian and military authorities concerned.

Article 7: In the case of an accident incurred by an agricultural worker outside of the place of work for which he has been hired, the CEA agrees to report it within five (5) days to the Haitian Embassy in the Dominican Republic in order to disclaim its responsibility.

Article 8: The Haitian agricultural worker hired by the State Sugar Council will be employed to work exclusively in the Dominican State sugar factory for which he has been engaged.

The State Sugar Council agrees, with the collaboration of the supervisors and inspectors appointed by the Haitian Embassy in Santo Domingo, to take all necessary measures to avoid having the worker transferred to a private work center having no obligation to the Haitian Government.

Article 9: The Haitian agricultural worker hired by the State Sugar Council will benefit generally by all the other advantages provided for by the Agreement of 14 November 1966.

Article 10: In order to cover the expenses brought about by the hiring of the 15,000 agricultural workers and their transportation from the hiring centers in Haiti to Malpasse, the State Sugar Council agrees to pay the Haitian Government the sum of one million, two hundred twenty five thousand dollars ($1,225,000) in American currency. This sum will be paid in two equal issues: the first payment will be made immediately after the Haitian Government's acceptance of the request submitted by the State Sugar Council has been communicated to the above-mentioned Council; the rest will be paid within fifteen (15) days from the opening date of the hiring operations or before this deadline if the State Sugar Council has already hired half of all the solicited agricultural workers.

Article 11: The Haitian Government authorizes the State Sugar Council to deduct one (1) dollar every two weeks from the wages of each Haitian worker; the sums deducted in such a way will be converted to American dollars and will be given to the Haitian Ambassador in the Dominican Republic at the end of the harvest, to be distributed to the Haitian workers as withheld wages upon their return to Haiti.

Article 12: The Supervisors and the Inspectors of the Haitian Embassy whose primary concern is the protection and defense of the Haitian agricultural workers will be remunerated by the State Sugar Council.

Article 13: Fifteen (15) days before the expiration of the period for which the Haitian agricultural workers have been engaged, the State Sugar Council will notify the Haitian Embassy by letter of the repatriation date. The State Sugar council agrees to repatriate, at the end of the sugar season, the 15,000 Haitian agricultural workers who must be the same individuals who were hired in the different hiring centers established in Haiti for this purpose. The Haitian Embassy will immediately inform the Haitian government. The Haitian agricultural workers will be repatriated at the expense of the State Sugar Council.

The transportation will be carried out in buses providing the same guarantees of comfort and security.

The State Sugar Council will pay the Haitian government the sum of eighty-five thousand dollars ($85,000) to cover the transportation expenses of the 15,000 Haitian workers from Malpasse to the centers in which they were hired.

Article 14: It is agreed that the Haitian Embassy in the Dominican Republic has the privilege of appointing 75 (seventy-five) inspectors and fifteen (15) supervisors in order to protect the Haitian agricultural workers.

Article 15: The Director of the Division of Labor and Manpower of the State Bureau of Social Affairs of the Haitian Republic is authorized to designate civil employees from the State Employment and Placement Bureau, whose number will not exceed five (5), who may be sent to the Dominican Republic with the agreement of the Dominican Government in order to survey the working conditions and relations in conformity with the dispositions of this contract.

Article 16: The supervisors and inspectors, together with the civil servants and employees of the State Sugar Council, must be at the Malpasse-Jimani border, from the beginning to the end of the arrival of the Haitian agricultural workers in the Dominican Republic. Also in the different work centers, where they will assure that the above mentioned workers not be transferred to a work center for which they were not hired.

Article 17: The supervisors and inspectors will visit the dwelling units to be occupied by the Haitian agricultural workers before their arrival in the Dominican Republic, and will be entitled to appear before any civil servant or civilian, military or paramilitary employee in the said factories, in order to solve any problem that might concern the Haitian agricultural worker.

Article 18: The supervisors and inspectors will be free to visit, without restriction, the cane fields where the Haitian agricultural workers work, the cane-weighing sites, and the centers where payment is made. They will be entitled to intervene to defend the interests of the Haitian agricultural workers any time it is needed, irrespective of the rank of the employee concerned.

Article 19: The supervisors and the inspectors will be provided with a suitable house in the village (batey) where they work for an optimum execution of their function.

Article 20: The standard salary of each supervisor will be $350 D.R. (three hundred and fifty dollars) a month, and the standard salary of each inspector will be $200 D.R. (two hundred dollars) a month during the harvest. The sum total of these salaries will be sent directly to the Haitian Embassy, according to the instructions of the Haitian Government, in order to be paid to its recipient.

Article 21: From the commencement of the arrival of the Haitian agricultural workers in Dominican territory, the State Sugar Council will put at the disposal of the supervisors and inspectors two (2) chauffered vehicles in working order for optimum execution of their duties. It remains understood that the State Sugar Council will undertake the expense of the lubrication and maintenance of the above-mentioned vehicles; it will deliver monthly 600 gallons of gasoline or 300 gallons of diesel fuel and a sufficient number of toll tickets to the Haitian Embassy in Santo Domingo for the transportation of the supervisors and inspectors.

Article 22: The State Sugar Council agrees to instruct the State sugar factories to grant the Haitian agricultural workers free time from 12:00 p.m. to 1:30 p.m. for a meal. Also, Sunday will be a holiday. The State Sugar Council will also put at the disposal of the Haitian agricultural workers recreation centers organized by the Department of Social Affairs of this organism.

Article 23: The Haitian agricultural worker who, upon his arrival in the Dominican State sugar factories, is temporarily not given work, will receive an allotment of .75 peso a day for his food.

Article 24: The State Sugar Council will notify the Haitian Embassy by letter of the exact date of the opening of the harvest in each factory of the Dominican State.

Article 25: In the event that a Haitian agricultural worker is the victim of an accident, the State Sugar Council agrees to provide him with free transportation from the site of the accident to a Health Center where he must be treated.

Article 26: The State Sugar Council agrees to pay the Haitian agricultural worker the sum of 1 peso 35 in Dominican currency for each short ton of cane cut. It is understood that in the event of a wage increase paid to the Dominican worker, in accordance with the Dominican laws, the Haitian agricultural worker will be granted the same advantages, and the Haitian Embassy in Santo Domingo will be so informed.

Article 27: In the unforeseen case of a devaluation of the Dominican peso during the duration of the contract, the State Sugar Council will compensate in the same proportion the wages of the Haitian agricultural workers and also those of the supervisors and inspectors who work in the sugar factories of the Dominican State.

Article 28: Sums deducted from the salaries of each Haitian agricultural worker for the Social Security will in no case exceed the values strictly established by the laws concerning this subject.

Article 29: The Company agrees to pay the day laborer, concurrently with the payment of the last fifteen days work's wages, the amount of the annual bonus provided for by the Work Code of the Dominican Republic.

Article 30: The State Sugar Council agrees to guarantee the conversion to American currency of the savings realized by the Haitian agricultural workers in the Dominican Republic at the time of their repatriation.

In witness whereof the Plenipotentiaries have signed the present contract in two copies, one in French and the other one in Spanish, the two texts having the same juridical value. Signed in Port-au-Prince, Haiti, 14 October 1978.

For the Haitian Government
Achille Salvant, Secretary of
 Social Affairs
François Guillaume,
 Ambassador of Haiti in the
 Dominican Republic

For the State Sugar Council
Dr. Milton Ray Guevara,
 Secretary of State
Rafael Adrano Valdoz Hilario,
 Secretary of State of the
 Dominican Armed Forces
Pedro Purcell Peña,
 Secretary of State
Porfirio Brito, Deputy Director
 of the CEA
Porfirio Basora Puello, Exec.
 Director of the CEA

The 79-80 contract comprises the following differences:

Article 4: Payment to the Haitian worker between his arrival and the effective start of his work: one peso a day.

Article 14: The office of the Secretary of Social Affairs of the Republic of Haiti is entitled to designate state agents whose number will not exceed five (5) and an International Labor Representative (OIT) chosen by the Haitian Government. They will be delegated to the Dominican Republic with the approval of the Dominican Government, in order to investigate working conditions as stated in the present contract.

Article 15: The Haitian Embassy may appoint 80 inspectors and 17 supervisors (instead of 75 and 15).

Article 20: Salary of each supervisor: 385 pesos/month (instead of 350); salary of each inspector: 220 pesos/month (instead of 200).

Article 26: The CEA agrees to pay the Haitian worker 1 peso 55 for each short ton of cut cane.

Finally, in Article 10, mention of the total amount of the transaction between the CEA and the Haitian Government, 1,225,000 dollars, has disappeared.